WHY STATES MATTER
An Introduction to State Politics

Gary F. Moncrief and Peverill Squire

Second Edition

ROWMAN & LITTLEFIELD
Lanham • Boulder • New York • London

Published by Rowman & Littlefield
A wholly owned subsidiary of The Rowman & Littlefield Publishing Group, Inc.
4501 Forbes Boulevard, Suite 200, Lanham, Maryland 20706
www.rowman.com

Unit A, Whitacre Mews, 26-34 Stannary Street, London SE11 4AB

British Library Cataloguing in Publication Information Available

Library of Congress Cataloging-in-Publication Data Available

ISBN 978-1-4422-6805-0 (cloth : alk. paper)
ISBN 978-1-4422-6806-7 (pbk : alk. paper)
ISBN 978-1-4422-6807-4 (electronic)

∞™ The paper used in this publication meets the minimum requirements of American National Standard for Information Sciences—Permanence of Paper for Printed Library Materials, ANSI/NISO Z39.48-1992.

Printed in the United States of America

Contents

Preface to the Second Edition

Just as we were winding up work on this second edition of *Why States Matter*, the campaign and election for the U.S. presidency was winding down. As everyone knows, it was a grinding, brutal, and ugly campaign. It was fought out state by state, just as the long nomination process had been. The importance of the states was obvious to everyone who viewed an election map.

Given the results of the 2016 election, we expect most attention will be focused on the national stage for a while. This is not surprising. With a Republican-controlled Congress seeking to pursue its preferred policies, a potentially mercurial president who ran against the political establishment, and a wide range of important decisions to make, there is much at stake. The role of the states as policymaking units is not going to be the lead story for the national media; they will focus, even more than usual, on the unfolding drama in Washington, DC.

Nonetheless, the states remain important and, we would argue, are likely to become even more central in a number of policy areas. In a rare fit of bipartisanship, Congress passed and President Obama signed into law the Every Student Succeeds Act in December 2015. According to the *Washington Post*, the new law "effectively ends heavy federal involvement in public schools and sends much of that authority back to states and local school districts."[1] Public education has long been the largest expenditure at the state and local level, but the states had lost a chunk of their policy control over it to the federal government under President Bush's No Child Left Behind Act. Now, the states will largely have control once again.

In addition, it is likely that states will gain greater freedom over health policy as well. Important changes, if not outright repeal, of the Affordable Care Act (ACA, also known as "Obamacare") will be a priority of the Trump administration. It is also possible that Medicaid will be converted to a block grant, affording greater policy control to the states over healthcare programs for lower income individuals.[2] Of course, such increased policy control for the states will also mean that the states will likely receive fewer federal dollars to help pay for the cost of such programs.

Indeed, changes in fiscal federalism are almost certainly on the horizon. This means states will be faced with critical choices about the type and level of services they provide and the way such services are funded. And different states will make different choices. The fact that so many states now have unified government (one party in control of both the executive and legislative branches) makes it easier for those states to adopt policies that diverge significantly from the status quo.[3] In other words, states will continue to matter, and in some ways they will matter even more.

For many years, political scientists have noted a trend whereby voters in state elections appear to make decisions based on national trends and issues. We think that it is imperative that citizens understand that states and their local governments are not mere extensions of the national government. It is only then that we can act as responsible citizens in a federal system.

Notes

1. Lindsey Layton, "Obama Signs New K-12 Education Law That Ends No Child Left Behind," *The Washington Post*, December 10, 2015.

2 Robert Pear, "Expect Medicaid to Change, Not Shrivel Under Donald Trump," *The New York Times*, November 15, 2016.

3 Alan Greenblatt, "With Control of More States, Conservatives Plan," *Governing*, November 11, 2016.

1

Making a Case for the States

Introduction: Why Did the Chicken Cross the Road?

THROUGH KANSAS CITY AND BEYOND, State Line Road runs in a north-south direction for about twelve miles. Along that stretch, the road literally runs atop the state line, so that on the east side of the road is Missouri and on the west side of the road is Kansas. That means that if you buy gasoline on the west side of State Line Road, you are buying in Kansas and you are paying a gasoline tax of 25 cents per gallon. But if you pull into a station on the east side of the road, you are in Missouri and pay the Missouri motor fuels tax of 17 cents. On the Kansas side you also pay higher sales tax on groceries and a higher tax on beer. And you pay substantially more in tobacco tax for a pack of cigarettes; Missouri has the lowest cigarette tax (17 cents) in the country, while the rate in Kansas is $1.29 per pack. One answer to the age-old question, "Why did the chicken cross the road?" may be "because the taxes were lower."

There are other meaningful differences between the two states (see table 1.1). For example, Missouri is one of only five states that still allow texting while driving (as long as the driver is twenty-one years of age or older). Texting and driving is illegal for everyone in Kansas.[1] Kansas permits common-law marriage, while Missouri does not. Kansas requires radiologic technologists to be licensed; Missouri does not. In fact, the licensure requirements and standards differ for real estate agents, cosmetologists and barbers, funeral directors, and nail technicians. Kansas allows the practice of naturopathic medicine; Missouri does not.

TABLE 1.1
Kansas City, Kansas, versus Kansas City, Missouri, December 2015

	Kansas	Missouri
State Income Taxes		
Rate Range	2.7% to 4.6%	1.5% to 6.0%
Number of Brackets	2	10
Lowest Bracket	$15,000	$1,000
Highest Bracket	$15,000	$9,001
Federal Tax Deductible	No	Yes
State Corporate Tax Rate	7.0%	6.25%
State Sales Tax Rate	6.5%	4.225%
Applied to Food?	Yes	Yes, 1.225%
Applied to Prescription Drugs?	No	No
Applied to Nonprescription Drugs?	Yes	Yes
State Gas Tax	$0.2503 per gallon	$0.173 per gallon
Tobacco Tax	$1.29 per pack	$0.17 per pack
Beer Tax	$0.18 per gallon	$0.06 per gallon
Sales Tax also Applied?	Yes	Yes
Medicaid Eligibility Limit (Parents Family of Three)	38% of federal poverty rate	22% of federal poverty rate
Child Health Insurance Program (CHIP) Monthly Income Eligibility Limit, Child Age 6 to 18	138% of federal poverty rate	155% of federal poverty rate
Motorcycle Helmet Mandatory?	Only for riders under 18 years old	Mandatory for all riders
Speed Limits, Maximum Posted		
Rural Interstates	75 mph	70 mph
Urban Interstates	70 mph	60 mph
State Marijuana Laws	Possession of less than 450 grams first offense is a misdemeanor, punishable by one year in jail and a maximum $2,500 fine	Possession of less than 35 grams first offense is a misdemeanor, punishable by one year in jail and a maximum $1,000 fine
	Subsequent possession of any amount is a felony punishable by 10 months to 3.5 years in jail and a $100,000 fine	Possession of more than 35 grams is a felony

Kansans found in possession of more than 1.2 ounces of marijuana can be charged with a misdemeanor (up to one year in jail) for a first offense. Walk across the street into Missouri and they can be charged with a felony (up to seven years in prison). Traffic laws differ; whether you have to wear a motorcycle helmet and the maximum speed at which you can drive are different. Medicaid eligibility standards differ. The same is true for state-administered health insurance for children.

The Kansas City case is just one of many instances of neighboring communities in different states with consequential policy differences. Take as another example LaCrosse, Wisconsin, and LaCrescent, Minnesota. Separated only by the width of the Mississippi River, the residents of these two cities share the same physical world—the same climate and geography. What is not the same for these residents is their public policy world. In recent years, the state government of Wisconsin cut income taxes, reduced collective bargaining rights for public employees, decreased public school spending, and declined to expand Medicaid. At the same time, Minnesota increased some business taxes, raised the income tax rate for high-income earners, expanded the right to unionize to include in-home child care workers, increased per-student K–12 spending, expanded Medicaid coverage, and created a state-based health exchange.[2] These two states, which for generations were so similar in ethnicity, economic base, and ideology that they were described as "cousins" or "two peas in a pod," are now following contrasting policy paths.[3] As one political scientist observes, Minnesota and Wisconsin "have begun a natural experiment that compares the agendas of modern progressivism and the new right."[4] Knowingly or otherwise, the citizens of LaCrosse and LaCrescent are part of that experiment.

Such examples are not restricted to the Midwest. Among other contrasting pairs are Easton, Pennsylvania, and Phillipsburg, New Jersey; Phenix City, Alabama, and Columbus, Georgia; and Wendover, Utah, and West Wendover, Nevada. To varying degrees, border towns across the United States are subject to different state laws than their neighbor right across the state line. Perhaps the most dramatic example of neighbors living in two different policy worlds is Lewiston, Idaho, and Clarkston, Washington. Less than four hundred yards separates those who live in a state (Washington) where the citizens have legal access to recreational marijuana, doctor-assisted suicide for the terminally ill, labor union friendly laws, and a state-mandated minimum wage of at least $11 per hour from a state (Idaho) with none of those policies.[5]

Clearly, states matter. When it comes to voting, taxes, environmental regulation, social services, education, criminal justice, political parties, property rights, gun control, marriage and divorce laws, and just about anything else other than national defense, the state in which you reside makes a difference, often a big difference. This idea—that states matter—is the fundamental idea behind this book. So much attention is paid by the media to the national government and what the president and Congress are doing—or not doing—that it is easy to lose sight of the fact that states are different, their policies are different, and these differences have a real, direct effect on the lives of their citizens. Indeed, a strong case can be made that, as one Republican official recently commented, "the real action is happening in the states."[6] To take just one example: under the headline "States Step Up as Washington Stalls on Immigration," one journalist wrote that while the national government remained deadlocked on the issue, "lawmakers in virtually every state in the union aren't waiting," and they enacted over two hundred laws in 2015 that impacted immigrants.[7] As a federalism expert notes, "State legislatures . . . often enact statutes intended to fill a perceived void in congressional law making. This longstanding feature of the U.S. federal system has been particularly on display in the 2000s."[8] While a Republican Congress and a nominal Republican in the White House may ease gridlock in 2017 and beyond, nevertheless, much of the policymaking authority will reside in the states.

Increasingly, states are the first to address the problems and uncertainties induced by emerging technologies. Telemedicine is an example. Recent developments include electronic health care consultations that allow online chats or videoconferences between medical professionals and patients. This in turn raises questions about diagnostic protocols and insurance reimbursement requirements for "virtual visits" to the doctor. And these are questions that involve the role of the state in both regulation and public health.

Today, states are at the forefront of such issues as the safety and regulation of hoverboards and the rights of civilian drone owners compared to the right of privacy. Recently, states have been called upon to make policies in regard to ballot selfies, ride-sharing apps, and fantasy sports wagering. It is the states— or at least some states—that are trying to be responsive to these new issues.

The Historical Context

To claim that states matter does not require us to argue that they matter in quite the same way as in the past. It would be foolish to believe that states hold the same position, relative to the national government, that they did in 1790. Clearly, the world has changed over the last two centuries.

We think it foolish to even argue that states *should* hold precisely the same position as they did in 1790; after all, hardly anything in the world is as it was in 1790. Certainly, the international role of the U.S. government was far different than today. The role of all governments was much smaller then; there were few large cities, virtually no public education, health, or welfare, and few public roads.[9] Industrialization had not yet occurred on a significant scale. The vast majority of labor and commerce in the United States was associated with farming and maritime trade. Many people died of diseases that today are controllable. The average life span was about forty-five years, compared to about seventy-nine years today. The infant mortality rate (well below 1 percent today) was as high as 15 percent in 1790.

The first U.S. Census, conducted in 1790, indicated the total population of the thirteen states was 3.9 million, which is barely more than 1 percent of the population of the United States today. Of that 3.9 million, the largest urban area was New York City, with a population of 33,131.[10] Today, there are more than a thousand cities in the United States with a population greater than New York City in 1790.[11] In fact, by 2016 fourteen metropolitan areas in the United States each had a population greater than that of the entire country in 1790.

Of the 3.9 million people counted in the 1790 census, almost 700,000 were slaves. The usual estimate is that about 90 percent of the workforce was employed in agriculture in 1790, while today less than 2 percent works in that sector.

Obviously, the nature of society was different. The population was small, residing almost entirely on family farms and homesteads, with considerably less interaction or interdependence among people than we find today. The role of government—all governments, regardless of national, state, or local level—was limited. And the relationship between these levels of government differed. Scholars often characterize the original relationship between the states and the federal government as "dual federalism"—by which they mean the national and state governments operated in separate policy spheres. For the most part, however, neither sphere was very large.

From the founding it was unclear exactly what the relationship between the national and state governments ought to be. The Articles of Confederation—the first system under which the nation operated—gave the states the upper hand. But that system failed, leaving open the question of how the different levels of government were to relate. When the Constitution was adopted, there was still considerable uncertainty. There were those, such as Alexander Hamilton, who argued forcefully for a nationalist perspective—contending that the primary constituents of the new system were the people and that it was "the people" as a collection of individuals who were sovereign grantors of authority to the new government. Under this view, the national government would hold a preeminent position. A second view was that the federal system was agreed to by the states themselves, not individuals. In this view, the states were the sovereign grantors of authority to the new government and as such retained the ultimate sovereignty themselves. Proponents of this view saw the federal system as an agreement—a compact—of sovereign states. Obviously, this tug between two views—the nationalist and the compact—is still with us today. In 2010, governors or legislatures in several states invoked the "compact theory" as they argued that states had the constitutional authority to reject the newly enacted federal health care law. These claims were largely unsuccessful, but they highlight the fact that such arguments have been central to some of the most historic moments in the country's history.

James Madison, one of the key architects of the new system, argued that both the nationalist and the compact theories were correct—or at least they were partially and equally correct. Madison described the system as a "compound republic." As Martha Derthick noted, "It is a pity that Madison's term *compound republic* did not survive in our political language for it conveys the complicated and ambiguous intent of the framing generation and helps to make comprehensible what otherwise is bewildering to the modern citizenry."[12]

Madison's compound republic was a system that "sought to assemble majorities of two different kinds: one composed of individual voters, the other, of the states as distinct political societies."[13] The individual voters, by forming an "association of people, under a constitution of government, uniting their power" provide the nationalist perspective.[14] The states, as "distinct political societies" forming together, provide the compact perspective.

We will explore the various interpretations and mutations of federalism in greater detail in chapter 2. For now, it is enough to note that whatever the "proper" federal relationship was at the time the Constitution was ratified, it has changed substantially over our history. Certainly, the Civil War resulted in a different version of federalism than that which had existed previously.

But the most dramatic changes in the federal relationship occurred in the twentieth century. The expansive role undertaken by the national government during the Great Depression of the 1930s and Civil Rights era of the 1960s is particularly important in redefining the nature of American federalism. The changes do not end there; the U.S. Congress and an activist U.S. Supreme Court continued to push the limits in redefining the acceptable reach of national power through most of the century.[15]

If the national government usurped some policymaking roles traditionally left to the states, it was largely in reaction to the states' incapacity in exercising their responsibilities and inability to meet the needs of their citizens. Robert Allen, in a pointed criticism of the states in the middle of the twentieth century, wrote, "Since 1930, state government has dismally failed to meet responsibilities and obligations in every field. . . . The federal government has not encroached upon state government. State government has failed."[16]

To put it bluntly, it was largely the states' own fault they lost relative power to the national government. Most states were unwilling or unable to devise modern revenue systems until forced to do so by the economic collapse wrought by the Great Depression. And when states did change, it was often too little too late to have a meaningful effect, leaving the national government's "New Deal" programs to carry the burden.[17] As former North Carolina governor Terry Sanford wrote in 1967, "Out of the ordeal of the depression came damaging blows to the states. From the viewpoint of the efficacy of state government, the states lost their confidence, and the people their faith in the states; the news media became cynical, the political scientists neglectful, and the critics became harsh."[18] Borne of this era was a dramatic expansion of federal aid to the states, the phenomenon known as "fiscal federalism." Between 1930 and 1980, fiscal federalism was central to redefining the relationship between the states and national government.

Furthermore, many states had neglected to redistrict their legislatures for decades, leaving rural interests with disproportionate political power. State officials were poorly paid; state government was poorly staffed and poorly rated. In the most hyperbolic muckraking tradition, one journalist wrote in mid-century that "state government is the tawdriest, most incompetent, and most stultifying unit of the nation's political structure. In state government are to be found in their most extreme and vicious forms all the worst evils of misrule in the country."[19] Among the evils attributed to state governments he specifically identified "low-grade and corrupt Legislatures."[20]

Meanwhile, under the revived rubric of "State's Rights," government officials of the southern states resisted a national desire to end segregation and ensure civil rights for racial minorities, especially African Americans. It was an ugly time, pitting citizen against citizen, and the national government against some of the state governments. As one historian put it, "By the 1950s and 1960s, the only time state action made headlines was when a racist governor stood in the schoolhouse door."[21]

It is easy to dismiss the bulk of the twentieth century as a "lost era" for the states. But some argue that, despite the obvious shortcomings of the states, they were doing innovative work at various times during the century.[22] One can make that case for some states during the Progressive Era, early in the twentieth century, and again at the end of the century.

Starting with the "reapportionment revolution" of the 1960s and 1970s, and facilitated by reformist-minded groups like the Citizen's Conference on State Legislatures, the National Conference of State Legislative Leaders, the Eagleton Institute of Politics at Rutgers University, the Ford Foundation, Carnegie Corporation, and the Twentieth-Century Fund, state governments were pressed to modernize and develop their institutional and policymaking capacities.[23] Some of this story is told in greater detail in chapter 4. For now, it is worth noting that state governments generally—and state legislatures in particular—became more capable policymaking institutions during the modernizing period often known as the "legislative professionalization revolution" in the 1960s and 1970s.[24]

To put it simply, out of all the turmoil, state governments were pushed to become much more capable governing partners in the federal system. This may not often be recognized by the media or even by members of Congress (many of whom are themselves former state legislators but seem to forget this as soon as they get inside the Beltway). But apparently the general public recognizes it on some fundamental level, as evidenced by the fact that surveys consistently demonstrate a higher level of trust for state government than national government. A 2012 Pew Research Center poll indicated that far more people (51 percent to 33 percent) held a favorable view of their state government compared to the federal government and the gap has been increasing over time.[25] In a 2014 poll, Pew found that only 24 percent of the respondents indicated trust in the national government, while 57 percent said they trusted their state government.[26] Furthermore, on questions about "honesty in government," "addressing people's needs," "careful with the people's money," and "is generally efficient," the states consistently receive higher marks than the federal government.[27]

Arguably most telling, however, is a question posed at three points in time over the last eighty years. When asked, "Which theory of government do you favor: concentration of power in the state government or concentration of power in the federal government," 56 percent of respondents in 1936 chose the federal government. As we will see in chapter 2, having a majority take this stance in the middle of the Great Depression does not come as a surprise because at that time state governments were unable to respond to the economic crises, leaving the governing field to the federal government. When the question was asked again in 1981 during the first year of the Reagan administration, 56 percent of respondents preferred to concentrate power in state governments. Virtually the same response was given in 2016, with 55 percent of respondents opting for power to be at the state level. So for a generation Americans have expressed a clear preference for state government.[28]

Red States, Blue States, and Big Sorts

Red state, blue state is part of today's political lexicon. It developed from the desire in the visual media for a simple way to show how states were voting in the presidential election. Why? Because the presidential election is determined by the Electoral College and the vote units in the Electoral College are the states. If presidential elections were not decided in blocks of state units, perhaps no one would have conceived of red and blue states.

Nonetheless, the "red state, blue state" characterization works fairly well for a growing number of states, as the division of partisans across them is becoming more lopsided. In other words, political polarization is real and growing in many states. The authors of one book on the subject put it this way: "Geography matters politically. States are not merely organizational entities. . . . States have real, significant cultural and political differences. And despite the homogenizing tendencies of national media, drastically lower transportation costs, and a franchised economy, regional differences have not gone away."[29]

In other words, changes in technology, mobility, and mass consumerism have not eliminated state differences. Some argue, in fact, that the differences are growing as technology and mobility allow people to live where they want.[30]

In his book, *The Big Sort: Why the Clustering of Like-Minded America Is Tearing Us Apart*, Bill Bishop wrote that "people do not live in states. They live in communities." This is not an entirely accurate statement, of course. People do live in states. What Bishop meant was that people choose to live in particular communities, or particular neighborhoods that just happened to be in a particular state. His point is that people are "sorting" themselves by their religious and civic attitudes into like-minded local "tribes."[31]

But the fact of the matter is that cities and counties are creations of state governments. The way local governments operate—their taxing authority, their policymaking abilities, their governmental structures—is determined by state constitutions and by state legislatures. Our behaviors as citizens are constrained or encouraged by state legal codes far more than they are by the federal code. As Gimpel and Schukneckt note, "State boundaries have taken on great meaning partly because of the social and economic practices that are legally permitted or prohibited within them."[32] States are important in that they help structure civil society. So not only do people live in states, but it also matters in which state they live.

There is growing evidence in support of that assertion. Statisticians and political bloggers Harry Enten and Nate Silver find "the data is enough to suggest that the people moving away from a region are ideologically distinct from those who continue to live there. . . . Instead, movers have more in common with their new neighbors; liberals are attracted to liberal regions, and conservatives to conservative regions."[33] Political scientists Gerald Wright and Nathaniel Birkhead report something similar; they find that the correlation between ideology and party affiliation among the general public is growing in strength state by state. We have long known that party elites (elected officials and leaders) are polarizing at the state level. Wright and Birkhead conclude that as long as party elites are polarized, "the mass electorate will continue to sort and the macro-level manifestation of that are redder red states and bluer blue states."[34]

The Contemporary Context

It is interesting that in this time of globalization there remain dissimilarities among the states on an entire range of economic, demographic, cultural, and other dimensions. We are reminded that states do indeed represent different mixes of people, characteristics, and cultures and that is, in Elazar's phrase, "what transforms each state into a civil society, possessing a political system that is in some measure autonomous."[35] A glimpse at the differences among the states on several dimensions is provided in table 1.2. The contrasts are striking. California has sixty-five times more people within its borders than does Wyoming. In fact, there are fifteen counties in California, each of which has a larger population than the entire state of Wyoming. Los Angeles County alone has a larger population than at least forty states. As you can imagine, states as governing units face different policy and administrative demands.

States vary in many other meaningful ways. California's economy, measured as state gross domestic product, would rank sixth or seventh in the world around those of France and Brazil. In contrast, Vermont's would rank ninety-seventh, just ahead of Cameroon.[36] Per capita income varies widely across the states; Mississippi's is about half of Connecticut's. Of course, the source of state wealth differs; some states have been blessed with valuable natural resources while others have not. The proportion of college-educated individuals is much higher in some states than others (which is an important variable in explaining per capita income). Racial and ethnic makeups vary. Frequency of church attendance differs; regular church attendance is much higher in southern states (as well as Utah) than in the Pacific Northwest and New England states. A 2009 Gallup Poll found that at least 80 percent of the interviewees in Mississippi, Alabama, and South Carolina said that religion was an important part of their daily lives, while less than half of the people in New England states made that claim.[37] The depth of religious meaning to one's daily life is known as "religiosity" and has been linked to very specific policy preferences on issues such as abortion and same-sex marriage.

Given all of this variation, can any state be thought to be representative of the nation? One attempt to answer this question produced surprising answers. Looking at fifty-one different indicators, the most representative state was Kansas, followed by Oregon and Delaware. Isolating just economic variables, Iowa was the most representative, followed by Oregon and Georgia.[38]

The key point here is that the states are not just fifty shades of vanilla. They differ geographically, demographically, and economically. All of this adds up to the realization that the people in the different states have somewhat different political and social values—different civil societies. Students of comparative state political systems are familiar with the term "political culture" and the idea that different states have different political cultures. The old designation of individualistic, traditionalistic, and moralistic political cultures may no longer be an especially accurate or appropriate reflection of today's state-by-state differences in the United States.[39] But the idea that differences exist, and that they affect policy preferences differently, is still very real. Indeed, it is probably more accurate today than it was a generation or two ago. To some extent, sorting may contribute to this. And to some extent, the political stalemate at the national level means states are left with more latitude to pursue their own policy agendas on some issues—and what is considered sound policy in one state might not be in another.

These changes do not go unnoticed by policymakers and those who wish to influence the policymakers. As the *Wall Street Journal* recently declared, "with gridlock in Washington, lobbyists turn to statehouses."[40] State lawmakers have taken note as well. Complaining about inaction by the Republican-controlled Congress on internet sales, a Republican state senator from South Dakota justified her legislature's action on the issue by saying, "Since Congress has once again failed, it falls to us to fill that void."[41] A Republican state representative from Indiana expressed similar concerns in regard to regulating e-cigarettes: "The FDA is not addressing it, and I don't think the state of Indiana should sit on its heels and wait for the federal government."[42]

"Meanwhile," says Bill Bishop, "in states and cities where the Big Sort has resulted in increasingly larger majorities, there has been an explosion of innovation and legislation. Federal leadership has been replaced by a wild display of federalism, as like-minded communities put their beliefs into law."[43] Some states, notably Kansas and North Carolina, have adopted conservative policies, while others such as California have moved to a liberal agenda.

We are likely to see further divergences in state policies, as some states increasingly fall under one political party's control. For the past decade we have more states with unified control of government (that is, the governor, the state senate, and the state house all controlled by the same party) than at any time since 1962. After the 2014 election, the number of unified state governments declined from a historical high of thirty-eight to twenty-nine (thirty if we were to count Nebraska, which is officially nonpartisan but in practice

TABLE 1.2

Top Five, Bottom Five, and Median States, Selected Demographic and Socioeconomic Variables

Rank	Population 2015 (millions)	Gross State Product, 2015 (in millions $)	Per Capita Income 2015 (thousands $)	Percent Hispanic 2013	Percent Black 2014	Percent Weekly Church Attendance 2014	Percent College Degree	Percent Under 18 Years Old 2013
1	CA	CA	CT	NM	MS	UT	MA	UT
	39.1	2,424,033	66.9	47.3	38	51	38.1	30.9
2	TX	TX	MA	CA	LA	MS	CO	TX
	27.4	1,648,007	61.0	38.4	33	47	35.6	26.6
3	FL	NY	NJ	TX	GA	AL	CT	ID
	20.2	1,444,406	59.8	38.4	33	46	35.6	26.5
4	NY	FL	NY	AZ	MD	LA	MD	AK
	19.8	883,735	57.7	30.3	32	46	35.2	25.6
5	IL	IL	MD	NV	SC	AR	NJ	KS
	12.9	764,817	56.1	27.5	29	45	34.4	25.0
MEDIAN	LA, KY	OR, AL	IA, SD	NC, DE	KY	IA, MI	NC, PA	AL, MO
	4.5	225,661	45.0	8.8	9	32	26.2	23.0

46	SD	0.8	ND	53,686	NM	38.4	MS	2.9	ME	3	WA,OR	24	LA	20.3	WV	20.6
47	ND	0.7	MT	45,799	SC	38.0	ND	2.9	WY	2	MA	22	KY	19.7	NH	20.5
48	AK	0.7	SD	45,415	ID	37.5	VT	1.7	VT	2	ME	20	MS	19.4	RI	20.4
49	VT	0.6	WY	40,170	WV	37.0	ME	1.4	ID	1	NH	20	AR	18.8	ME	19.7
50	WY	0.6	VT	29,750	MS	35.4	WV	1.4	MT	1	VT	17	WV	17.1	VT	19.6

Sources:

1. Population and per capita income are Census Bureau 2015 estimates.
2. Gross State Data from U.S. Department of Commerce, Bureau of Economic Analysis, http://www.bea.gov/iTable/drilldown.cfm?.
3. Data for black population based on U.S. Census Bureau estimates for 2014 found at http://blackdemographics.com/population/black-state-population/.
4. Data for Hispanic population from "United States–Hispanic or Latino Origin Population Percentages 2013 By State" at www.indexmundi.com.
5. Percent weekly church attendance data from 2014 Gallup Poll and *Washington Post* at https://www.washingtonpost.com/blogs/govbeat/wp/2015/02/18/map-the-most-religious-states-in-america/.
6. Percent college degrees at www.census.gov/compendia/statab/rankings.html.
7. Percent under eighteen from U.S. Census Bureau population estimates, found at http://www.indexmundi.com/facts/united-states/quick-facts/all-states/percent-of-population-under-18#chart.

is a unified Republican government). After the 2016 election, the number of unified states was thirty, well over half of the states. Figure 1.1 shows these trends since 1960.

In 1960, 63 percent of the states operated under unified government; in 1962 the figure reached 65 percent (thirty-two states). But over the next forty years there was a steady decline in the number of states with unified government, as southern states and some northeastern states began the slow process of partisan realignment. Fewer than half of the states experienced unified government in any given electoral cycle between 1984 and 2006. In other words, divided government became the norm. On several occasions between 1986 and 1996, over 60 percent of the states had divided government. Starting around 2006, however, a new and dramatic trend occurs. There is a clear increase in the percentage of states with unified government.

And it is not simply that states are now more apt to have unified governments. In many states the majority party enjoys unchallenged dominance. After the 2016 elections, Democrats, for example, controlled over 80 percent of the state legislative seats in Hawaii and Rhode Island, while the Republicans held at least 80 percent of the seats in each chamber in Idaho and Wyoming. The proportion of legislative chambers in which one party dominates (defined here as holding at least two-thirds of the chamber seats) is very high today. Although party competition can still be found in some states, many clearly tilt heavily in one party's favor. Given that Republicans dominate in some states while the Democrats are in clear control in others, we can expect

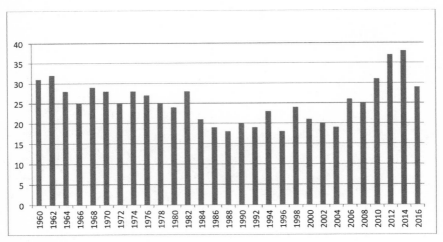

FIGURE 1.1
Number of States with Unified Government

contrasting approaches to governance to emerge. And that is exactly what we have seen in the past few years.

The Federal Government and the Future

There is little doubt that the federal budget will be under considerable pressure for the foreseeable future. The federal debt to national economic output (GDP) ratio has fluctuated considerably over the past seventy years, but it has grown since 2000. As the baby boom generation retires, federal budget obligations to social insurance programs like Medicare and Social Security mean that in the absence of substantial changes to those programs the debt will increase, putting greater pressure on the federal budget. One of the implications for the states is that they almost certainly will see a decline in federal aid to programs outside of health care. As a long-time National Governors' Association official noted, there will "have to be significant cuts in grants to state and local governments over the next decade."[44] In other words, in the future states are likely to have to deal with more problems using only their own resources. This is not going to be a painless transition. One option for state policymakers will be to increase taxes—almost never a popular option among the voting public. Another choice will be to cut back or completely eliminate some programs. In some cases this means eliminating programs relied on heavily by the poor and most vulnerable segments of society, another option that the public usually resists. A third alternative will be for states to try innovative—some might say "radical"—solutions by drastically changing the way that services are provided and the manner in which costs are borne. Major changes to education, corrections, welfare, and transportation can be expected. For the American states, the next decade will be a time of significant changes. Those changes will probably not look the same from one state to another. But it should be pointed out that change is nothing new to the states.

A Need for Citizen Awareness

Sometimes state governments fail their citizens. Ask the people of Flint, Michigan, who learned in late 2015 that their water was tainted. To be fair, it appears that all levels of government—local, state, and federal—had a hand in the tragedy that resulted in over six thousand children being exposed to lead poisoning due to a severely contaminated water supply.

But the role of Michigan state officials is central to the story. Under state authority, the governor had appointed an emergency manager of Flint who then authorized the switch in the municipal water source that resulted in the contamination problem. Complaints from Flint residents and warnings from a Flint pediatrician and a Virginia Tech civil engineer who tested the water went unheeded by city and state officials. Ultimately, several managers in the Michigan Department of Environmental Quality resigned or were dismissed. The governor issued apologies for the state's role in creating this crisis. Petitions to recall the governor circulated.

State governments make important decisions that affect their citizens. Sometimes their actions—or inactions—can have serious long-term consequences. It is essential that citizens pay attention to what their state officials are doing and act to hold those officials accountable. Unfortunately, accountability appears to be waning. For example, about 40 percent of state legislators do not face competition in the general election. And even if there is an opposing candidate, only a small percentage of races are truly competitive. Furthermore, voters in such elections appear to be remarkably ill-informed. Research by Steven Rogers shows that less than half of citizens know which party controls their state legislature. He also finds that voters appear to choose state legislative candidates not on the basis of state or local issues but on the basis of their reaction to the president's performance.[45] Other researchers have confirmed these findings.[46] If state legislators are being held accountable for anything at all, it is for things the national government did, not what they did at the state level.[47]

Part of our task in writing this book is to make the case that states matter as governing institutions. If we are convincing in this argument, perhaps the reader will recognize that we as citizens have an obligation to attend to those institutions and to hold them accountable.

In the remainder of this book we discuss some key areas in which states matter and ways in which changes have occurred. In chapter 2, we start at the beginning by discussing the adoption of the U.S. Constitution, the establishment of the federal system, and the continual tug between national and state influences on policymaking. We will also see how federalism has played out differently in other countries. While most of the discussion in chapter 2 concerns the interplay between national and state levels, we will also look at the relationship between state and local governments.

Chapter 3 examines how the basic structures of state government developed and makes the case for why these governments are important in specific policy arenas. While states are clearly constrained by the U.S. Constitution, U.S. Supreme Court decisions, and actions by the president, the Congress, and the federal agencies, there are plenty of areas in which states have authority to chart their own courses.

As mentioned earlier, states face major challenges in the immediate future. Much of the burden to meet these challenges falls on the institutions of state government—the executive, legislative, and judicial branches. Chapter 4 demonstrates how these instruments of state government, which were so inadequate sixty years ago, are much better prepared to take on increased responsibilities today. The overall capacity of the states to govern effectively is much greater today than two generations ago.

In chapter 5 we make the case that states are significant policymakers in many functional areas. For example, state governments make most of the relevant decisions about publicly funded schools, at both the K–12 level and higher education. Often states are out in front of the national government in developing innovative, imaginative solutions to public problems. In some cases, they are far out in front of the national government. And in many instances, the variation in public policy from one state to another is real.

One of the ways that states matter most is in the electoral arena. Unfortunately, this is not often appreciated by the general public, except when incredibly close contests expose the reality. Chapter 6 provides an explanation of the critical role states play in national electoral politics. We also discuss the various instruments of direct democracy that play a critical role in some state policymaking but which are nonexistent at the national level. Some of the innovative policies discussed in chapter 5 are driven by the referendum and initiative processes that exist in many states.

Some of the most important and least understood aspects of state governments are their fiscal systems. It is a complicated topic, but one that is critical for students and citizens of the states to grasp. In chapter 7, we tackle this crucial topic. It is especially important today because federal budget difficulties will continue to have significant effects on state fiscal policies. Finally, in chapter 8, we conclude with an assessment of how the world of state government and politics is changing and why states will remain important for the foreseeable future—that is, why states matter.

Notes

1. National Conference of State Legislatures, "Cellular Phone Use and Texting While Driving Laws." www.ncsl.org/research/transportation/cellular-phone-use-texting-while-driving-laws.aspx.

2. Monica Davey, "Twinned Cities Now Following Different Paths," *New York Times*, January 12, 2014, http:www.nytimes.com/2014/01/13/us/twinned-cities-now-following-different-paths.html? r=0.

3. Lawrence R. Jacobs referred to them as "cousins" in "Right vs. Left in the Midwest," a Sunday Opinion piece in the *New York Times*, November 23, 2013, http://www.nytimes.com/2013/11/24/opinion/sunday/right-vs-left-in-the-midwest.html?_r=0. Roger Feldman called them "two peas in a pod" in an opinion piece

called "Minnesota and Wisconsin: How Did Two Peas in a Pod Grow Apart?" in the Minneapolis *Star Tribune* on March 7, 2015, http://www.startribune.com/minnesota -and-wisconsin-how-did-two-peas-in-a-pod-grow-apart/295426901/.

4. Jacobs, "Right vs. Left in the Midwest."

5. We are not the first to point out the policy differences affecting the citizens of these two cities. See James Gimpel and Jason E. Schuknect, *Patchwork Nation* (Ann Arbor: University of Michigan Press, 2004), 7.

6. Reid Wilson, "Taxes, Marijuana, Legislatures at Stake in November," *Morning Consult*, October 11, 2015, http://morningconsult.com/2015/10/taxes-marijuana -legislatures-at-stake-in-november/. The quote is from Matt Walter, President of the Republican State Leadership Committee.

7. Richard Gonzales, "States Step Up As Washington Stalls on Immigration," *National Public Radio*, February 16, 2010, http://www.npr.org/sections/thetwo way/2016/02/16/466989955/states-step-up-as-washington-stalls-on-immigration. Also see Robert McCartney, "How States and Localities Are Filling the Gaps Left by Washington's Gridlock," *Washington Post*, September 26, 2015, https://www .washingtonpost.com/local/how-states-and-localities-are-filling-the-gaps-left-by -washingtons-gridlock/2015/09/26/e43c5b58-63b8-11e5-b38e-06883aacba64_story. html.

8. John Dinan, "Relations Between State and National Governments," in *The Oxford Handbook of State and Local Government*, ed. Donald Haider-Markel (New York: Oxford University Press, 2014), 17.

9. The 1790 Pennsylvania Constitution actually required free public education for those who could not afford it on their own, but legislation creating such public schools did not pass for some years.

10. U.S. Census Bureau, "1790 Fast Facts," http://www.census.gov/history/www .through_the_decades/fast_facts/1.

11. "Biggest US Cities By Population," http://www.google.com/url?sa=t&rct=j& q=&esrc=s&source=web&cd=8&ved=0CE8QFjAH&url=http%3A%2F%2Fwww.big gestuscities.com%2F&ei=Shd7UK7uCObtigLos4HwDQ&usg=AFQjCNHxmog_dU 1pRYE146_KMD_KN3C-Ng.

12. Martha Derthick, *Keeping the Compound Republic: Essays on American Federalism* (Washington, DC: Brookings Institution Press, 2001), 3.

13. Derthick, *Keeping the Compound Republic*, 3.

14. The quote is from Daniel Webster, as cited in Samuel Beer, *To Make a Nation: The Rediscovery of American Federalism* (Cambridge, MA: The Belknap Press of Harvard University Press, 1993), 12.

15. For a thoughtful summary of these events and the changes they wrought, see Martha Derthick, "Federalism," in *Understanding America*, ed. Peter H. Schuck and James Q. Wilson (New York: PublicAffairs, 2008), 121–45.

16. Robert Allen, ed., *Our Sovereign State* (New York: Vanguard Press, 1949), xxix.

17. See James T. Patterson, *The New Deal: Federalism in Transition* (Princeton, NJ: Princeton University Press, 1969).

18. Terry Sanford, *Storm Over the States* (New York: McGraw-Hill, 1967), 21.

19. Robert Allen, "The Shame of the States," in *Our Sovereign State*, ed. Robert S. Allen (New York: Vanguard Press, 1949), i.

20. Allen, "The Shame of the States," iii.

21. Jon C. Teaford, *The Rise of the States* (Baltimore, MD: Johns Hopkins University Press, 2002), 2.

22. See Teaford, *The Rise of the States*.

23. Alan Rosenthal, *Heavy Lifting: The Job of the American Legislature* (Washington, DC: CQ Press, 2004), 7–8.

24. Peverill Squire, *The Evolution of American Legislatures: Colonies, Territories and States, 1619–2009* (Ann Arbor: University of Michigan Press, 2012), chap. 7.

25. The Pew Research Center, "Growing Gap in favorable Views of Federal, State Government," April 26, 2012, http://www.people-press.org/2012/04/26/growing -gap-in-favorable-views-of-federal-state-governments/. See also Gallup, "Trust in Government, September 2012," October 19, 2012, http://www.gallup.com/poll/5392/ trust-government.aspx.

26. Pew Research Center, "Public Trust in Government, 1958–2014," http://www. people-press.org/2014/11/13/public-trust-in-government/.

27. This varies by state, of course. A recent Gallup poll indicated that only 25 percent of Illinois respondents were confident in their state government, while 81 percent of North Dakotans were confident in their state government. See Jeffrey M. Jones, "Illinois Residents Least Confident in Their State Government," *Gallup Daily Tracking*, February 17, 2016, http://www.gallup.com/poll/189281/illinois-residents -least-confident-state-government.aspx?version=print.

28. Justin McCarthy, "Majority in U.S. Prefer State Over Federal Government Power," July 11, 2016, http://www.gallup.com/poll/193595/majority-prefer-state -federal-government-power.aspx?version=print.

29. Andrew Gelman, David Park, Boris Shor, Joseph Bafumi, and Jeronimo Cortina, *Red State, Blue State, Rich State, Poor State* (Princeton, NJ: Princeton University Press, 2008), 21–22.

30. This point is often made in the context of the growing polarization in the United States. See, for example, Alan Abramowitz, *The Disappearing Center* (New Haven, CT: Yale University Press, 2010).

31. Bill Bishop, *The Big Sort: Why the Clustering of Like-Minded Americans Is Tearing Us Apart* (New York: Mariner, 2009). A good discussion of the evidence, pro and con, of sorting can be found in Steven Schier and Todd Eberly, *Polarized: The Rise of Ideology in American Politics* (Lanham: Rowman & Littlefield, 2016), esp. 47–62.

32. Gimple and Schuknecht, *Patchwork Nation*, 9.

33. Harry Enten and Nate Silver, "Migration Isn't Turning Red States Blue," August 29, 2014, http://fivethirtyeight.com/features/immigration-isnt-turning-red -states-blue/.

34. Gerald Wright and Nathaniel Birkhead, "The Macro Sort of the State Electorates," *Political Research Quarterly* 67 (2014): 436.

35. Daniel Elazar, *American Federalism: A View from the States* (New York: Thomas Crowell Co., 1966), 6.

36. Gross state product is from the Department of Commerce, Bureau of Economic Analysis, http://www.bea.gov/newsreleases/regional/gdp_state/gsp_newsrelease.htm. Gross National Product is taken from the World Bank, http://databank.worldbank .org/data/download/GDP.pdf. See also http://www.newsweek.com/economic-out put-if-states-were-countries-california-would-be-france-467614.

37. Frank Newport, "State of the States: Importance of Religion," October 20, 2012, http://www.gallup.com/poll/114022/state-states-importance-religion.aspx.

38. Michael S. Lewis-Beck and Peverill Squire, "Iowa: The Most Representative State?" *PS: Political Science and Politics* 42 (2009): 39–44.

39. For a description of the three ideal types of state political culture, see Elazar, *American Federalism*.

40. Dante Chinni, "With Gridlock in Washington, Lobbyists Turn to Statehouses," *Wall Street Journal*, January 14, 2016.

41. Richard Rubin, "States Set Up Fight Over Web Sales Tax," *Wall Street Journal*, February 24, 2016.

42. Tripp Mickle, "States Dash to Regulate E-Cigarettes," *Wall Street Journal*, January 31–February 1, 2015.

43. Bill Bishop, *The Big Sort*, 222.

44. Raymond Scheppach, "The Intergovernmental Grant System," in *The Oxford Handbook of State and Local Government Finance*, ed. Robert Ebel and John Petersen (New York: Oxford University Press, 2012), 955. See also Rudolph Penner, "Fiscal Austerity and the Future of Federalism," in the same volume.

45. Steven Michael Rogers, "Accountability in a Federal System" (PhD dissertation, Princeton University, 2013).

46. Carl E. Klarner and Heather Evans, "The Polarization and Nationalization of State Elections, 1971–2014," unpublished manuscript.

47. Seth Masket, "Why We're Not Holding State Legislators Accountable," *Pacific Standard*, September 2, 2014, http://www.psmag.com/politics-and-law/voting-accountability-state-legislators-politics-election-89974.

2

States and the Federal System

States matter because

- They are an essential part of the federal system
- They still have primary responsibility for policymaking in many issue areas
- They employ more government workers than the national government
- They have authority to define the nature of local government operations
- Citizens look to the states when there is stalemate at the national level
- Efforts to address the federal deficit will put a greater burden on the states

Introduction

IN THE SPRING OF 2016 IN NORTH CAROLINA, a skirmish broke out between city, state, and national government over "the bathroom bill." It is a story that touches several of the important themes of this book, including the relationship between local and state governments, the tension inherent in federalism, and the polarizing effect of many issues in today's politically charged environment.

The story began on February 22, when hundreds of citizens showed up to a Charlotte city council meeting. On the agenda was a proposed change to the city's existing nondiscrimination ordinance; the change would extend protections against discrimination to lesbian, gay, bisexual, and transgender (LGBT) individuals. Included in the protections would be a specific stipulation that a transgender individual had the right to use the bathroom of the sex with which they identified, not necessarily the sex to which they were assigned at birth. While there were a variety of protections provided in the proposed amendment, it was this particular policy aspect that drew the most attention—so much so that the ordinance (and subsequent legislative reaction) became known as "the bathroom bill."

As reported in the state's largest newspaper, "After more than three hours of impassioned public comment . . . Charlotte City Council approved new legal protections for gay, lesbian and transgender people—a decision that will likely provoke a battle with the General Assembly, which could nullify the city's historic vote."[1] Indeed, within a matter of weeks the North Carolina state legislature (officially known as the General Assembly) acted. As one newspaper account held, "In a one-day specially convened session Wednesday, North Carolina's legislature passed a sweeping law that reverses a Charlotte ordinance . . . [and] also nullified local ordinances around the state that would have expanded protections for the LGBT community."[2] The bill was designated as House Bill 2 (HB2) and was signed by the governor almost immediately after its passage by the legislature on March 23. Essentially, HB2 reaffirmed the statewide definition of classes of people who are protected from discrimination. That definition does not include sexual orientation. The state law prevents local governments from establishing their own, more inclusive standards. In other words, the state of North Carolina not only nullified the actions of the City of Charlotte, it prohibited all local governments in North Carolina from passing similar ordinances.

On May 4, the national government intervened, with the U.S. Justice Department announcing that it considered HB2 a violation of the 1964 Civil Rights Act. The Justice Department informed North Carolina governor Pat McCrory that unless the law was rescinded North Carolina stood to lose millions—perhaps hundreds of millions—of dollars in federal funding.[3] Four days later, the governor sued the U.S. Justice Department, arguing that the federal agency had exceeded its authority because the U.S. Congress had never passed a law extending civil rights protections to transgender individuals.[4] "It's the federal government being a bully," exclaimed Governor McCrory. The U.S. Justice Department responded that same day with a countersuit, saying the North Carolina law required "public agencies to follow a facially discriminatory policy."[5] Several days later, the U.S. Departments of Justice and Education sent letters to public school districts in all fifty states arguing that transgendered individuals were protected under the federal 1964 Civil Rights Act and providing guidance on how to implement these protections as they apply to public school bathrooms. By May, eleven states had filed legal briefs in support of North Carolina's challenge to the national government.[6]

This story highlights several features of today's domestic policymaking environment in the United States. First, it demonstrates the tension that often exists between local governments and state governments. This strain is especially apparent between large cities, which are often progressive in social policy, and state legislatures, which are often more conservative. One thing that is clear, however, is that the state does indeed have the legal authority to void local government rules, as HB2 does, *unless that action by the state itself violates federal law.* In other words, while there are often political disagreements between city and state, the tension is almost always resolved in favor of the state. Local governments are created by the state and are therefore subject to the authority of the state. In the last few years, we have seen numerous instances of the tension between local ordinances and state law; indeed, we have seen many cases in which state legislatures voided the actions of local governments—especially cities. To cite just one example for now: On Earth Day 2014, the small town of Bisbee, Arizona, passed a local ordinance banning plastic shopping bags from retail stores. When it became evident that other cities, including Tucson, were looking at passing similar ordinances, the Arizona state legislature intervened and passed a law in 2015 prohibiting local governments from enacting plastic bag bans. Many such examples exist across numerous states and policy areas, and we will return to this tension between local communities and the states later in this chapter.

A second feature is that contemporary policymaking in the United States is often intertwined with partisan and ideological considerations. With a Democratic administration at the national level and a Republican state government (the governorship and both chambers of the North Carolina General Assembly were held by Republicans during this period), and with state and national elections to occur in 2016, the issue was quickly politicized.

Finally, the issue became defined as a federalism matter. The state of North Carolina asserted that it had the right to determine whether LGBT individuals should be a protected class, while the national government, through the U.S. Department of Justice, claimed that the federal Civil Rights Act is the prevailing authority, arguing that HB2 violates federal law and should not stand. This is far from the only instance in which a state or states have confronted the national government lately. Recent headlines such as "States Rise Up Against Washington," "In States, a Legislative Rush to Nullify Federal Gun

Laws," and "Minnesota Lawmakers Resist Federal Security Requirements" are in the news more and more.[7] On matters of gun control, federal land ownership, health care policy, same-sex marriage, immigration, internet sales tax, and many other issues, states—at least some states—are increasingly assertive. As a legal scholar has aptly observed, "Federalism today is front-page news."[8]

A vivid illustration is the reaction of some state governments to the passage of the Patient Protection and Affordable Care Act (PPACA, also known as the ACA, or "Obamacare"), passed by Congress in 2010. Idaho is a case in point. In 2011, the state legislature passed House Bill 117, which stated,

> The Legislature of the state of Idaho, therefore, on behalf of the citizens of this state and to secure the blessings of liberty, hereby asserts its legitimate authority to interpose between said citizens and the federal government, when it has exceeded its constitutional authority and declares that the state shall not participate in and considers void and of no effect the PPACA.[9]

Supporters of the Idaho bill contended that states have the authority to nullify laws passed by the national government. This argument for "interposition and nullification" has been around since the adoption of the U.S. Constitution. It is, in effect, an interpretation of federalism that gives primacy to states' rights. While the U.S. Supreme Court has never accepted the "nullification" doctrine, the phrase is resurrected from time to time. In 2011 and 2012, it was in the news often, as "Obamacare" nullification bills were introduced in more than a dozen state legislatures. Attorneys General in twenty-six states filed a lawsuit challenging the law and three governors vowed to block its implementation in their states.[10] Eventually the U.S. Supreme Court upheld the core component of the law, affirming that the national government did indeed have the authority to enforce the new health care law.[11] But the Court struck down the federal mandate that the states must extend Medicaid health care insurance to their citizens to continue receiving Medicaid funds. As of June 2016, nineteen states had declined to set up their own state programs, constituting a milder form of resistance.

The "Endless Argument"

One cannot talk about the role of the states without talking about federalism. Federalism is defined as "a political system in which power and authority are divided between two or more levels of government."[12] That is a pretty imprecise definition because federalism is a pretty imprecise arrangement. What does it mean to say "authority is divided between levels of government?" Divided in what proportion to which level: 50/50, 80/20, 20/80? Is authority divided differently for different policy areas, so that the division is different on transportation policy compared to welfare policy? These and similar questions have been around since the debates over the drafting and adoption of the U.S. Constitution. And here is the key point: the questions are never resolved. As John Donahue wrote in *Disunited States*, "The Framers at Philadelphia launched not only a nation, but an appropriately endless argument over the proper balance between federal and state authority—an argument whose intensity ebbs and flows and whose content evolves, but which is never really settled."[13]

Federalism is always a complicated arrangement. It is further muddled in the United States because the division or sharing of power involves fifty subnational (regional) units. Whether they are called states, provinces, cantons, or *länder* (the German word for "lands," in this case meaning states), no other federal system in the world has as many regional units as the United States. Australia has but six; Canada ten. There are thirteen states in Malaysia, while Germany has sixteen, Brazil has twenty-six, and India has twenty-nine.[14] The only countries besides the United States with more than thirty regional governments are Mexico (thirty-one) and Nigeria (thirty-six).

Given the complexity of federal systems, it is no surprise that relatively few countries adopt this arrangement. There are some two hundred sovereign nations in the world today and only about twenty-five of them have a federal system. Federal systems are relatively common among countries with a large geographic size (for example, Argentina, Australia, Canada, Brazil, India, the United States) or with a large population (for example, Brazil, Germany, India, Mexico, Nigeria, Pakistan, the United States). Federal systems are found in six of the eight geographically largest and five of the eight most populous countries. The ways that these federal systems operate differ from one another depending on a whole host of variables including size, ethnic and racial diversity, history, and economy. And some are very new and not necessarily stable federations at this point.

One recent study maintains that if we impose some conditions such as stability and the presence of truly democratic elections, the number of functioning federal systems is only eleven.[15] Federal systems are difficult to maintain because of the chronic tension between the central (national-level) government and the peripheral (state, regional, provincial) governments. As one federal systems scholar puts it, "Characteristic of federal systems is the simultaneous existence of powerful motives for constituent units to be united (for certain shared purposes) and their deep-rooted desires for self-government (for other purposes)."[16] To put it another way, there are both centrifugal (pulling away from the center) and centripetal (pulling toward the center) tendencies. Such propensities vary across federal systems and over time or by policy area within a particular federal system.

While there are now about twenty-five federal systems worldwide, most emerged only after World War II. According to one authority, there were only four countries with true federal systems of government prior to the twentieth century.[17] The oldest continuous federal system in the world is the United States; inaugurated in 1789, it celebrated its 225th anniversary in 2014. But the federal system in the United States today hardly looks like the federal system of 1789. Of course, the United States itself hardly looks like the country of two centuries ago, as table 2.1 makes clear. We have evolved from a small, rural, and agrarian nation of four million people and thirteen states to a sprawling, urban, and economically complex country with fifty states. The population is almost one hundred times greater; the number of states has quadrupled; the shift from rural to urban and now to suburban locations has been dramatic. The 1790 census indicated that almost 20 percent of the enumerated population was black (of which 8 percent were free and 92 percent were slaves). The remainder of the enumerated population was almost entirely of European descent.[18] American Indians were not included as a category in the first census, but probably numbered at least 600,000, mostly in the territory beyond the settled borders of the thirteen states.[19]

One quick measure of the magnitude of change is travel time. Consider, for example, a trip from one end of the original country to the other; basically that would have been from Boston to Savannah (note that Atlanta did not yet exist; it wasn't founded until 1837). Today, by air travel, it is about a two-hour flight between these two cities. In 1789, if a person owned a horse and chose to ride from Savannah to Boston, he could expect the journey to take at least three weeks, if the weather was decent and the roads were passable. The fastest mode of travel would have been by ship, and with luck could be accomplished in five or six days. It would also be quite expensive. Obviously, most people did not travel much at all. Each community, and certainly each state, was something of a world unto itself. This bears no resemblance at all to the world we know today.

Table 2.1 represents five eras in the United States. These roughly half-century intervals were characterized by significant constitutional changes. Indeed, all but six of the amendments to the U.S. Constitution occurred during the periods represented in table 2.1. The federal relationship has changed as well—a theme of much of the rest of this chapter.

The U.S. Constitution and the Roots of Federalism

Conflict and controversy are endemic to a federal system. Recall that under the Articles of Confederation the states were widely understood to be sover-

TABLE 2.1
The Evolution of a Federal System

Date	National Population	Percent rural population	Population of Largest Cities	Number of States	Constitutional Amendments
1790	4 million	95	33,181 (New York) 28,552 (Philadelphia)	13	1–10 (1791)
1860	31 million	80	813,559 (New York) 565,529 (Philadelphia)	33	13–15 (1865–1870)
1910	92 million	44	3 cities over 1 million*	46	16–19 (1913–1920)
1960	179 million	30	5 cities over 1 million**	50	23–26 (1960–1971)
2010	308 million	16	9 cities over 1 million***	50	None since 1992

*New York, Chicago, Philadelphia (in descending order of population)
**New York, Chicago, Los Angeles, Philadelphia, Detroit
***New York, Los Angeles, Chicago, Houston, Philadelphia, Phoenix, San Antonio, San Diego, Dallas
Source: U.S. Census Bureau, various tables.

eign and functionally independent of one another. The confederation was little more than a treaty among thirteen sovereign entities. But to say the states were sovereign does not necessarily mean they were effective or powerful. It was their ineffectiveness that led some to call for a formal meeting in Philadelphia to discuss ways to salvage the system. Nonetheless, giving up some portion of their state's sovereignty was not something most did willingly. Even with the serious problems the nation experienced under the Articles, there were many citizens and political elites in the states who did not want to relinquish any sovereign power to another, "higher" government.

At the Constitutional Convention there was controversy, disagreement, and different interpretations of the "proper" relationship between the national government and the states. And many of those disagreements and differences of interpretation have never been resolved. This is a core characteristic of American federalism.

The emphasis, quite understandably, in contemporary high school history and civics courses is on the debates, the various plans, and the compromises that resulted in the drafting of the Constitution. But we should remember that not all who participated in the Philadelphia convention agreed with those compromises. When it came time to affix their names to the document, three people in the room at Independence Hall refused to sign. All were notables in their day and are still known even in our time: George Mason and Edmund Randolph of Virginia and Elbridge Gerry of Massachusetts. At least four delegates left the convention in protest of the proceedings and nine others left early, claiming they were needed at home.

Another twenty-one individuals who were invited to attend declined to show up at all—including the entire Rhode Island delegation. Some were simply unable to attend, but others assuredly boycotted the convention because they were opposed to any effort to reduce the independence of the states. Patrick Henry was among those who was invited but refused to attend, later claiming he declined because "I smelt a rat."[20]

Controversy certainly did not end with the convention's adjournment. While some states, like Delaware, ratified the new form of government almost immediately, others took convincing. Recall that the mechanism for adoption of the new constitution was not the various state legislatures, but ratifying conventions to be held in each state. For our purpose, this is significant for two reasons. First, it was assumed that a number of state legislatures would be opposed to the new government because it clearly diminished the power of the states. And as the key decision-making units in the states under the Articles, the state legislatures would principally be diminished by the new system. Second, under the Articles, the state legislature was in effect the government of the state. In other words, the legislature represented the state as a sovereign entity. In contrast, the ratifying conventions could be thought of as representing the people of the state. For many, this is a crucial distinction.

From the outset, then, there was disagreement as to whether the Constitution was adopted by the people or by the states.[21] To reiterate, at core the question comes down to the nature of the ratification assemblies called in the various states to consider and act upon the newly proposed constitution. The Federalist argument was that the delegates to the various ratification assemblies represented the people of the various states, and thus it was the people—the citizens themselves—who chose to discard the government under the Articles of Confederation and to adopt a new government with a more robust national presence.

The Antifederalist argument was that the ratification assemblies represented the sovereign states, not the people directly. Because the states themselves were the sovereign units under the Articles, only the states had the authority to accept, reject, or modify the conditions of the proposed arrangement under the Constitution. In this view, the Constitution was a compact among sovereign states. And because a compact is little more than a voluntary association, any state that agrees to the compact has the right to disassociate when it feels the policies of the compact government—in this case the federal government—are not in the interests of the aggrieved state.

Thus the conflicting views over whether "the people" or "the sovereign states" are the true adopters of the Constitution and therefore of the new federal arrangement are at the heart of the "states' rights" argument and a key rationale in the argument for "interposition and nullification." Typical of this reasoning is the statement adopted by one state legislature in 1814, "Whenever the national compact is violated, and the citizens of this state are oppressed by cruel and unauthorized laws, this Legislature is bound to interpose its power, and wrest from the oppressor his victim."[22]

While we usually associate such a sentiment with the southern states, this quotation is from a report of the Massachusetts state legislature in reaction to an embargo placed on American ships by President James Madison. Similar expressions of the right to interposition (and nullification) can be found among other New England states over the embargo and over the efforts to draft state militia during the War of 1812. It is worth pointing out the irony here; these northern states were using the principles of interposition and nullification against the actions of Presidents Thomas Jefferson and James Madison—the authors of the original drafts of the Kentucky and Virginia Resolutions. By late 1814 the dissatisfaction with the embargo and the War of 1812 (1812–1815) led representatives of several New England states to meet to discuss their grievances. This was the Hartford Convention, which met in secret for several weeks during the winter of 1814–15. Most of the Hartford delegates were members of the Federalist Party, so it is surprising that both nullification and secession were apparently discussed.

Discussion of nullification usually begins with the Kentucky and Virginia Resolutions (1798–1799), drafted by Thomas Jefferson and James Madison, respectively. The state legislatures of Kentucky and Virginia, controlled by Antifederalists, adopted these statements in response to the Alien and Sedition Acts of 1798, which were passed into law by the Federalist Party–controlled U.S. Congress. These laws were viewed by many as a severe restriction on the right to free speech. Alarmed by what they considered the national government's unconstitutional usurpation of power, the Kentucky and Virginia state legislatures argued they had the authority—indeed, the duty—to resist the repressive tendencies of the national government on behalf of their state citizens. In other words, a state had the right to "intervene" between its citizens and the national government to protect the rights of its citizens. Kentucky further argued that it had the right to nullify the federal action, while the Virginia resolution did not go quite this far.[23] These sentiments express a thread that runs through the fabric of American history.

The words "interposition" and "nullification" appear in the public discourse surrounding the Kentucky and Virginia Resolutions (1798–1799); the New England resistance (c. 1805–1815); the "nullification crisis" of 1832 involving John C. Calhoun, South Carolina, and the congressional tariff laws; the period immediately prior to the Civil War; the desegregation and Civil Rights period (c. 1954–1965); and the reaction in some quarters recently to the Real ID Act of 2005 and the Affordable Care Act (2005–present).

Because the terms have reappeared in response to several issues recently, it is worth explaining the terms in their historical context. The terms "interposition" and "nullification" are often used interchangeably, but they do not have the same meaning. As used by Madison and others of his time, "interposition" meant a state should intervene on behalf of its citizens when the national government exceeded its constitutional authority. Basically, this was an oversight function, a calling of attention to an act or policy that deserved resistance or questioning. Moreover, "interposition" was viewed as a collective endeavor, something that several or many states would undertake, and together they might exert sufficient pressure to get the national government to reconsider or amend the policy in question. Within this context, then, interposition is a legitimate action; whether it is successful in getting the egregious act repealed is another matter. It is a procedure by which states can "converse" and perhaps bargain with the national government. Political scientist John Dinan speaks of the "various ways that states can 'talk back' to federal officials," which we think captures the spirit of interposition as conceived by Madison.[24]

Thus the Kentucky and Virginia Resolutions called upon other states to join them in resisting the congressional laws. But no other state did.

The act of voiding or rejecting the application of a congressional or presidential act or federal judicial decree within a specific state is "nullification." It is an act of defiance meant to nullify a national policy within the confines of a particular state. Nullification has been consistently rejected by the federal courts as unconstitutional.[25] This does not preclude the term from finding its way into public discourse. One 2015 news story claimed that more than two hundred bills were introduced in state legislatures "aiming to nullify regulations and laws coming out of Washington, D.C."[26]

The Evolution of American Federalism

While "interposition" and "nullification" are instruments that have been argued over since the Constitution's ratification, we should not lose sight of the fact they are remedial instruments designed to correct a perceived transgression on the part of the national government vis-à-vis the state governments. The period surrounding the Constitutional Convention and the ratification process demonstrate considerable resistance by Antifederalists because they feared what they saw as the centralizing tendencies in the document.[27]

A half-century ago, Cecelia Kenyon described the Antifederalists as "men of little faith." She was not referring to their religious attitudes but to the fact that they were, from the outset, distrustful of the constitutional arrangement and were unconvinced that under the new arrangement the states would be able to hold the national government in check. Their argument rested on "four great pillars of consolidation."[28] The four features of the Constitution that most concerned these defenders of the states were 1) the power of the national government to tax, 2) the power of the national government to raise and maintain a military force, 3) the necessary and proper clause at the end of Article I, Section 8, and 4) the national supremacy clause in Article VI. From the point of view of those who believed the states were the essential sovereigns and preferred it that way, their fears that the Constitution provided for national consolidation were both real and eventually realized.

For the most part, the centralization process has been slow and it is by no means complete. Some historical events were instrumental in redefining the relationship between the national and state governments: the Civil War and the Great Depression are the two most obvious. Many other events or trends contributed to the changing relationship over 225 years. A list would include, at a minimum, the following.

1. The Supreme Court's adoption of the implied powers doctrine in 1819

The Antifederalists' concern that the "necessary and proper" clause could be a vehicle for the expansion of the role of the national government seems prescient with the U.S. Supreme Court's 1819 decision in the case of *McCulloch v. Maryland*.[29] As Cecelia Kenyon noted, "This was a clause so sweeping in its possible implications . . . that the Antifederalists could see no logical limit to the powers of the central government."[30]

The issue in *McCulloch* involved the authority of the national government to establish a national bank.[31] Creation of such a bank is not one of the specific enumerated powers of the national government stipulated in Article I, Section 8 of the Constitution; some states therefore argued that the creation of banks was a state power and not a power held by the national government. Chief Justice John Marshall argued the "general government" (by which he means the national government) is a government of enumerated powers,

> But the question respecting the extent of the powers actually granted is perpetually arising, and will probably continue to arise so long as our system shall exist. In discussing these questions, the conflicting powers of the General and State Governments must be brought into view, and the supremacy of their respective laws, when they are in opposition, must be settled.[32]

Marshall went on to note that the enumerated powers are supported by a variety of actions and means that are not necessarily listed and, he noted, this is one of the ways in which the system established under the Constitution clearly differed from that under the Articles of Confederation.

> Among the enumerated powers, we do not find that of establishing a bank or creating a corporation. But there is no phrase in the instrument which, like the Articles of Confederation, excludes incidental or implied powers and which requires that everything granted shall be expressly and minutely described.[33]
>
> Let the end be legitimate, let it be within the scope of the Constitution, and all means which are appropriate, which are plainly adapted to that end, which are not prohibited, but consist with the letter and spirit of the Constitution, are Constitutional.[34]

The expansion of national powers through the implied powers doctrine did not occur on a grand scale immediately. But the precedent was established with *McCulloch* and this becomes critical almost a century later when one of the enumerated powers—the power to regulate interstate commerce—is broadly interpreted.

2. The Union victory in the Civil War and the passage of the Civil Rights Amendments

The victory of the Union over the Confederacy was essential to the maintenance of the federal system. Virtually by definition, a right to secede would reduce a federal system to a confederation. One immediate result of the Union victory was the nationalization of the rights of former slaves through the adoption of the Thirteenth, Fourteenth, and Fifteenth Amendments between 1865 and 1870. While these amendments were enforced during Reconstruction, the application of the Fourteenth and Fifteenth soon waned. By the end of the nineteenth century, a return to the "dual federalism" of the first half of the century was evident in such cases as *Plessy v. Ferguson* (1896) and *Williams v. Mississippi* (1898). Nonetheless they returned to prominence and became instrumental in redefining the federal relationship in the Civil Rights era of the mid-twentieth century. As one observer notes, "These amendments would become the instruments for a recasting of federal-state relations"[35]

3. The adoption of a broad interpretation of congressional authority to regulate interstate commerce

Since the close of the nineteenth century, one of the most important channels for the expansion of national power has been the interstate commerce clause. Article I, Section 8 of the Constitution says, in part, Congress has the power to regulate commerce "among the several states." Unlike many aspects of the Constitution, this particular power was not contested by Antifederalists.[36] Perhaps this was because they recognized the need for some regulation, given the disastrous situation under the Articles of Confederation.

The pivotal case for our purposes is *Wickard v. Filburn* (1942), in which the U.S. Supreme Court determined that economic activity that is not ostensibly interstate may nonetheless be regulated by Congress.[37] It marks the beginning of a period in which the Court gave free reign to congressional action in the name of regulating interstate commerce. Indeed, the Court found no limit to congressional authority to regulate via the interstate commerce clause until 1995.[38]

4. The adoption of the Sixteenth Amendment (1913) and the development of fiscal federalism

Earlier, we noted that Antifederalists were concerned about the centralizing effect of granting the national government the right to tax under Article I, Section 8 of the Constitution. Previously, under the Articles, the central government had no authority to tax. Many of the Framers, notably Alexander

Hamilton, recognized a need for the new national government to be able to raise revenue on its own.

Although some opponents of the Constitution feared granting the national government such authority, the fact is that the states (and their local governments) exercised most of the taxing authority until well into the twentieth century. With the passage of the Sixteenth Amendment, creating an annual federal income tax, the fiscal dynamics begin to change. In particular, the development of fiscal federalism on a significant scale was not possible until the national government had a substantial and steady source of revenue through the income tax. Later we will discuss fiscal federalism in more detail, but now it is enough to point out that federal grants-in-aid give the national government considerable leverage in the policymaking arena. Federal aid represents about 30 percent of the general revenue for all states combined. The dependence on such fiscal aid varies quite a bit by state, however, with some states relying much more on federal aid than others. About 40 percent of the total state budget comes from federal aid in Mississippi, Louisiana, and Tennessee, while only about 20 percent of the North Dakota, Hawaii, and Alaska budgets flow from the federal government.[39]

5. The adoption of the Seventeenth Amendment (1913) and direct primaries

In 2016, the Utah state legislature passed a resolution calling for the repeal of the Seventeenth Amendment.[40] Ratified at the height of the Progressive Reform era, this amendment mandates the direct popular election of U.S. senators. The Constitution originally stated (Article I, Section 3), "The Senate of the United States shall be composed of two Senators from each State, chosen by the Legislature thereof for six Years; and each Senator shall have one Vote." In the context of the role of the states in the new federal system, there are two important components to this provision. The first is that the states have an equal representation in the Senate. As Madison notes in *Federalist* 62, "The equal vote allowed to each State is at once a constitutional recognition of the portion of sovereignty remaining in the individual States, and an instrument for preserving that residuary sovereignty."[41]

The second point is the legislature of each state would select the U.S. senators. The Framers assumed this would ensure that the states had some influence over Congress because the senators would be accountable to their state legislatures. Once the Seventeenth Amendment was ratified and direct elections of senators were in effect, the power of state legislatures to control their senators was removed.[42] Some see this as being of "transcendent importance to federalism" because it marked the abandonment of one of the key constitutional protections for the states.[43]

But as William Riker noted, this power of the states over their senators was never as strong as some would believe. Central to this effort on the part of these legislatures to control their U.S. senators was the doctrine of instructions.[44] This doctrine held that the state legislatures could instruct their U.S. senators how to vote on important issues. As William Riker demonstrates, the doctrine of instructions was applied, off and on, for about 120 years, but was never entirely successful because there was no firm way to enforce sanctions against senators who ignored instructions. The ratification of the Seventeenth Amendment diminished what leverage states, through their state legislatures, held in the U.S. Senate, even if such leverage was never as strong as the Founders had anticipated it would be. The call to repeal the Seventeenth Amendment was especially popular when the "Tea Party" movement emerged within the Republican Party around 2010. One of the key supporting organizations, the American Legislative Exchange Council (ALEC), an organization that drafts and offers conservative "model legislation" to Republican state legislators, declined to support the effort to repeal; meanwhile, direct election of the U.S. senators remains popular among the general public.[45] So despite recent efforts, repeal of the amendment remains "quixotic."[46]

The Seventeenth Amendment was part of the agenda of the Progressive reform movement to weaken the state- and city-based political party organizations, which were seen as corrupt, undemocratic, and controlled by party bosses and machines. Another such reform was the direct primary, instituted in most states by 1915. Primary elections "stripped the parties of a critical source of power: control over nominations."[47] Control over who gets the party's nomination for the general election is an important power; if a small group or a single "boss" controls the nomination phase, they have the opportunity to influence the nominee's behavior once elected. The combined effect of direct primaries and the Seventeenth Amendment was to weaken the linkage between the state party organizations and members of Congress.

6. The Great Depression and the development of national social welfare policy

Prior to the 1930s the domestic policy reach of the national government was quite limited. Until that point in time, the activities of the national government and the state governments did not often intersect. The history of U.S. federalism up to the 1930s is often described as "dual federalism" in which the national government had primary authority over foreign affairs and some regulation of economic activity and state governments had primary authority in other policy arenas. This is a generalization and not entirely accurate, but it is not far from the reality of the way things operated. It ended markedly, however, with the crushing effects of the Great Depression.

For those who did not live through the Great Depression of the 1930s, it is difficult to imagine its harshness and the hardships it imposed. True, the recent "Great Recession" of 2007–2009 and its lingering effects for the next several years was a difficult time for citizens and governments. But the Great Depression was much worse. The stock market crash of October 1929 put the American economy into a years-long tailspin. Unemployment rates reached 25 percent (compared to under 10 percent in the recent recession) and the decline in the domestic economy (GDP) was –25 percent (compared to –3.3 percent in the recent recession). While fewer than one hundred banks failed in the recent recession, over nine thousand banks went under during the Great Depression. The point is that the Great Depression resulted in economic devastation and social disruption of greater magnitude than what we recently experienced. By 1931 and early 1932, state and local governments were struggling to cope. States were slashing their budgets; Illinois, Texas, and Vermont each cut their budgets by 25 percent; Arizona's was cut by an astounding 35 percent. Almost 20 percent of New Jersey's municipalities were bankrupt. Several southern states were on the verge of defaulting on their debts.[48] Officials in many states were timid and often shortsighted in their response to the crisis, as historian James Patterson describes, "Legislators . . . often compounded problems with factionalism, mindless criticism, and deadly doses of partisan politics. The result before 1933 was a sadly unproductive record."[49]

It is on this basis that we must understand the actions of the national government under Franklin Roosevelt. Martha Derthick sees this period as one that fundamentally changed the nature of federalism in the United States: "In response to a catastrophic economic collapse . . . [a] new constitutional law emerged after 1937 that swept away previous limits on Congress's power to regulate commerce and solidified its power to tax and spend for any purpose associated with the general welfare."[50] Patterson concurs: "The combination of national policy and depression forever transformed federal-state relations."[51]

7. The Civil Rights/Great Society Era (c. 1954–1968)

It is important to remember that it was just a bit more than fifty years ago, in 1963, that George Wallace, in his inaugural address as the newly elected governor of Alabama, said, "I draw the line in the dust and toss the gauntlet before the feet of tyranny and I say segregation now, segregation tomorrow, segregation forever."[52]

This period involved more than civil rights. But it was the drive to desegregate and expand the civil and voting rights of African Americans that led the national government into a more activist role in the domestic affairs of the states, unprecedented since Reconstruction. It is a period in which the Fourteenth and Fifteenth Amendments were rediscovered and reinvigorated. The *Brown v. Topeka Board of Education* (1954) school desegregation case, the use of federal troops by Presidents Eisenhower and Kennedy to enforce this court decision in southern cities such as Little Rock, Tuscaloosa, and Oxford, and the passage of landmark legislation such as the Civil Rights Act (1964) and the Voting Rights Act (1965) demonstrated a strong commitment by all branches of the national government to end the pernicious activities of both private citizens and public entities in the South.

The words "interposition" and "nullification" reappeared during this time, as politicians in several southern states invoked the right of the state to disregard the actions of the Supreme Court and the Congress.[53] Within two years of the U.S. Supreme Court's decision in *Brown*, eight southern states adopted resolutions invoking interposition and declaring the Court's ruling to have no standing within their specific state.[54]

Beyond the civil rights question, this period found the national government, driven by an activist Congress, developing preemptive policies. As Joseph Zimmerman notes, "A revolution in national-subnational relations commenced in 1965 when the Congress enacted the first minimum standards preemption statute—the Water Quality Act of 1965. . . . Minimum standards statutes regulate private and subnational governmental activities."[55] What this means is that the national government sets standards that all states must meet or exceed; otherwise, the national government will take over the administrative or regulatory control of that policy area from the state. This allows Congress—and the federal bureaucracy to which Congress often delegates power—major policy influence in areas previously left to the states.

This was also a period in which fiscal federalism increased at warp speed. During the decade of the 1960s federal aid tripled, and it continued to grow at a rapid rate in the following decade. It was not just the amount of money distributed to subnational governments but the expansion in functional areas for which the money was intended. In 1960 there were only 132 federal grant programs available to state or local governments. By 1968 there were 387 and by 1978 there were almost 500 separate and distinct grants.[56] The development of fiscal federalism as both a carrot and stick to facilitate state compliance with expanding national goals was a defining feature of this period.

At the center of this active period was the U.S. Supreme Court. Writing about its role, Derthick stated, "It emerged as a reformer, and the institutions it chose to change were those of state governments."[57] This is an intriguing statement because it points to the fact that many states were slow to change and adapt to a new political and social environment. Many states were poorly funded and ineffectively administered. As we show in chapters 3 and 4, the capacities of states today are substantially greater than they were in 1960.

The Court, focusing on issues of equality of rights for American citizens, rendered transformative decisions involving school segregation, criminal justice and the rights of the accused, public school prayer, and the "one person, one vote" definition of voting equality. When one looks at the totality of the national effort—the activist role of the U.S. Supreme Court and the efforts on the part of Congress and the president to end segregation, guarantee individual rights, and expand the reach of minimal national standards through statute and fiscal federalism—this period stands out as one in which the fundamental character of federalism in the United States changed more than any other period except the New Deal.

8. The new century

Toward the end of the twentieth century much was being written about a rolling back of the national government's influence—a devolution in the federal relationship. There were certainly some signs pointing in that direction, as indicated by a study published in 1986 by two political scientists titled "The Resurgence of the States."[58]

One of the distinguishing features of Ronald Reagan's presidency (1981–1989) was an effort to slow the growth of federal domestic spending. In part, this effort focused on reducing state and local reliance on federal aid. As a result, federal grants to state and local governments declined as a percentage of GDP and as a percentage of total federal spending and in inflation-adjusted dollars.[59]

The landmark agreement between the GOP Congress and President Bill Clinton that restructured a key component of social welfare policy and shifted more control to states was another such sign. Numerous decisions by the Rehnquist Court that signaled a rethinking of the unfettered use of the interstate commerce clause as a rationale for congressional policymaking in traditionally state arenas is another. The election of a Republican president, George W. Bush—a former governor—coupled with a Republican-controlled Congress, led many to expect an administration sympathetic to a state-oriented version of federalism.

Whatever devolutionary momentum existed was stopped by the events of September 11, 2001. In response to 9/11, President Bush and the Congress pushed for a strong antiterrorism role for the national government in domestic policy. The Patriot Act (2001) and the Real ID Act (2005) were centerpieces of this centralization effort. Additionally, President Bush successfully pushed a major educational reform effort, the No Child Left Behind Act (2001), which broadened national control over what has always been viewed as a state function—public education.[60]

The Great Recession weakened the states further and, as we discuss in chapter 7, led to a substantial increase in the reliance on federal financial assistance for several years. The main domestic policy of the first Obama administration, the Affordable Care Act, extended national policymaking over health insurance policy in dramatic ways. About half the states challenged the Congress' authority to establish an individual mandate to purchase health insurance. The Supreme Court's decision in this regard was much anticipated. The result, in a complex decision with multiple opinions, was a blow to state sovereign power in that the Court upheld the national government's authority to require such a mandate. The victory was not complete, however, as the Court also ruled that the national government did not have the power to force the states to expand Medicaid coverage, which was part of the health care act.

Beyond the health care issue, tension between the national government and the states remains high today. Much of it is a result of the ideological polarization that currently exists between the two major political parties. For most of the Obama administration, Congress was gridlocked, unable to reach policy agreements. Over the course of the Obama years, Republicans made great strides in winning state elections and thus gaining control of more and more state legislatures and governorships. Consequently, federalism became viewed as a contest between a Democratic president and Republican-controlled state governments. In this sense, as David Brian Robertson points out, we can think of "American federalism as a political weapon," to be wielded as a call for a national standards or states' rights, depending on the issue and the issue position of the various players. As Robertson notes, "The conflicts over federalism have fractured into many narrower issues even as the battlefield of federalism expanded into thousands of controversies over jobs, health care, race, education, environmental protection, immigration, abortion, gay marriage, energy, roads, taxes, and many more."[61]

To put it another way, the tensions inherent in federalism are even greater in times of political polarization, especially so when the forces of polarization have captured different levels of government. When the Republicans control the national government policy apparatus, states with Democratic regimes will resist the policy proposals they view as most egregious. And when the Democrats control the national level, Republican-controlled states will do the same. That is the nature of federalism in a highly politicized and polarized environment.

The Inherent Tensions with Federalism

The federal system created under the U.S. Constitution is remarkably complex. It fashions a complicated structure with distinct yet overlapping executive, legislative, and judicial powers and two levels of government, each with a claim to sovereignty, or at least partial sovereignty. The structure, as created in Philadelphia, was new to the world. And because it was new and unfamiliar, there was room for competing interpretations. This was true in 1789 and it remains true today. Martha Derthick, an astute analyst of the American form of federalism, noted, "It is, however, a very confusing form of government, with authority widely diffused and obscurely allocated. And it requires much tending. Issues of intergovernmental relations consume a great deal of official attention, including that of the Supreme Court."[62] And as we argue in chapter 6, it is a system that requires citizens to distinguish between the levels of government in elections—a requirement that some voters today seem to ignore.

Under the Constitution, the federation seeks to balance a number of values such as national interests and state interests, majority power and minority rights. Larry Gerston points out that two values our federal system constantly struggles to balance are liberty and equality.[63] Liberty is an expression of the freedom to pursue individual self-interest. It was a value emphasized by the Antifederalists, who feared the loss of liberty under a strong national government. Equality, or fairness, is a value best fostered by a central government that can guarantee uniformity of policy across the states. Finding the balance between these values is almost impossible; according to Gerston, "To the extent that government institutions promote liberty, the public policy rules are bound to differ from state to state. And to the extent that government institutions endorse equality, states are disallowed from behaving in ways unique to their individual existences. Therein lies a conundrum of American federalism."[64] The North Carolina "bathroom bill" discussed in the introduction to this chapter is a prime example of this conundrum.

Martha Derthick made a similar point, arguing that the primary tension is between "place-based groups" such as states and communities and the rights of individuals as guaranteed by the national constitution. She concluded that "one type of group—the place-based group that federalism had honored— yielded to groups otherwise defined, as by race, age, disability or orientation to an issue or cause."[65]

It also is, as David Walker noted, a "conflicted" system—one in which both centripetal and centrifugal forces may occur at once: "The system is conflicted insofar as it reflects simultaneously centralizing and decentralizing, cooperative and competitive, co-optive and more discretionary, and activist as well as retrenching tendencies."[66]

This is the case because the operation of federalism may be different in different policy areas at different times. Furthermore, it can be the case because different institutions may pull in different directions or be constrained in different ways during the same time period; for example, Congress and the bureaucracy may seek to expand control through fiscal federalism at a time when the Supreme Court may seek to limit the reach of the national government in certain domestic arenas. It can be the case because, while the general public professes to distrust and dislike the growth of the national government, that same public advocates for the expansion of specific programs funded and administered by the national government. It can also be the case because we focus so much on the formal measures of who is "winning" (the Supreme Court's rulings on federalism, the broadening of congressional statutory authority, the expansion of fiscal federalism) when there are more informal, less obvious trends at work. Relevant in this regard is the argument made by John Nugent that states have learned how to influence national policymakers.[67] In particular, state officials are involved in what Nugent calls "constructive engagement" with members of Congress and federal agencies over 1) the shape of future policy, 2) the conditions associated with federal grants, and 3) the amount and shape of administrative discretion given to the state agencies that often are the primary implementers of federal policies.

While some of this negotiation occurs in a series of single-state to national official interactions, a good deal of it occurs through associations of state officials. These associations essentially serve as interest groups on behalf of the states and their local governments. One group of such organizations is known as "The Big Seven" and is especially active and influential on behalf of state and local governments, with a substantial lobbying presence in Washington, DC. The Big Seven are the National Governors Association (NGA), the National Conference of State Legislatures (NCSL), the Council of State Governments (CSG), the U.S. Conference of Mayors (USCM), the National Association of Counties (NACo), the National League of Cities (NLC), and the International City/County Management Association (ICMA). Other groups representing various state officials and interests include the National Association of State Budget Officers (NASBO), the National Association of Attorneys General (NAAG), and the National Association of Secretaries of State (NASS). The activities of these organizations are often overlooked in discussions of federalism. Perhaps this is because they involve organized interest group activity and the policy discretion of administrative agencies, two developments not generally anticipated by the Founders (*Federalist* 10 notwithstanding).

Nugent further argues, and as we show in chapters 3 and 4, that state governments today are far more competent and sophisticated and have dramatically increased their capacity for effective governance. They have, in Nugent's terms, "developed a robust set of institutions to facilitate interstate cooperation and to strengthen their individual and collective hands in dealing with federal officials."[68] This is an important point often overlooked; the states today are not the states as they existed in the middle of the twentieth century.

Even when the national government is perceived to have won a struggle with the states over policymaking, the victory is not necessarily total. A good example is the decision in *NFIB v. Sebelius*, the 2012 Supreme Court decision on the constitutionality of the ACA (Obamacare). The Court upheld the national government's right to require that states enforce the congressional requirement that health insurance be mandated of all citizens, and this decision became the focus of virtually all media reports on the SCOTUS decision. But another provision of the ACA required states to expand Medicaid coverage by stipulating that states must accept people into the program who might not otherwise be eligible. These are the "working poor," those who make too much money to qualify for certain programs because their income is above the federal poverty line but who do not make enough money to easily afford health insurance. To ensure that states would comply, the national government threatened the loss of federal aid if a state balked. But the *NFIB* decision struck down this provision. States cannot be penalized if they choose not to expand Medicaid coverage to the working poor in their state. As *Governing* magazine observed, "That means states have a real choice about whether to participate."[69] Indeed, as of November 2016, nineteen states had chosen not to expand Medicaid coverage. With the election of Donald Trump and a Republican Congress, substantial changes to the law are likely, and we may see a wide variety of approaches taken by the states.

As we trace the historical events and eras that over more than 225 years have led to a more nation-centered federalism, we might despair of the states and their roles. But that would be a mistake. Without a doubt, the role of the national government has grown substantially. But in many respects, so too has the role of the states. It is tempting to think of the federal relationship as a zero-sum game; if the national government expands its power, the states must be losing power. But this assumes that the size of the game itself remains constant—that the sum of all national and state power is a constant. But it is not. Governments at all levels—national, state, and local—are a bigger part of the citizens' lives now than previously. They are certainly a much bigger part of life than any or all government was in 1789. How could it be otherwise in a society as large, complex, and technological as today's? Furthermore, as Joseph Zimmerman notes, while it is clear that the authority of the national government to make policy in the domestic arena has expanded dramatically, such authority is often enacted in such a way as to increase the implementation and regulatory authority of state governments.[70]

It is also the case that states can resist some initiatives of the national government by refusing to accept federal funds for such policies. For example, some states declined funds for "abstinence-only" sex education pressed by the administration of George W. Bush, while more recently others refused to accept hundreds of millions of dollars in federal grants for planning and construction of high-speed rails systems.[71]

Let us be clear on the message here: We are not saying that government *ought* to be as big a presence in citizens' lives as it is. We are certainly not saying that the federal system in the United States today *ought* to be as centralized as it has become. But we are saying that limited government in the way the Founders understood it—in a rural, agrarian society with a relatively small population and few technological advances beyond the printing press and rudimentary steam engines—is not feasible today.

It is also worth keeping in mind that, while the role of the national government in today's American federation is clearly central, it has not eliminated the need for the states. States retain significant policymaking power in most areas of domestic policy. Indeed, states are often ahead of the national government when it comes to innovation. As one analyst has pointed out, "State governments are usually first to act in response to new problems or issues, of which many arise in a time of rapid technological and cultural change."[72] Examples include immigration policies in a number of states, California's tougher auto-emissions standards enacted in the 1990s, and state laws addressing cybersecurity and opioid addiction. These are but a few areas in which the states have moved ahead, "otherwise taking over duties that Congress is too paralyzed to handle," as the *Washington Post* observed.[73]

The National Governors Association (NGA) conducts an annual "State of the States" address in Washington, DC. The NGA president in 2014 was Oklahoma governor Mary Fallin. She effectively summarized the current position of governors and other state officials when she said, "States are leading, and we encourage our federal partners to work more closely with us and to take note of and use the policy ideas coming from their state partners. Above all, please do not get in our way."[74]

Federalism Elsewhere

The United States is not the world's only federal system. As noted earlier, of the approximately two hundred sovereign nations in the world, about twenty-five have a federal system. By now it should be evident that there are many gradations of federalism, with some leaning toward a regional- or state-centered system and some more toward a nation-centered federalism. Because each is a product of the culture, history, and specific geographical, political, and economic conditions within a country, each federal system is unique. And even within a single country the federal relationship shifts over time, as we have demonstrated in this chapter.

Any comparison of federal systems leads to the conclusion that there are numerous ways in which the power is distributed between the center and the periphery. On the one hand, some federal systems (for example, Argentina, Spain, and South Africa) are clearly more centralized than the American federation. On the other hand, a few federations are less centralized and more oriented toward the peripheral, regional-level governments, with examples being Canada and Germany.

In Germany, the basis for a federal system was established after World War II and extended with the 1990 reunification of East and West Germany. As one textbook notes, "Its 16 states, or Länder, exercise a great deal of power, far more than states do in the United States. . . . The central government has exclusive authority over foreign affairs, money, immigration and telecommunications. But the Länder retain residual powers over all other matters."[75] This includes education, health and welfare, and civil and criminal law.

Canada is another federal system in which the balance between center and the periphery is tipped toward the latter. In Canada, it is the regions—the provinces—that enjoy substantial autonomy. Canada is arguably the most periphery-oriented federal system in the world. In part this is because of the mosaic cultures that characterize Canada. The bargain for keeping francophone Quebec in the system is substantial autonomy for provinces on many matters. This includes the fact that the provinces tax and spend at a higher rate than the federal government.[76] Moreover, there is a significant distribution of federal revenues to the provinces but without a heavy burden of national mandates attached to the funds.

The State and Local Relationship

Federalism focuses on the relationship between the national government and the states. By now it should be clear that it is a complex relationship, ever changing, inconsistent, and often variable by policy area. It is also clear that today's federalism is different from that of 1789, or even from the federalism of 1930 or 1960. Federalism—here meaning the political and constitutional arrangement between the national and state governments—is just one intergovernmental relationship involving the states. States must also interact with local governments. The difference is that, while states may claim some measure of sovereign authority vis-à-vis the national government—the federal and state governments each have constitutional standing—local governments can make no such claim. They are creatures of the state government—meaning they were created by the state and derive their powers from it. From a legal perspective, local governments in their various incarnations—counties, cities, special districts, school districts, townships, etc.—are entirely dependent on state governments for their policing, regulatory, and taxing authority.[77]

While the local governments are "creatures of the state," they are also "agents of the state" in that they carry out state powers at the local level.[78] They provide services authorized by the state and they regulate behavior as mandated by the state. Precisely how these activities are divided between the state and the local governments is highly variable. For example, in some states most of the welfare function is carried out at the local—usually county—level, while elsewhere it is centralized at the state level. One study found that the proportion of public services delivered by the state (rather than by the local governments) ranged from almost 80 percent (Vermont) to less than 40 percent (Nevada).[79]

Technically, then, the relationship between the state and its local governments is a unitary system, not a federal one. Local governments are not sovereign; they owe their claim to govern to a grant of authority, called a charter, from the state government. The charter stipulates what local governments can or cannot do and what they are required to do. Some states, either through the state constitution or legislative statute, determine the precise organizational structure that a county or municipality (city) must have. The degree of latitude offered to local governments by the state authority differs from one state to another and differs over time within each state. In some, local governments are permitted a fair amount of freedom to operate as they see fit (home rule). In others, the state—especially through the state legislature—places strict limits or constraints on the powers and the taxing authority of local governments. Sometimes this brings local governments—especially school districts and cities—into conflict with the state legislature. One particularly salient example is public school funding, a topic discussed in some detail in chapter 7.

Although states have the legal authority over local governments, it is the case that for at least the first half of this country's existence, local governments were where most of the "governing" occurred. Political scientist (and future U.S. president) Woodrow Wilson observed this fact in 1898.[80] It remained true into the early part of the next century: "At the turn of the twentieth century, local governments were raising more revenue, doing more spending, and had more debt than the federal and state governments *combined*."[81] The relevant point is that states are much more engaged in the activities of local governments today than they were one hundred years ago. In some ways, this is where the role of states has increased most dramatically. Because the focus so often is on the relationship between the states and the national government, the stronger role today of the states vis-à-vis their local governments is often overlooked. This is a powerful point once we recognize the pervasiveness of local governments; currently there are about 90,000 such units in the various states. There are almost 7,000 local governments in Illinois and more than 4,000 in Pennsylvania, Texas, and California.

This engagement of states in local government administration extends increasingly over time to funding. For decades the primary source of revenue for local governments was the property tax, a cumbersome revenue source that is stable but inefficient and unpopular. Consequently, states have shifted some of the local reliance on the property tax to other revenue instruments. These include local option sales taxes and user fees. It also includes state aid to local governments. This is especially true of local school districts, which receive over half their revenue from the state in many instances. Cities and counties also receive revenue transfers from the state. Just how much of the financial burden for local government is undertaken at the state level varies by state. Nonetheless, it is clearly the case that states are now far more actively involved in assisting local governments, as well as regulating local governments, than they were in the past.

Recently, a great deal has been written about the regulatory tension between some states and their local governments. As one intergovernmental relations text notes, "Because states have vast legal powers over local governments, a state may order its local units to do all sorts of things: regulate private activities, provide services, refrain from using some types of taxes, limit tax rates, utilize a particular personnel system—the possibilities are enormous."[82] The tension can be especially acute between state legislatures and the larger cities and more urban counties within the state. Currently, most state legislatures are in the hands of Republican majorities and therefore have conservative policy preferences. But many urban areas elect liberal officials who pursue a progressive political agenda, in part because cities tend to have a younger and better educated population compared to the rest of the state.[83] The potential for conflict is clear, and recent examples abound. Since 2012, for example, thirty-three cities and counties have passed legislation raising their minimum wage above the federal level.[84] When Birmingham, Alabama, adopted such a measure, the GOP-controlled state legislature passed a bill blocking any local government's power to raise its minimum wage. A Republican state representative conceded, "While we say we want local control of certain things, I don't believe the minimum wage is one of those. . . . No one ever envisioned that cities would do this."[85]

Such state measures are called "preemption laws" and they appear to be increasing in frequency. Recently we have seen state legislatures pass preemption laws to curb local governments (usually cities) from enacting plastic bag bans, firearms restrictions, paid sick leave mandates, and occupational licensing requirements. Some states have prevented local governments from banning or regulating Uber drivers or the use of e-cigarettes. In 2015, Oklahoma passed a bill that prevents local governments from barring hydraulic fracturing (fracking), and Texas did the same after the city of Denton passed an antifracking ordinance.

It is clear that states have the legal authority to pass such laws. But local government officials bristle at them. When Columbia, Missouri, contemplated banning plastic bags, the Republican-dominated legislature passed a bill blocking any such efforts. A Columbia city council member who had been a Republican candidate for the state house responded, "While I'm opposed to local governments, or anyone, banning useful products, I am even more opposed to our state representatives getting involved in our local issues."[86] Similar sentiments were expressed by local government officials in North Carolina in the wake of the "bathroom bill" controversy. The mayor of Greensboro complained, "It's frustrating when you have a legislature, who instead of taking care of their business, is sticking their nose in our business." A Republican legislator countered, "The state government is the government that's closest to the people. . . . If you don't like it, run for state government and try and change it."[87] For local governments and local government officials, state governments and state elected officials really do matter.

Conclusion

Early in this chapter we related the story of the resistance by some states to the controversial health care reform legislation passed by a Democrat-controlled Congress, at the Democratic president's urging, in 2010. Almost all the resistance was from Republican governors and Republican-controlled state legislatures. Partisanship and ideology are often part of the "endless argument" over federalism. In today's highly polarized political environment, federalism is often a political weapon and a rhetorical gambit. It is indeed an endless argument, a contest that is never entirely resolved, but a fight with real consequences for citizens.

It is clear that the role of the national government in domestic policymaking has grown substantially over the centuries. We have outlined a number of trends and events that led to the current configuration. While states have less power today relative to the national government, this does not mean that states are powerless—far from it. As David Brian Robertson notes, "Political opponents use federalism as a weapon because the states have enormous authority, because they use that authority in different ways, and because they produce different results."[88] In other words, states still matter and they matter in important ways. In many functional areas, states are energetic, imaginative, and primary policymakers, as we will demonstrate in chapter 5. The institutions of state government today are clearly more capable and competent than fifty years ago, as we will demonstrate in chapters 3 and 4.

Furthermore, while states may have less relative power compared to the national government, one can make a case that they have more absolute power than previously—certainly more so than in 1789. Everyday life was fundamentally different then, and the need for regulation and public services was minimal. In today's society of 320 million people, living in urban environments experiencing rapid technological and social change, government at all levels—including state governments—has a much larger role to play.

Moreover, because of the emphasis on the most visible institutions and most salient issues, we often underappreciate the ability of states to influence federal policies in a meaningful way. Much of this is done through bureaucratic channels.

Finally, we should note that increased concern over the national government's fiscal policies and the growth in the federal debt almost certainly will require a recalibration of the relationship between the national and state governments. As Alice Rivlin observes, "A thorough rethinking of fiscal federalism is in order. A clearer demarcation of responsibilities between the federal and state levels could improve efficiency, accountability, and performance at both levels."[89] Others have made similar calls for a rethinking of the roles of the national and state governments.[90]

The extent to which these prescriptions are honored or ignored remains to be seen. The next few years will be especially important in terms of the relative role of the states in the federal system. As we show in the following chapters, states are better prepared than ever, despite the growing challenges of governing in our federal system.

Notes

1. Steve Harrison, "Charlotte City Council Approves LGBT protections in 7–4 vote," *Charlotte Observer*, http://www.charlotteobserver.com/news/politics -government/article61786967.html.

2. Michael Gordon, Mark S. Price, and Katie Peralta, "Understanding HB2: North Carolina's Newest Law Solidifies State's Role in Defining Discrimination," *Charlotte Observer*, March 26, 2016, http://www.charlotteobserver.com/news/politics -government/article68401147.html.

3. Matt Zapotosky and Mark Berman, "Justice Dept. to North Carolina: Law Limiting Protections for LGBT People Violates Federal Law," *Washington Post*, May 4, 2016, https://www.washingtonpost.com/politics/justice-dept-to-north-carolina-law

-limiting-protections-for-lgbt-people-violates-federal-law/2016/05/04/c11fa75a
-1237-11e6-81b4-581a5c4c42df_story.html.

4. Alan Blinder, Richard Pérez-Peña, and Eric Lichtblau, "Countersuits over North Carolina's Bias Law," *New York Times*, May 9, 2016, http://www.nytimes.com/2016/05/10/us/north-carolina-governor-sues-justice-department-over-bias-law.html?_r=0.

5. Blinder, Pérez-Peña, and Lichtblau, "Countersuits over North Carolina's Bias Law."

6. Nolan McCaskill and Caitlin Emma, "11 States Sue Obama over Transgender Bathroom Directive," *Politico*, May 25, 2016, http://www.politico.com/story/2016/05/texas-lawsuit-obama-transgender-bathroom-223569.

7. *The Hill* (congressional newspaper), February 19, 2015, thehill.com/regulation/legislation/232255-states-rising-up-against-washington; *Washington Post*, August 29, 2014, https://www.washingtonpost.com/blogs/govbeat/wp/2014/09/20/in-states-a-legislative-rush-to-nullify-federal-gun-laws/; Carrie McDermott, "MN Lawmakers Resist Federal Security Requirements," Wahpeton, North Dakota, *Daily News*, December 18, 2015, http://www.wahpetondailynews.com/news/mn-lawmakers-resist-federal-security-requirements/article_4ebe4b1e-a5a2-11e5-9ad7-8346146ca72b.html.

8. Alison LaCroix, "How the Noisy Debate Over States' Rights Distorts History and the Intent of Federalism," *Washington Post*, March 25, 2010.

9. Sixty-First Legislature of the State of Idaho, HB 117, page 2, lines 39–44.

10. Florida v. Sibelius (2010), No. 3:10-CV-91-RV-EMT (N.D. Fla. March 23, 2010).

11. National Federation of Independent Businesses v Sibelius, 132 S.Ct. 2566 (2012).

12. Mahalley D. Allen, "Federalism," in *Political Encyclopedia of U.S. States and Regions*, ed. Donald Haider-Markel (Washington, DC: CQ Press, 2009), 766.

13. John D. Donahue, *Disunited States* (New York: Basic Books, 1997), 17.

14. For purposes of simplicity, we use the term "states" here as the conventional term for regional government; it is not necessarily the term used in some of the federal systems we have identified.

15. Nicole Bolleyer and Lori Thorlakson, "Beyond Decentralization—the Comparative Study of Interdependence in Federal Systems," *Publius: The Journal of Federalism* 42, no. 4 (2012): 576. The eleven countries that meet their criteria are Argentina, Australia, Austria, Belgium, Canada, Germany, India, South Africa, Spain, Switzerland, and the United States.

16. Ronald L. Watts, "Federalism, Federal Political Systems, and Federations," *Annual Review of Political Science* 1 (1998): 123–24.

17. The four are the United States, Switzerland, Canada, and Australia. David E. Smith, *Federalism and the Constitution of Canada* (Toronto: University of Toronto Press, 2010), 17.

18. Campbell Gibson and Kay Jung, "Historical Census Statistics on Population Totals By Race, 1790 to 1990" (U.S. Census Bureau, Working Paper #56, September 2002).

19. The figure is from Russell Thornton, *American Indian Holocaust and Survival: A Population History Since 1492* (Norman: University of Oklahoma Press, 1987), 133.

20. Thomas S. Kidd, *Patrick Henry, First Among Patriots* (New York: Basic Books, 2011), 183.

21. This discussion relies, in part, on William J. Bennett, *American Theories of Federalism* (Tuscaloosa: University of Alabama Press, 1964), 128, chap. 3.

22. "The General Court of Massachusetts on the Embargo, February 22, 1814," in *State Documents on Federal Relations* (Department of History, University of Pennsylvania, Philadelphia, 1911), 71–72.

23. Bennett, *American Theories of Federalism*, 92–100.

24. John Dinan, "Contemporary Assertions of State Sovereignty and the Safeguards of American Federalism," *Albany Law Review* 74 (2011): 1665.

25. See Christian G. Fritz, "Interposition and the Heresy of Nullification: James Madison and the Exercise of Sovereign Constitutional Powers" (Washington DC: Heritage Foundation, 2012). This is Number 41 of the "First Principles" series of the Heritage Foundation and can be found at http://report.heritage.org/fp41. See also Bennett, *American Theories of Federalism*, especially 98–100.

26. Lydia Wheeler, "States Rise Up Against Washington," *The Hill*, February 10, 2015, thehill.com/regulation/legislation/232255-states-rising-up-against-washington.

27. See, for example, Jack N. Rakove, *Original Meanings* (New York: Vintage Books, 1996), chap. 7.

28. Cecelia M. Kenyon, ed., *The Antifederalists* (Indianapolis: Bobbs-Merrill, 1966), xxi–cxvi.

29. 17 U.S. 316.

30. Kenyon, *The Antifederalists*, xliii.

31. There is also the issue of national supremacy in this case, but for our purposes the question of the meaning of the necessary and proper clause is most important.

32. McCulloch v Maryland, 17 U.S. 316 (1819), 405.

33. McCulloch v. Maryland, 406.

34. McCulloch v. Maryland, 421.

35. Martha Derthick, "Federalism," in *Understanding America*, ed. Peter H. Schuck and James Q. Wilson (New York: Public Affairs, 2008), 127.

36. Kenyon, *The Antifederalists*, xliii.

37. 317 US 111 (1942).

38. United States v. Lopez, 514 US 549 (1995).

39. Jared Walczak, "Which States Rely the Most on Federal Aid?" *The Tax Foundation*, January 6, 2016. The analysis relies on U.S. Bureau of Census data from FY 2013. http://taxfoundation.org/blog/which-states-rely-most-federal-aid-0.

40. http://www.deseretnews.com/article/865649135/Legislature-passes-resolution-calling-for-repeal-of-17th-Amendment.html?pg=all.

41. *The Federalist* (Cleveland: The World Publishing Co., 1961), 417.

42. The German federal system retains a system similar to that originally established in the U.S. Senate. In the German instance, the upper chamber, the Federal Council, is composed of members chosen by the legislatures of the *Länder* (states).

43. Martha Derthick and John J. Dinan, "Progressivism and Federalism," in *Progressivism and the New Democracy*, ed. Sidney M. Milkis and Jerome M. Mileur (Amherst: University of Massachusetts Press, 1999), 81.

44. William Riker, "The Senate and American Federalism," *American Political Science Review* 49 (1955): 455.

45. http://www.huffingtonpost.com/2014/01/23/alec-legislation_n_4652051.html.

46. "Noble but quixotic" is the phrase used by the vice president of the conservative Cato Institute in an assessment of the movement to repeal the Seventeenth Amendment. See http://www.cato.org/publications/commentary/repeal-17th-amendment.

47. L. Sandy Maisel and Mark Brewer, *Parties and Elections in America*, 5th ed. (Lanham, MD: Rowman & Littlefield, 2008), 47.

48. These figures are reported in James T. Patterson, *The New Deal: Federalism in Transition* (Princeton, NJ: Princeton University Press, 1969), 31, 47.

49. Patterson, *The New Deal*, 38.

50. Derthick, "Federalism," 128.

51. Patterson, *The New Deal*, 198.

52. As quoted in Christopher Sullivan, "1963 at 50: A Year's Tumult Echoes Still," *Associated Press*, January 14, 2013.

53. This was especially the case in Mississippi. For a history of the resistance to segregation in Mississippi, see Joseph Crespino, *In Search of Another Country: Mississippi and the Conservative Counterrevolution* (Princeton, NJ: Princeton University Press, 2007) or Neil McMillen, *The Citizens Council* (Champaign: University of Illinois Press, 1994).

54. See footnote 16 in Dinan, "Contemporary Assertions of State Sovereignty and the Safeguards of American Federalism."

55. Joseph F. Zimmerman, *Contemporary American Federalism: The Growth of National Power* (Westport, CT: Praeger, 1992), 11.

56. See Table 4 of the Congressional Research Service report, "Federal Grants to State and Local Governments: A Historical Perspective on Contemporary Issues," March 3, 2015, https://www.fas.org/sgp/crs/misc/R40638.pdf.

57. Derthick, "Federalism," 130.

58. Ann O'M. Bowman and Richard Kearney, *The Resurgence of the States* (Englewood Cliffs, NJ: Prentice Hall, 1986).

59. Congressional Research Service, "Federal Grants to State and Local Governments," Table 3.

60. While most Republican presidents at least pay some lip service to restoring the role of the states in the federal system, George W. Bush seemed reluctant to even make the symbolic gesture. As one observer noted, "He paid no honor to federalism." In addition to meeting substantial state resistance to his efforts to nationalize education policy and to create a national identification card, the cost of the expansion of prescription drug benefits to Medicare resulted in substantial cost increases to the states. See Derthick, "Federalism," 136.

61. David Brian Robertson, "American Federalism as a Political Weapon," in *New Directions in American Politics*, ed. Raymond La Raja (New York: Routledge, 2013),

23. For a more detailed discussion of Robertson's argument, see Brian D. Robertson, *Federalism and the Making of America* (New York: Routledge, 2012).

62. Derthick, "Federalism," 123.

63. Larry N. Gerston, *American Federalism: A Concise Introduction* (Armonk, NY: M. E. Sharpe, 2007).

64. Gerston, *American Federalism*, 32.

65. Martha Derthick, *Keeping the Compound Republic* (Washington, DC: Brookings Institution Press, 2001), 140.

66. David Walker, *The Rebirth of Federalism* (Chatham: Chatham House Publishers, Inc., 1995), xii.

67. John D. Nugent, *Safeguarding Federalism: How States Protect Their Interests in National Policymaking* (Norman: University of Oklahoma Press, 2009).

68. Nugent, *Safeguarding Federalism*, 225.

69. Dylan Scott, "Medicaid: What Now?" *Governing* (December 2012): 48.

70. Zimmerman, *Contemporary American Federalism*, 196.

71. These and other examples are discussed in Sean Nicholson-Crotty, "Leaving Money on the Table: Learning from Recent Refusals of Federal Grants in the American States," *Publius: The Journal of Federalism* 42 (2012): 449–66.

72. Derthick, "Federalism," 140.

73. Robert McCartney, "How States and Localities Are Filling the Gaps Left by Washington Gridlock," *Washington Post*, September 26, 2015, https://www.washingtonpost.com/local/how-states-and-localities-are-filling-the-gaps-left-by-washingtons-gridlock/2015/09/26/e43c5b58-63b8-11e5-b38e-06883aacba64_story.html.

74. Rick Lyman, "Governors Criticize Gridlock in Congress," *New York Times*, January 15, 2014, http://www.nytimes.com/2014/01/16/us/politics/from-governors-to-congress-a-blunt-message-do-something.html?_r=0.

75. James MacGregor Burns, J. W. Peltason, Thomas Cronin, David Magleby, and David M. O'Brien, *Government by the People* (Upper Saddle River, NJ: Prentice Hall, 2002), 61.

76. David M. Thomas, "Past Futures: The Development and Evolution of American and Canadian Federalism," in *Canada and the United States: Differences That Count*, ed. David M. Thomas and Barbara Boyle Torrey, 3rd ed. (Peterborough, ON, Canada: Broadview Press, 2008), 28.

77. Elizabeth Fredericksen, Stephanie Witt, and David Nice, *The Politics of Intergovernmental Relations*, 3rd ed. (San Diego: Birkdale Publishers, 2016), chap. 6.

78. Zimmerman, *Contemporary American Federalism*, 164.

79. Zimmerman, *Contemporary American Federalism*, 176. Also see chapter 7 of this volume.

80. As discussed in Derthick, "Federalism," 125.

81. Derthick, "Federalism," 125; italics added.

82. Fredericksen, Witt, and Nice, *The Politics of Intergovernmental Relations*, 204.

83. Tim Henderson, "Age Gap Fuels City-State Clashes," *Stateline*, July 12, 2016, http://www.pewtrusts.org/en/research-and-analysis/blogs/stateline/2016/07/12/age-gap-fuels-city-state-clashes.

84. Alan Blinder, "When a State Balks at a City's Minimum Wage," *New York Times*, February 21, 2016. See also http://laborcenter.berkeley.edu/minimum-wage-living-wage-resources/inventory-of-us-city-and-county-minimum-wage-ordinances/.

85. Blinder, "When a State Balks at a City's Minimum Wage."

86. Jack Suntrup, "Columbia City Council Members Take On State Lawmakers' Proposals," *Columbia Missourian*, April 20, 2015.

87. Valerie Bauerlein and Jon Kamp, "Cities, States Clash on Social Policy," *Wall Street Journal*, July 8, 2016.

88. Robertson, "American Federalism as a Political Weapon," 23.

89. Alice Rivlin, "Rethinking Federalism for More Effective Governance," *Publius: The Journal of Federalism* 42 (2012): 299.

90. See, for example, Erin Ryan, *Federalism and the Tug of War Within* (New York: Oxford University Press, 2011).

3

The Policymaking Environment in the States

States matter because

- State government structures are distinctive from those of the national government
- State legislatures are very different one from another and operate with a variety of structures and resource levels
- Governors have become powerful political actors, with great influence over the policymaking process
- Bureaucracies have evolved to handle the policy burdens required by the states
- State courts operate with different structures and different methods of selection to the bench

IT IS EASY TO THINK OF THE FIFTY STATE governments as being smaller versions of the federal government. In this view, the governors are simply minor league versions of the president, state legislatures a pale imitation of the Congress, and state courts the judicial officials left to handle traffic violations and property disputes while their federal colleagues tackle the heavy legal issues. But such a perspective is fundamentally misguided; state governments have their own histories and have developed their own governing structures, none of which mirror the federal experience. Moreover, as discussed in chapter 2, the lines of policy authority between the federal and state governments have never been clear and have been continually shifting. Thus it is critical to understand how the state governments we have today have come to be as they are and how their decision-making power over the endless number of policy decisions that shape our daily lives has developed because it is not self-evident from understanding government at the national level.

In this chapter we trace the development of the policymaking environment in the states. We discuss why over time legislatures came to lose power while the executive and courts increased their influence over policymaking. We then discuss why these changes matter and what difference they make to the policymaking process. Finally, we turn to an examination of which policies the states dominate and how the mix of policies over which the states govern has changed over time.

Designing Governments

It is essential to appreciate that the original thirteen states were governing entities before any national government was established. When the first states emerged during the early movement toward independence, they had to create ruling structures to replace the colonial structures against which they were rebelling without having any national model to emulate. The initial governing device employed in most of the emerging states was called the provincial congress. These bodies were representative assemblies that assumed legislative, executive, and, to a much lesser extent, judicial functions. They governed from roughly 1774 through early to mid-1776, when the newly written state constitutions started taking effect.[1]

In designing new governing structures, those who wrote these constitutions wanted systems that functioned more effectively than the provincial congresses had. Indeed, in the preamble to New York's 1777 constitution, the authors admitted, "And whereas many and great inconveniences attend the said mode of government by congress and committees, as of necessity, in many instances, legislative, judicial, and executive powers have been vested therein." Thus the new governments were created with the now familiar idea of separate legislative, executive, and judicial branches. But in reality this initial separation of powers was fuzzy and uneven. What was actually created in the first states was a system where the legislative branch clearly dominated the other two branches. Policymaking effectively rested entirely in the hands of each state's lawmakers, establishing legislative supremacy.

The Rise, Fall, and Resurrection of the State Legislatures

Explicit references to a separation of powers were present in about half of the original state constitutions. But only in New York and Massachusetts was the notion given much attention, and even in these constitutions clear lines dividing the branches were not to be found. The muddled nature of separation of power greatly bothered James Madison, who later complained in *Federalist* 47, "If we look into the constitutions of the several States we find that, not withstanding the emphatical and, in some instances, the unqualified terms in which this axiom has been laid down, there is not a single instance in which the several departments of power have been kept absolutely separate and distinct."[2] In designing the new federal government, Madison and his colleagues made a conscious effort to establish a more clearly defined and balanced distribution of power among the three branches.

In particular, those who wrote the federal Constitution were concerned that in the state constitutions too much power had been concentrated in the hands of state legislatures. There was considerable evidence to support their apprehensions. In eight of the new states, the legislature elected the governor. And in a slightly different set of eight states, the legislature selected judges. This meant that in a majority of the new states the governor and the judges were directly beholden to the legislature for their positions. Not surprisingly, legislatures used their dominant position to bully the other branches to do their bidding. In a celebrated 1786 legal case, Rhode Island's Supreme Court issued a decision declaring a measure passed by the legislature to be unconstitutional, the first time any state court had done so. Lawmakers responded by demanding that the justices appear before them to justify their decision. The justices' arguments were not persuasive and when their terms expired the following year, legislators voted to replace all of those who had supported the decision.

But the era of legislative supremacy did not last long in most states. As early as the 1780s efforts were made to rein in legislative powers, in part by taking away control over gubernatorial selection and also by giving greater independence to the judiciary.[3] When the original states replaced their initial constitutions, the newer documents included provisions that constrained lawmakers; when new states were admitted to the Union, their constitutions limited legislative power from the start. As will be discussed shortly, these changes unyoked governors and judges from legislative dominance. And constitutions also came to place explicit limits on the kinds of laws the legislature could pass. Article IV, section 27 of the 1865 Missouri constitution, for example, contained specific prohibitions against the legislature "establishing, locating, altering the course, or affecting the construction of roads, or the building or repairing of bridges; or establishing, altering, or vacating any street, avenue, or alley in any city or town" and "extending the time for the assessment or collection of taxes, or otherwise relieving any assessor or collector of taxes from the due performance of his official duties." Such limitations appeared in most nineteenth-century state constitutions.[4]

Perhaps the most prominent among the constitutional restraints imposed were provisions allowing legislatures to meet only once every other year. In the original states, legislatures were required to meet every year because it was thought frequent meetings promoted closer ties between representatives and the represented and also gave the legislature greater control over the executive.[5] When legislative supremacy began to fall out of favor, the rationale behind legislative sessions shifted. Because it was thought that legislatures abused their powers, holding sessions only every other year came to be preferred because it was calculated that lawmakers would be able to cause less trouble, the system of laws would become more stable, and the cost of running the legislature would be reduced.[6] As documented in table 3.1, the trend over the course of the nineteenth century was unmistakable. At the beginning of the century, almost every state had annual sessions. By the end of the century, almost every state had biennial sessions. In 1901, Alabama even went so far as to institute quadrennial sessions. As we will discuss later, governors were the main beneficiaries of the trend toward having legislature meet less often. In essence, a power vacuum was created and the executive filled it.

The trend toward less frequent legislative sessions reversed course in the twentieth century, as public pressure on the states to perform better began to build. As more demands were made of state government, it seemed prudent to have the legislature meet annually. It was also thought that, echoing ideas

TABLE 3.1
The Rise, Fall, and Resurrection of Legislative Power

Year	Number of States	Number of States with:		
		Annual Sessions	Biennial Sessions	Quadrennial Sessions
1777	13	13		
1832	24	21	3	
1861	33	15	18	
1889	38	6	32	
1931	48	6	41	1
1960	50	19	31	
1999	50	43	7	
2016	50	46	4	

Source: Adapted from Peverill Squire, *The Evolution of American Legislatures: Colonies, Territories, and States, 1619–2009* (Ann Arbor: University of Michigan Press, 2012), 243–49, 270–73.

in the original constitutions, annual sessions would help rein in gubernatorial power.[7] As table 3.1 documents, by 2016 only four states still meet every other year; the rest have annual sessions.

State legislatures, of course, underwent other important changes during the twentieth century, as will be detailed in chapter 4. Most important, as they came to meet annually, their sessions also became longer and they met for more days. Because legislative service became more demanding, legislative compensation and benefits improved. Staff also increased, giving lawmakers a greater ability to generate and evaluate information needed to make decisions. Facilities generally improved as well; members came to have private offices and access to computers and other technological innovations that improved their capacity to do their job. All of these changes are subsumed under the concept of legislative professionalization. The idea driving these changes was to make the legislatures more competitive with the governor and the executive branch in the policymaking process. Thus during the American federal experience, state legislatures have traveled from being the dominant governing institution to being weakened to the point of near irrelevancy to being rehabilitated to once again be important actors in policymaking.

The Increasing Importance of the Governor and the Executive Branch

The American colonies had governors who were, in all but two cases, appointed and imbued with impressive formal powers. But in reality, their ability to exercise those powers was greatly constricted by the fact that control over taxing and spending came to be asserted by the colonial assemblies. As noted earlier, when the new states wrote their constitutions, they opted to make the legislatures powerful and the governors (called presidents in several states) weak. Indeed, New Hampshire chose to go without any chief executive at all until its 1784 constitution! As James Madison noted during the Constitutional Convention, "The executives of the states are in general little more than ciphers; the legislatures omnipotent."[8] The original governors' lack of power can be documented in two ways, as shown in table 3.2. First, in eight of the states the governor was elected by the legislature. This method of election put the executive under the legislature's thumb. Governors who wanted to retain office had to appease lawmakers. Second, in nine of the states the governor was given only a one-year term, leaving them little time to accomplish any significant policy goals. Election by the legislature and short terms of office were adopted to ensure that all important decisions were made by the legislature.

TABLE 3.2
Gubernatorial Terms of Office over Time

		Length of Gubernatorial Term by State							
Year	Number of States		One-Year		Two-Year		Three-Year		Four-Year
1776–77	13*	9	CT, **GA**, **MD**, MA, **NJ**, **NC**, **PA**, RI, **VA**	1	SC	2	**DE**, NY	0	
1789	13	8	CT, **MD**, MA, NH, NJ, NC, **PA**, RI	1	SC	4	**DE**, **GA**, NY, **VA**	0	
1833	24	9	CT, ME, **MD**, MA, NH, **NJ**, **NC**, RI, VT	6	AL, GA, MS, NY, OH, **SC**	3	IN, PA, **VA**	6	DE, IL, KY, LA, MO, TN
1889	42	2	MA, RI	20	AL, AR, CO, CT, GA, IA, KS, ME, MI, MN, NE, NH, ND, OH, SC, SD, TN, TX, VT, WI	2	NJ, NY	18	CA, DE, FL, IL, IN, KY, LA, MD, MS, MO, MT, NV, NC, OR, PA, VA, WA, WV

Year	Total							
1933	48	0	24	AZ, AR, CO, CT, GA, ID, IA, KS, ME, MA, MI, MN, NE, NH, NY, NM, ND, OH, RI, SD, TN, TX, VT, WI	1	NJ	23	AL, CA, DE, FL, IL, IN, KY, LA, MD, MS, MO, MT, NV, NC, OK, OR, PA, SC, UT, VA, WA, WV, WY
1989	50	0	3	NH, RI, VT	0		47	AL, AK, AZ, AR, CA, CO, CT, DE, FL, GA, HI, ID, IL, IN, IA, KS, KY, LA, ME, MD, MA, MI, MN, MS, MO, MT, NE, NV, NJ, NM, NY, NC, ND, OH, OK, OR, PA, SC, SD, TN, TX, UT, VA, WA, WV, WI, WY
2016	50	0	2	NH, VT	0		48	AL, AK, AZ, AR, CA, CO, CT, DE, FL, GA, HI, ID, IL, IN, IA, KS, KY, LA, ME, MD, MA, MI, MN, MS, MO, MT, NE, NV, NJ, NM, NY, NC, ND, OH, OK, OR, PA, RI, SC, SD, TN, TX, UT, VA, WV, WI, WY

*New Hampshire did not have a formal executive until 1784. Pennsylvania operated with a Supreme Executive Council headed by a president until 1790. Massachusetts did not adopt its constitution until 1780.

States in **bold** indicate executive was elected by the legislature.

Sources: Gathered by the authors from state constitutions.

The flaws of this institutional design became apparent relatively quickly. Those who wrote the federal constitution, for example, decided against having Congress elect the president and gave the office a four-year term. In the states, as legislatures came to be seen as be abusing their exalted position, power was taken from them and given largely to the executive.[9] By 1833, only four of the twenty-four governors were still elected by the legislature, meaning most of them were put into office by the voters. Indeed, every state that entered the union following the first thirteen states required its governor to be elected by the people. By 1889, all governors were directly elected, with South Carolina being the last state to give way on this score in 1866. Being directly elected gave governors an independent political base, which in turn could be leveraged to increase their ability to influence policy decisions.

Governors also came to enjoy longer terms, affording them more time to accomplish their objectives. In 1833, less than half the states still retained one-year terms, while a quarter of them allowed their governor four years in office. A century later, no state had one-year terms; half had two-year terms and the other half either three- or four-year terms. The trend toward longer terms has continued. Currently only two states (New Hampshire and Vermont) have two-year terms; the rest have four-year terms. Governors now have more time to pursue their agendas and lawmakers and others in the political process have to take that fact into account.

The second way it can be shown that governors have increased their powers is through the veto. Today, every governor enjoys some variant of the veto—the power to prevent legislation that has passed the legislature from becoming law.[10] The veto gives the executive the ability to greatly influence the legislative process. Most colonial governors had exercised an absolute veto, one that the legislature had no ability to override. In reaction, in the majority of the new states the writers of their constitutions shied away from endowing the governor with any veto power. South Carolina's governor briefly enjoyed a veto of the sort his colonial predecessors had, but that was taken away completely within two years. In New York, the veto power was exercised collectively by the governor jointly with the council and the court. The only state with a veto that would be familiar today was Massachusetts, whose veto power was the model for the veto given the president in the U.S. Constitution.

Relatively quickly, however, most governors acquired a veto power, as voters came to fear legislative overreach more than arbitrary decisions by a monarchial chief executive. Among the original thirteen states, most gave their governor a veto as soon as they replaced their first constitutions. A few of them, however, lagged, most notably North Carolina, which did not grant its governor a veto until 1996. Among the states admitted after the original thirteen, almost all of them gave their governor a veto in their initial constitutions. Thus all governors today have some ability to veto measures passed by their legislatures, giving them significant leverage in the legislative process.

But of course, not all vetoes are created equal. A line-item veto gives an executive the ability to pick and choose which provisions of a bill to accept and which to block. The original veto power in the Massachusetts constitution (and the one still in the U.S. Constitution) is a package veto; an all or nothing proposition in which the chief executive either accepts an entire measure or loses it all. A line-item veto gives a governor even greater leverage over the legislature by allowing him or her to threaten specific provisions that matter greatly to lawmakers without risking losing things that he or she wants.

The line-item veto first appeared in American politics in, of all places, the Confederate constitution. Georgia put one into its 1861 Confederate constitution a few days later. The line-item veto proved to be of sufficient interest that by the end of the nineteenth century a majority of states had given their governor a version of it, as shown in table 3.3. Maine was the most recent to institute a line-item veto in 1995.

Governors in forty-four states now enjoy some ability to pick and choose provisions of legislation they wish to sign into law. Of course, within line-item vetoes some are more powerful than others—Wisconsin's "partial" veto is usually thought to be the most powerful.[11] Even with its reach whittled down over the last few decades, Wisconsin's governor can still strike entire words and individual digits from appropriations bills and appropriated sums

TABLE 3.3
The Adoption of the Line-Item Veto

Century Line-Item Veto Adopted	Number of States	States (Year Adopted)
1800–1899	28	GA (1861), TX (1866), WV (1872), PA (1873), AR (1874), NY (1874), AL (1875), FL (1875), MO (1875), NE (1875), NJ (1875), CO (1876), MN (1876), CA (1879), LA (1879), IL (1884), ND (1889), MT (1889), SD (1889), WA (1889), ID (1890), MS (1890), WY (1890), KY (1891), MD (1891), SC (1895), UT (1896), DE (1897)
1900–1999	16	VA (1902), OH (1903), KS (1904), MI (1905), OK (1907), AZ (1912), NM (1912), OR (1916), MA (1918), CT (1924), WI (1930), TN (1953), AK (1959), HI (1959), IA (1968), ME (1995)
No Line-Item Veto	6	IN, NC, NH, NV, RI, VT

Sources: Rui J. P. de Figueredo Jr., "Budget Institutions and Political Insulation: Why States Adopt the Item Veto," *Journal of Public Economics* 87 (2003): 2677–701; John A. Fairlie, "The Veto Power of the Governor," *American Political Science Review* 11 (1917): 473–93; National Conference of State Legislatures, *Inside the Legislative Process*, Table 98-6.10, http://www.ncsl.org/documents/legismgt/ILP/98Tab6Pt3.pdf; various state constitutions.

may be stricken with lower sums substituted.[12] Maryland's line-item veto is the most limited. It applies only to projects in the capital budget and not to appropriations in the larger general operating budget.[13]

The power behind a governor's veto hinges on the ability of the state legislature to override it. All gubernatorial vetoes are subject to being overridden. The question is how many votes are required to do so. Gubernatorial veto power is strongest where a higher percentage of lawmakers have to agree to an override. The most stringent override requirement is two-thirds of the elected membership, as at the federal level. The weakest requirement is a majority of the elected membership. When in 2013 the Alabama Constitutional Revision Commission contemplated increasing the vote required to override a gubernatorial veto in that state to three-fifths from a simple majority, the Republican governor appeared personally to complain, "Only five states have a veto as weak as the [Alabama] governor's office does." But Republican legislators sitting on the commission rejected the proposal, saying the lower threshold allows them to protect their constituents' interests.[14] More likely, they were concerned with protecting the legislatures' power relative to the governor.

Being directly elected to long terms and armed with sweeping veto powers makes governors today much more powerful than their predecessors. But as is always the case with the states, some governors are granted greater formal powers than are others. Along with their veto powers, governors also vary in the degree to which they can influence the budget process and in their appointment powers. In addition, while some governors can serve for an unlimited number of terms, most can only hold the post for two terms, and Virginia's governor is limited to a single four-year term.[15] Thus the role a governor can play in his or her state's policymaking process will vary across the states.

Another reason governors today exercise considerable power is because they each sit atop a large bureaucracy. As noted in earlier chapters, government at all levels did relatively little when the country was young. Thus state bureaucracies were almost nonexistent. But as state populations increased and as their economies grew and diversified, more demands were made on government. The bureaucracy grew in response as, over time, more agencies were created to administer the programs demanded by voters.

The early growth of the bureaucracy can be demonstrated by the changes in New York between 1800 and 1925. At the beginning of the nineteenth century, New York had just ten state agencies. By 1850, another ten agencies had been added. At that point, state government growth accelerated: by 1900 there were eighty-one agencies, and another eighty agencies were established by 1925. This dramatic increase was driven by changes in society. As education came to be seen as an important governmental function, New York responded by creating a superintendent of public instruction in 1854. The state started agencies to regulate banking in 1829, insurance in 1859, and public utilities in 1882. As the Industrial Revolution took hold, a commissioner of statistics of labor was established in 1883. Urbanization raised sanitation issues and a public health department was fashioned in 1880. Environmental issues also surfaced and in response game and fish protectors were created in 1880, followed by a forest commission in 1885, a fisheries commission in 1892, and a state water commission in 1905. All were eventually swept into a single conservation department in 1926. Similar growth trajectories driven by similar social trends were found in other states.[16]

Indeed, the growth of state government continued unabated over the rest of the twentieth century and the first decade of the twenty-first century, as documented in table 3.4. Again, state agencies were added as new problems appeared on the public agenda. In 1959, there were fifty-one agencies that existed in at least thirty-eight (or three-quarters) of the states. These were units

TABLE 3.4
Growth in State Agencies, 1959–2009

Year	Number of State Administrative Agencies Present in Thirty-Eight or More States	Notable Examples
1959	51	Corrections Education Highways

Year	Number of New State Administrative Agencies Created in Thirty-Eight or More States during Previous Decade	Notable Examples
1969	12	Air Quality Economic Development Highway Safety
1979	29	Civil Rights Consumer Affairs Mass Transit
1989	8	Ground Water Management Hazardous Waste Underground Storage Tanks
1999	8	Lotteries Mining Reclamation Public Broadcasting Systems
2009	7	Campaign Finance Recycling State Data Center

Sources: Adapted from Cynthia J. Bowling and Deil S. Wright, "Public Administration in the Fifty States: A Half-Century Administrative Revolution," *State & Local Government Review* 30 (1998): 52–64, and various editions of the *Book of the States.*

devoted to what most would agree were core governmental activities, such as corrections, education, and highways. As fresh issues emerged, states responded by creating bureaucracies to deal with them. Thus among the twelve agencies initiated in most of the states in the 1960s were ones devoted to air quality, economic development, and highway safety. The 1970s saw a significant increase in the size of government, in addition to agencies overseeing civil rights, consumer affairs, and mass transit, arts councils, energy departments, and women's commissions were also added. Growth rates subsided in the 1980s and 1990s, but state governments still created agencies to oversee ground water management, hazardous waste, lotteries, mining reclamation, public broadcasting systems, and underground storage tanks. Over the most recent decade, campaign finance, recycling agencies, and state data centers were added.

By 2016, state government bureaucracies touched on an extraordinary array of policy areas. Consider the list compiled by the Council of State Governments of *selected* state agencies found in almost every state: administration, agriculture, auditor, banking, budget, civil rights, commerce, community affairs, comptroller, consumer affairs, corrections, economic development, education, election administration, emergency management, employment services, energy, environmental protection, finance, fish and wildlife, general services, health, higher education, highways, information systems, insurance, labor, licensing, mental health, natural resources, parks and recreation, personnel, planning, post-audit, pre-audit, public library development, public utility regulation, purchasing, revenue, social services, solid waste management, state police, tourism, transportation, and welfare.[17] In one way or another, state governments are now involved with almost every aspect of daily life. As the state's chief executive, this reality makes the governor more important today than in the past.

But it is again important to appreciate that although states have departments, agencies, and bureaus devoted to most of the same policy issues, the way the bureaucracies are configured across the states varies. In New Jersey, for example, the governor appoints the heads of most agencies, in some cases with the approval of the state senate. Occasionally, an agency head is allowed to make the appointment of subsidiary bureau leaders, but of course, the agency head is a gubernatorial appointee. Thus in New Jersey the state bureaucracy is under the governor's control. In contrast, in North Dakota a large number of agency heads are elected by the voters, giving each of them independent political standing. Thus where the New Jersey Commissioner of Education is nominated by the governor, subject to state senate confirmation, and serves at the governor's discretion, the North Dakota Superintendent of Public Instruction is elected by the voters, leaving a recent officeholder to boast on his website that as "an extremely popular public official, Dr. Sanstead received more votes in his 1988 re-election than any other candidate for any office in the history of North Dakota."[18] Clearly, New Jersey's education leader has to be responsive to the governor's wishes in a way that North Dakota's educational leader does not.

The Courts as a Parallel Dimension of Federalism

Perhaps nowhere is the American federal system of government on better display than in the judicial system. American courts operate on parallel tracks, one federal and the other state. Their similarities are largely superficial. Although the U.S. Constitution's supremacy clause means that any conflict between federal and state law will be resolved in the former's favor, the design and scope of the two systems differs, and the laws and the interpretation of those laws also vary.

Courts existed during the colonial era, but what we take today to be exclusively judicial powers were actually shared among different governing institutions. Legislatures, for example, often heard legal cases and rendered decisions. Indeed, the archaic name still used by the state legislatures in Massachusetts and New Hampshire, the General Court, harkens back to this reality. The first state constitutions did little to give the newly created state courts clearly defined jurisdictions. Indeed, as with the drafting of the U.S. Constitution a decade later, the design of the court system was treated as something of an afterthought. Thus under New Jersey's original constitution, the governor and his council functioned as the state's court of last resort. Final judicial authority was not granted to the state's court of last resort (or supreme court) until the constitution of 1844. Similar final authority power was only granted to every state's court of last resort in the middle of the nineteenth century.[19]

The separation of trial courts from appellate courts was also slow in developing in the states. Initially, appellate court judges also served as trial court judges, devoting part of their time each year to riding their circuit, moving from town to town in their district along with lawyers and court clerks, in something of a legal road show. The burden this system placed on judges proved great. But the system really changed only in response to the increased demands made on a state's legal system as populations and economies grew. Thus during the nineteenth century, trial courts and appellate courts eventually became distinct operations, and later appellate courts usually split into a court of last resort with some subsidiary court of appeals, all to accommodate the increased demands being made on the legal system.[20]

As state judicial systems have continued to evolve, they have come to look different from the federal system and often from each other. In simplified form, the federal court system consists of three levels, with trial courts, courts of appeal, and the Supreme Court. Similar unified court systems, where trial courts handle all matter of civil and criminal cases, are only found in five states: California, Illinois, Iowa, Minnesota, and South Dakota. The other states have constructed more complicated systems.[21] New York has eight limited jurisdiction courts, with different systems for New York City (separate civil and criminal courts), Nassau and Suffolk Counties on Long Island, and the rest of the state (Surrogates' Courts in sixty-two counties and close to 1,300 Town and Village Courts), along with a specialized Family Court and a Court of Claims. Such complexity is not unusual. There are separate civil and criminal courts of last resort in Oklahoma and Texas. Water Courts were established in Colorado and Montana in the late 1960s and early 1970s to handle special issues involving water rights in those states. Vermont's Superior (or trial) Court has an Environmental Division that "hears appeals from state land use permit decisions . . . from state environmental permits and other decisions of the Agency of Natural Resources, and from municipal land use zoning and planning decisions."[22] Some states have separate courts that try cases involving taxes, workers' compensation, and probate matters. Maryland has an Orphan's Court. In terms of structures, then, each state has largely devised its own system to handle legal cases. These structures continue to evolve. In 2010, for example, Vermont completely reorganized and simplified its court structure.[23]

Another structural difference is the membership size of the state courts of last resort. They vary from five judges (seventeen courts of last resort), to seven judges (twenty-eight courts), to nine judges (seven courts).[24] Note that all have odd numbered memberships, which is important because they make decisions collectively by voting. What happens when a vacancy leaves a state appellate court with an even number of judges? When the U.S. Supreme Court was left with only eight members in 2016, it handed down a number of tied decisions on four to four votes. This meant the Court set no legal precedent. If lower courts had reached conflicting decisions on the case in question, different regions of the country were left to live under different interpretations of the law. Supreme courts in sixteen states operate like the U.S. Supreme Court and hand down tied votes. The remaining thirty-four state courts of last resort employ procedures whereby a temporary judge is appointed, allowing any ties to be broken. The particular selection procedures used to appoint the temporary member vary—in Louisiana the court clerk "plucks [judges] names from a plastic Halloween Jack-o'-Lantern," while North Dakota and Utah take the first lower court judge who volunteers—but they all allow those courts to avoid the predicament in which the U.S. Supreme Court found itself.[25]

In recent years, a number of states have debated whether to expand or contract the size of their courts of last resort. In 2016, Arizona expanded its court of last resort to seven members from five members, while Georgia went to nine members from seven members. Superficially, these debates have centered on workloads and the number of judges needed to manage it. In most cases, however, partisan politics was the real motivator, with each party angling to have a court composed of the number of judges it calculated was more likely to produce the decisions it prefers.[26]

State courts also vary in the way they reach decisions. The U.S. Supreme Court makes all decisions by majority vote. While all state courts of last resort have the right to overturn state laws, those in Nebraska and North Dakota require a supermajority vote instead of a simple majority vote to do so.[27] When in 2015 the Nebraska Supreme Court voted 4 to 3 to overturn a state law allowing construction of the controversial Keystone XL pipeline, a simple majority was not sufficient. Under the Nebraska constitution, the court needed five out of the seven votes to do so.[28] State courts also do not have to have a unanimous jury verdict for criminal convictions. Federal courts and those in forty-eight states require all jurors to agree. But juries in Oregon can convict on an 11 to 1 vote for any offense except first-degree murder (which requires a unanimous vote). Louisiana juries can convict on a 10 to 2 vote.[29]

States have also developed a range of approaches to judicial selection. Even the original thirteen states split in the way they put judges on the bench, as shown in table 3.5. In five states, governors appointed judges with the consent of the council; in the other eight states they were elected by the legislature. As noted earlier, legislative election made judges beholden to lawmakers. In contrast, gubernatorial appointment hinted at greater judicial independence. The Framers of the U.S. Constitution opted for this latter approach, allowing the president to nominate and the Senate to confirm federal judges to life terms. The idea that judges should enjoy independence from the political branches of government never gained complete favor in the states. By 1833, roughly half the states used gubernatorial appointment, but, with one exception, the rest employed legislative election.

And that one exception proved enormously important. In its 1832 constitution, Mississippi became the first state to have its judges elected by the voters. New York followed suit in 1846, and by 1889 the vast majority of states elected their judges. The move to judicial elections was triggered in large part by dissatisfaction with the performance of the judicial branch, which many voters thought catered too much to elite and moneyed interests. They preferred to make the courts more responsive to the interests of the voters. Thus

TABLE 3.5

State Judicial Selection Procedures Over Time

Year	Number of States	Selection Procedure for Court of Last Resort:						
		Gubernatorial Appointment		Legislative Election		Popular Election	
1789	13	5	MD, MA, NY, PA*, NH	8	CT, DE, GA, NJ, NC, RI, SC, VA	0	
1833	24	11	DE, IN, KY, LA, ME, MD, MA, MO, NH, NY, PA	12	AL, CT, GA, IL, NJ, NC, OH, RI, SC, TN, VT, VA	1	MS
1889	42	7	CT, DE, ME, MA, MS, NH, NJ	6	GA, LA, RI, SC, VT, VA	29	AL, AZ, AR, CA, CO, FL, IL, IN, IA, KS, KY, MD, MN, MO, MT, NE, NY, NC, ND, OH, OR, PA, SD, TN, TX, WA, WV, WI
1933	48	6	CT, DE, ME, MA, NH, NJ	4	RI, SC, VT, VA	38	AL, AZ, AR, CA, CO, FL, GA, ID, IL, IN, IA, KS, KY, LA, MD, MI, MN, MS, MO, MT, NE, NV, NM, NY, NC, ND, OH, OK, OR, PA, SD, TN, TX, UT, WA, WV, WI, WY
1989	50	23	AK, CA, CO, CT, DE, FL, HI, IN, IA, KS, ME, MD, MA, MO, NE, NH, NJ, NY, OK, SD, UT, VT, WY	3	RI, SC, VA	24	AL, AZ, AR, GA, ID, IL, KY, LA, MI, MN, MS, MT, NV, NM, NC, ND, OH, OR, PA, TN, TX, WA, WV, WI
2016	50	25	AK, CA, CO, CT, DE, FL, HI, IN, IA, KS, ME, MD, MA, MO, NE, NH, NJ, NY, OK, RI, SD, TN, UT, VT, WY	2	SC, VA	23	AL, AZ, AR, GA, ID, IL, KY, LA, MI, MN, MS, MT, NV, NM, NC, ND, OH, OR, PA, TX, WA, WV, WI

*In Pennsylvania, judges were appointed by executive council. In the other states the council consented to gubernatorial selections.
Sources: Data gathered by authors from http://www.judicialselection.us/.

instead of promoting judicial independence, the states opted for elections that accentuated accountability. Judges would have to be able to defend their decisions to the public to retain their place on the bench.

Judicial elections proved popular and every state that entered the Union between 1846 and 1912 required them in their constitutions. But a backlash against the use of elections to name judges developed over the second half of the nineteenth century. The concern was that elected judges were nothing more than another cog in the political machines that dominated state politics. Judges were now thought to be beholden to party bosses and therefore susceptible to corruption.

An altogether new alternative approach to naming judges was proposed in 1914 by Albert Kales, a Northwestern University law professor. Kales devised a system that placed great value on merit. Under his plan, a governor would fill a judgeship by naming one of the people suggested by a panel of lawyers and lay persons who would evaluate the qualifications of candidates who applied. The people selected to be a judge would serve for a year or two and then face the voters in a retention election, a contest in which the voters would only decide whether or not they wanted that judge to serve a full term. The idea was that this system would improve the legal qualifications of the people named as judges, while still giving the voters, but not the parties, a say in whether they would stay on the bench. It was also reasoned that judges would be able to focus on the cases before them and not have to devote time and effort to campaigning.

It took a quarter century before a state opted to implement any variant of what came to be called the "merit plan." In 1940, Missouri became the first state to adopt a version of it. No state followed suit until 1958, and then over the next two decades nineteen states adopted what was now becoming referred to as the "Missouri Plan." By 1989, roughly half the states selected their judges through some merit system.

Today, the variation in state judicial selection procedures is substantial. The governor nominates judges for the court of last resort, usually through a merit system, in twenty-seven states. Legislative election is still used in South Carolina and Virginia. The voters select judges in the rest of the states; partisan contests are held in five states, nonpartisan elections are employed in fourteen states, and in a curious hybrid approach, judicial candidates in Michigan and Ohio are nominated through partisan mechanisms but elected in nonpartisan elections. It is important to realize that with the provision of simple information about the candidates nonpartisan judicial elections are easily turned into partisan contests.[30] This happened in West Virginia's 2016 election for a state supreme court judgeship. The contest was the first nonpartisan race under a law passed in 2014. But the infusion of more than

$3 million to one of the candidates from the Republican State Leadership Committee thwarted the law's objective.[31] To further complicate selection matters, some states use one system to select judges for the court of last resort and another system to select lower court judges. Even in Missouri, the "Missouri Plan" is only used to select lower court judges in a handful of the largest counties; in the rest partisan elections are held.

There are two main points to take away from this discussion. First, few of the states follow the federal model of judicial selection in any significant way. Judges in Massachusetts, for example, used to be nominated by the governor for life terms, but in 1972 the voters passed a constitutional amendment requiring them to step down at age seventy. In addition, states vary selection procedures between court levels and sometimes by county. Second, state selection procedures place greater weight on judicial accountability, whereas the federal system places greater weight on judicial independence.

What, then, about the decisions judges make? As noted in this book's opening vignette, laws vary across the states. The way judges treat those laws also varies to some extent. In significant ways, states have developed their own legal histories. Perhaps the most significant development in the last half-century has been the appearance of the "New Judicial Federalism." Starting in the 1970s, state courts began looking to state constitutions rather than the federal Constitution to drive their decisions on a number of important questions about civil liberties.[32] From this perspective, the federal constitution and the way the U.S. Supreme Court interprets its provisions establishes the floor, or minimum standard, for civil liberties, while state courts interpreting state constitutional provisions have the opportunity expand and strengthen those liberties.[33]

The new judicial federalism has been the source of some significant policy changes in recent American history. In granting same-sex couples the right to marry in 2004, the Supreme Judicial Court of Massachusetts did so by finding that the ban against it violated provisions of the state constitution. There have, of course, been backlashes against such decisions, and it is critical to understand that state courts operate in a context in which their decisions can be resisted in ways that decisions by federal courts largely cannot. First, voters in some states can put measures on the ballot to overturn state court decisions. When the Supreme Court of California held same-sex marriage to be constitutional under that state's constitution in early 2008, opponents of the decision quickly launched a successful effort to overturn it at the ballot box. (An effort to allow the voters to overturn the Massachusetts court's decision failed because under that state's rules only the legislature could place such a measure on the ballot and lawmakers resisted calls to do so. In California, voters could gather signatures to get the measure put on the ballot.) Second, in many states voters get to pass judgment on judges. Thus after the Iowa Supreme Court found a ban against same-sex marriage to be unconstitutional under the state constitution in 2009, voters vented their displeasure by voting against retaining three of the judges when their names appeared on the ballot in 2010. (Iowa voters could not, as California voters could, place the decision itself on the ballot. As in Massachusetts, only lawmakers could do so, and Iowa legislators never did. And in Massachusetts, judges do not go before the voters, leaving them insulated from any voter displeasure.) Of course, the U.S. Supreme Court's 2015 decision legalizing same-sex marriage in all fifty states demonstrated the power of the Constitution's supremacy clause in the federal system. Although some states resisted, their efforts to override the Supreme Court's decision proved futile.[34]

The Design of State Governments

As they have evolved, the structures of state governments have come to look much like the federal government, with three separate branches. But as noted, upon closer inspection, there are notable differences, both between the federal government and the state governments and across the state governments themselves. Indeed, the notion of separation of powers means something slightly different in each system. In Rhode Island, for example, only since voters passed a constitutional amendment in 2004 has the era of legislative supremacy ended. Prior to the amendment's passage, the legislature dominated the executive branch through lawmakers' control over appointments to regulatory agencies.[35]

This leads to one final point that needs to be emphasized. Each state government is, in some fashion, unique. They operate under somewhat different sets of rules, with somewhat different structures. Thus the policy decisions they make are the products of different governmental structures and procedures.

State Governments and Policy Domains over Time

When they were first established, state governments did relatively little. But by their fifth decade, their involvement in various aspects of the economy and society was beginning to expand. Take, for example, the sorts of state laws passed in Georgia between 1819 and 1829.[36] Much legislative time was devoted to public education, both at the primary and higher levels. Transportation issues, mostly dealing with ferries and highways, were important.

Writing and refining criminal law consumed time, as did the creation and maintenance of a judicial system to administer it. Overseeing the conduct of elections was important. Regulation of the economy commanded attention. The legislature determined "the mode of granting a license to" physicians, while individual lawyers were "authorized to plead and practice." Banks and corporations were chartered. The state was also involved with gaming issues, authorizing a large number of lotteries, while determining the "punishment for keeping gambling-houses, tables, or rooms." A public health officer was authorized for Savannah.

What is of particular interest about these policy areas is that two centuries later they are still central to the policy jurisdictions of the states. As noted in chapters 2's discussion of federalism, although the U.S. Constitution established a federal system and in some instances allocated specific powers to each governmental level, there is sufficient ambiguity in the overall design that there has been an ongoing resorting of policy powers. The federal government has, over time, become more intimately involved in most of these areas. But as we assess the roster of policies that we still look to the states to deliver—education, transportation, the administration of justice, public health, and economic development—we find the same basic set that the states took responsibility for when they were first established.

Notes

1. See the discussion in Peverill Squire, *The Evolution of American Legislatures: Colonies, Territories, and States, 1619-2009* (Ann Arbor: University of Michigan Press, 2012), 72–83.

2. James Madison, Alexander Hamilton, and John Jay, *The Federalist Papers* (New York: New American Library, 1961), 303–4.

3. Horst Dippel, "The Changing Idea of Popular Sovereignty in Early America Constitutionalism: Breaking Away from European Patterns," *Journal of the Early Republic* 16 (1996): 21–45; Gordon S. Wood, *Creation of the American Republic 1776-1787* (Chapel Hill: University of North Carolina Press, 1969), 446–53.

4. John W. Burgess, "The American Commonwealth: Changes in its Relation to the Nation," *Political Science Quarterly* 1 (1886): 9–35.

5. Peverill Squire and Keith E. Hamm, *101 Chambers: Congress, State Legislatures, and the Future of Legislative Studies* (Columbus: Ohio State University Press, 2005), 68.

6. See the discussion in Squire, *The Evolution of American Legislatures*, 243–48.

7. Squire, *The Evolution of American Legislatures*, 271–73.

8. Jonathan Elliot, *Debates on the Adoption of the Federal Constitution, in the Convention Held at Philadelphia, in 1787; with a Diary of the Debates of the Congress of the Confederation; as Reported by James Madison, a Member and Deputy from Virginia* (Washington, DC: Jonathan Elliot, 1845), 327.

9. See the discussion in Leslie Lipson, *The American Governor from Figurehead to Leader* (Chicago: University of Chicago Press, 1939), 17–30.

10. The following discussion is drawn from Rui J. P. de Figueredo Jr., "Budget Institutions and Political Insulation: Why States Adopt the Item Veto," *Journal of Public Economics* 87 (2003): 2677–701; John A. Fairlie, "The Veto Power of the Governor," *American Political Science Review* 11 (1917): 473–93; National Conference of State Legislatures, *Inside the Legislative Process*, Table 98-6.10, http://www.ncsl.org/docu ments/legismgt/ILP/98Tab6Pt3.pdf, and various state constitutions.

11. See the discussion in Peverill Squire and Gary Moncrief, *State Legislatures Today: Politics Under the Domes* (Boston: Longman, 2010), 216–18.

12. Wisconsin Legislative Council, *Wisconsin Legislator Briefing Book 2015–16*, chap. 4.

13. http://www.ncsl.org/research/fiscal-policy/gubernatorial-veto-authority-with-respect-to-major.aspx.

14. Tim Lockette, "Alabama Constitutional Commission Debates Veto Override Power," *Anniston Star*, July 1, 2013.

15. See the discussion of gubernatorial power in Margaret Ferguson, "Governors and the Executive Branch," in *Politics in the American States*, ed. Virginia Gray, Russell L. Hanson, and Thad Kousser, 10th ed. (Los Angeles: Sage, 2013).

16. This discussion was taken from Finla Goff Crawford, *State Government* (New York: Henry Holt and Company, 1931), 181–82. See also Legislative Reference Bureau, *Constitutional Convention Bulletin No. 9, The Executive Department* (Springfield: Legislative Reference Bureau, 1920), 623–25.

17. This list is taken from *The Book of the States* (Lexington: Council of State Governments, 2015), 183–88.

18. http://www.dpi.state.nd.us/dept/bio.shtm.

19. Lawrence M. Friedman, *A History of American Law* (New York: Touchstone, 1973), 122–23.

20. Friedman, *A History of American Law*, 123–24.

21. Charts of current state court structures can be found at http://www.courtstatistics .org/Other-Pages/State_Court_Structure_Charts.aspx.

22. https://www.vermontjudiciary.org/GTC/Environmental/default.aspx.

23. http://www.ncsc.org/conferences-and-events/4th-symposium/~/media/Files/ PDF/Conferences%20and%20Events/4th%20Symposium/Davenport-VT.ashx.

24. The number adds to fifty-two because Oklahoma and Texas each have two courts of last resort.

25. Don Willett, "Chalices, Jack-o'-Lanterns and Other State Court Tiebreakers," *Wall Street Journal*, May 31, 2016.

26. Russell Berman, "Arizona Republicans Try to Bring Back Court-Packing," *The Atlantic*, May 10, 2016; Alan Greenblatt, "Does Size Matter? The Latest Battle Over State Supreme Courts," *Governing*, May 12, 2016.

27. Evan H. Caminker, "Thayerian Deference to Congress and Supreme Court Majority Rules: Lessons from the Past," *Indiana Law Journal* 78 (2003): 73–122.

28. Maria L. La Ganga, "Nebraska Supreme Court Rules on Keystone XL Pipeline," *Los Angeles Times*, January 9, 2015.

29. Andrew Cohen, "Will the Supreme Court Address Louisiana's Flawed Jury System?" *The Atlantic*, April 23, 2014.

30. Peverill Squire and Eric R. A. N. Smith, "The Effect of Partisan Information on Voters in Nonpartisan Elections," *Journal of Politics* 50 (1988): 169–79.

31. Phil Kabler, "Spending Sparks Criticism in Supreme Court Race," *Charleston Gazette-Mail*, May 12, 2016.

32. See G. Alan Tarr, "The Past and Future of the New Judicial Federalism," *Publius* 24 (1994): 63–79.

33. Robert W. Williams, "Introduction: The Third Stage of New Judicial Federalism," *NYU Annual Survey of American Law* 59 (2003): 211–19.

34. Alan Blinder, "Alabama Judge Defies Gay Marriage Law," *New York Times*, February 8, 2015.

35. See Carl T. Bogus, "The Battle for Separation of Powers in Rhode Island," *Administrative Law Review* 56 (2004): 77–134.

36. William C. Dawson, *A Compilation of the Laws of the State of Georgia, Passed by the General Assembly, Since the Year 1819 to the Year 1829, Inclusive* (Milledgeville, GA: Grantland and Orme, 1831).

4

The Policymaking
Capacity of State Governments

States matter because

- The policymaking capacity of state governments has increased markedly in the past two generations
- The training and preparation of elected officials today is far advanced over past generations
- The ability of governors to affect policymaking is substantial; many people believe being governor is "the best job in politics"
- Despite the deleterious effect of strict term limit laws in some states, today's legislatures are more capable partners in the policymaking process
- The standards for ethical behavior of elected officials appear to vary by state

OVER RECENT DECADES, an increasing number of policy decisions have been turned over to state governments to handle, as we have documented in earlier chapters. And as we have argued, in many regards this trend is positive. But one important question has been left unanswered. As more and more policy decisions are pushed onto state governments, do they have sufficient capacity to make competent decisions? By capacity, we mean the organizational resources to generate and analyze the information needed to make knowledgeable policy choices.

In this chapter, we assess the policymaking capacities of the four governmental institutions intimately involved in the policymaking process: the governor's office, the executive branch, the state legislature, and the state courts. Each institution is charged with making important policy decisions. The question to address is whether each has sufficient capacity to handle all that is now asked of it.

Before directly addressing these questions, we note a related trend. Today, there are numerous professional organizations that assist state officials. Examples include the Council of State Governments and the National Association of State Budget Officers. Some of these organizations, such as the National Governors Association, have been around for more than a century. Others, notably the National Conference of State Legislatures and the National Legislative Leaders Foundation, have existed for only a few decades. Regardless of when they were founded, all have become active in providing services, information, and training to state officials. Most are nonprofit organizations that the general public has never heard of and knows nothing about. But they are important support organizations that have helped state governments increase their capacity to govern. In addition, there are university-affiliated research and training operations, such as the Carl Vinson Institute of Government (University of Georgia) and the Hubert Humphrey School of Public Affairs (University of Minnesota) that devote many hours to the training and education of state and local officials. There are many such university-housed institutes or organizations, and they too have been an important part of the capacity-building efforts for state governments.

Gubernatorial Capacity

In the not so distant past, state governors were denigrated as being "good-time Charlies."[1] In 1962, for example, James Reston, an influential political columnist for the *New York Times*, lamented that "it is difficult to make a political swing around America these days without coming to the conclusion that the governors of the states, taken as a whole, are a poor lot."[2] Indeed, they often appeared to be less than engaged in the policymaking process. A reporter covering a National Governors Conference in 1970 noted with some hyperbole, "Most of the governors snored through dozens of 'policy statements.'"[3] Such characterizations suggested many governors were, at best, political hacks, interested more in the rough and tumble of elections than in the nitty-gritty of policymaking.

Over the following decade, that image began to improve. By the late 1970s, governors were seen as serious policymakers, focused on improving their state's lot. It is this latter image that appears to dominate today. In a recent treatise on governors, Alan Rosenthal chronicled the growth in policymaking influence of the governors over the past generation.[4] Interviews with numerous former governors led him to conclude that the governorship "according to nearly all of those who have held it, is now 'the best office in American politics.'"[5] For the most part, this is because state problems are more manageable than those at the national level and governors tend to have the resources necessary to address at least some of those problems. A particularly telling comparison comes from those who have served as both state governor and U.S. senator. Rosenthal claims that of the dozen members of the U.S. Senate in 2010 who were former governors, all but one "preferred their job as governor to their job as senator."[6]

Indeed, as former governors Jimmy Carter, Ronald Reagan, Bill Clinton, and George W. Bush have intimated, in many regards governors today may be better able to influence state policies than the president is able to influence national policies. There are three reasons why this might be the case. First, governors dominate state media. Between May 2015 and May 2016, for example, a search of Google News reveals 19,700 news stories mentioning Illinois governor Bruce Rauner compared to only 7,490 stories mentioning the state house speaker, Michael Madigan, even though Madigan is a powerful official who has held his important post for all but two years since 1983. Moreover, the two politicians were locked in an epic budget battle during this time period, yet the governor's actions got far more attention. Governors can exploit their media advantage to set their state's policy agenda, leaving legislators and others to only be in a position to react.

Second, governors enjoy a significant information advantage over their state legislatures. The governor's job is, of course, a full-time position. And as will be discussed shortly, governors now have large staffs to assist them, and they can draw on the state bureaucracy's expertise as well. In contrast, legislatures in most states are part-time and many have relatively meager staff resources. This disparity gives most governors the upper hand in policy debates that turn on facts and analyses. When in 2016 Kansas had to make significant cuts to balance its budget, the legislature allowed the governor to impose most of them. Their reasoning was explained by the vice chair of the state senate budget committee. He admitted, "We're a citizen Legislature. . . . We don't know the details of the agencies. The agency cabinet members, they work with the governor every day, so we just left it up to him and them to decide what they can do within their agencies."[7]

Third, as noted in chapter 3, most governors enjoy a powerful veto, one that gives them great leverage over the legislature. Unlike the president, who must take or leave an entire bill, governors in most states can pick and choose provisions that they wish to keep. Knowing that governors can pick and choose legislative provisions in a bill forces legislators to be more accommodating to them earlier in the legislative process. A veto threat provides governors considerable leverage in legislative negotiations.

Thus the evidence suggests that governors today are powerful. The question then becomes whether they are serious and capable policymakers. In table 4.1, we examine two personal characteristics of governors in 2016 that act as indicators of their capacity as policymakers. The first indicator is a governor's level of educational attainment. The idea behind this measure is simple: higher levels of educational attainment suggest that a governor has the academic training to analyze the vast amounts of information available on policy issues. Not surprisingly, as table 4.1 reveals, governors today are well educated. Almost all of the governors had at least an undergraduate degree. The two who did not—Gary Herbert (R-UT) and Scott Walker (R-WI)—attended college but left without graduating. Overall, a much higher percentage of governors graduated from college than did the general public.

TABLE 4.1
Capacity Indicators for Governors, 2016

Capacity Indicator	Number of Governors with Indicator
Highest Educational Attainment	
Some college	2
BA, BS, or other undergraduate degree	12
MA	2
JD	25
MBA	8*
MD	1
PhD	2*
Elective Office Experience	
City council, county supervisor	5
Mayor, county executive	8
District attorney	1
State legislature	20
State attorney general	6
Other statewide office	9
Lieutenant governor	8
U.S. House of Representatives	8
U.S. Senate	2
No elective office experience	9

*Governor Gina Raimondo (D-RI) has a JD and PhD. Governor Rick Snyder (R-MI) has a JD and MBA.

Perhaps even more impressively, over 70 percent of governors had a graduate degree of some sort. As might be anticipated, half of them had a law degree. Another eight had MBAs. Others held assorted degrees: Rick Snyder (R-MI) had both a JD and a MBA, Robert Bentley (R-AL) a MD, Gina Raimondo (D-RI) a JD and a PhD in sociology, and Tom Wolf (D-PA), a PhD in political science. These varied educational backgrounds indicate that governors have the intellectual training to handle the complex policy problems confronting state governments.

The second indicator of policymaking capacity is political experience as measured by other elective offices held previously. The notion that governors who have held other offices may be better positioned to navigate the complexities of policymaking in a governmental system characterized by the separation of powers is reasonably well accepted. Previous office holding, for example, is embedded in a widely used measure of gubernatorial power.[8] Governmental experience provides a governor with exposure to policy questions and a measure of expertise on some aspects of them, as well as a network of connections both within and outside of government that can be drawn upon to assist in policy development and evaluation. A legislative background can be especially helpful. A former Vermont governor and state representative remarked, "Legislative experience was a plus . . . lawmakers knew I had some of the same experiences they were having. I was familiar with the protocols and the committee process. I could relate to their problems, and they knew they couldn't snow me, either."[9]

Not surprisingly, the vast majority of governors—82 percent in 2016—had previous elective office experience. Some had served in local government, for example, John Hickenlooper (D-CO) as mayor of Denver and Bill Haslam (R-TN) as mayor of Knoxville. A number of others had served in the state legislature or in a statewide office. Governor Jerry Brown (D-CA) enjoyed a varied and impressive political résumé. The son of a California governor, he began his political career by being elected to the Los Angeles Community College Board of Trustees. Brown's next move was to a statewide office, California Secretary of State, and then he served as the state's governor from 1975 to 1983. He returned to elective office in 1999 as the mayor of Oakland and was elected California Attorney General in 2006. Brown returned to the governorship in 2010 and got reelected in 2014. Such varied experiences provide governors with extensive knowledge of the policy problems, policymaking processes, and policymakers in their states.

Just over half of the nine governors without elective office experience had some background in politics. Several had held appointed positions in earlier gubernatorial administrations, one had served as the chair of the Democratic National Committee, and two others were U.S. attorneys. All were familiar

with the way government works and therefore positioned to lead state policymaking.

The other governors were political neophytes and their tenures have not
always gone smoothly. Governor Bruce Rauner, a Republican, enjoyed great
success in finance, becoming extraordinarily wealthy in the process. But once
in office he quickly learned that government does not operate like the private
sector. A lengthy budget impasse with the Democrat-controlled legislature
led even his GOP predecessors as governor to publicly criticize him. One
noted Rauner "does not come from government. . . . He doesn't really come
from mainstream business. He comes from (being an) entrepreneur where
you buy a business, you tear it apart and you sell it. . . . I don't think you're
going to tear apart the state and sell it. He might want to, but you can't do
that."[10] Another counseled, "running government is not like running a business."[11] Legislative Democrats rebelled as well, with one representative complaining the governor "doesn't understand how the Legislature works. We're
not his middle management. He is not the boss of Illinois government."[12]

There are several reasons why running state government is not like running a business. First, although a governor is routinely referred to as the
state's chief executive, that does not mean the same things as being a chief
executive officer in the private sector. State government agencies operate in a
world with multiple masters. That is, while agencies need to be responsive to
the governor, it is the legislature that creates them, the legislature that funds
them, and it is the legislature that can abolish them. Lawmakers can expand
agency missions, contract agency missions, or change agency missions. Thus
bureaucrats have to be responsive to legislators as well as to the governor.
Second, private sector organizations are built around generating a profit, a
goal that, even with the complexities of accounting, is measured in a manner
most people understand and accept. Consequently, we can usually tell the
degree to which a business is successful. The same is not true with government. Government agencies perform a range of diverse activities and there
is little agreement about their goals and whether they have achieved them or
not. Finally, businesses enjoy the ability to make decisions out of public view.
In contrast, government decisions are almost always debated with the media
and interested parties watching. This greatly complicates decision making.

It must be pointed out, of course, that previous governing experience does
not guarantee success in office or that having only a business background
dooms a governor to failure. In North Dakota, John Hoeven had spent his
career in banking prior to winning the governorship. During his tenure,
he was enormously popular, in large part because of the state's strong economic performance. When he left the governorship he was elected to the
U.S. Senate. In contrast, Illinois governor Rod Blagojevich had impressive

political credentials before taking office, having served in the Illinois House of Representatives and the U.S. House of Representatives. Now he serves in the Federal Correctional Institution in Englewood, Colorado. He ended up being impeached and removed from office by a legislature controlled by his fellow Democrats and later convicted in federal court on corruption charges. But despite such aberrations, political experience is, on average, beneficial.[13]

It is also useful to look at the experience immediately prior to ascending to the governorship. Here we find an interesting temporal trend. As Margaret Ferguson shows, the proportion of governors who held some other statewide office prior to taking office has grown from about 20 percent in the period from 1900 to 1980 to 30 percent in the period from 1981 to 2011.[14] Thus not only do governors today have more experience, but the quality of that experience is higher. Even more telling is the fact that in the earlier period, from 1900 to 1980, less than 10 percent of governors were former members of Congress. During the most recent period, from 1981 to 2011, that number jumps to 18 percent. Almost one of every five governors left federal office and "came home" to become state governor. If we accept that politicians are progressively ambitious beings, then one implication of this move from federal office to state office is clear: states matter.[15]

Interestingly, the apparent attraction over the last several decades of better qualified people serving as governor has not been driven by the salaries paid to them. In 1959, the mean gubernatorial salary was $18,980, which is the equivalent of $156,054 in 2016. The mean salary paid governors in 2016 was $134,793. Gubernatorial salaries failed to keep up with inflation in thirty-four states, with the biggest losers being governors in many of the largest states: New York, California, and Pennsylvania. Governors reaping the greatest real increases since 1959 are actually in moderate-sized states: Tennessee, Washington, and Georgia.[16]

Today, one of the nation's best paid governors, New York's at $179,000, makes far less than many other state employees. Indeed, 1,797 New York state workers made more than their governor did in 2016.[17] Iowa governor Terry Branstad fared even worse: his $130,000 salary ranked 2,398th among his state employees.[18] In her final year as Hawaii governor in 2010, Linda Lingle earned $117,306. In 2015, she was hired as Illinois governor Bruce Rauner's chief of staff with a salary of $198,000.[19] Even with his vast experience in state government, California governor Jerry Brown makes 5 percent of what the state's highest paid employee—UCLA head football coach Jim Mora—is paid. At the lowest end, Maine's governor is paid only $70,000. In 2016, his wife took a job waiting tables, telling a reporter, "Oh honey, it's all about the money; it's all about the money. . . . I want to buy a car this summer."[20] Clearly, salary is not the cause of the improvement in the quality of state governors.

One positive change that has taken place over the last few decades is an expansion in the pool of potential candidates for the governorship. By the end of the 1960s, only three women had ever served as governor, each of them filling in, in one fashion or another, for their husband. Starting in the 1970s with Ella Grasso in Connecticut and Dixie Lee Ray in Washington, women who had worked their way up through the political ranks began winning the governorship on the basis of their own accomplishments. Similarly, by the 1980s, minority politicians in many states found the governorship open to them, further expanding the pool of possible contenders for the office. Allowing women and minorities to hold the office dramatically increases the prospects for electing high-quality candidates. Among recent examples are Susana Martinez (Republican governor of New Mexico, graduate of the University of Texas, El Paso, law degree from University of Oklahoma, former district attorney), Nikki Haley (Republican governor of South Carolina, graduate of Clemson University and former state representative), Maggie Hassan (Democratic governor of New Hampshire, graduate of Brown University, law degree from Northeastern Law School, former state senator), and Brian Sandoval (Republican governor of Nevada, graduate of the University of Nevada, Reno, law degree from Ohio State University, former state assembly member, former chair of the Nevada Gaming Commission, and former state attorney general).

There are two other noteworthy developments that have increased the policymaking capacity of governors. As noted in chapter 3, gubernatorial terms of office have changed over time. Currently, all but two states—New Hampshire and Vermont—have shifted their governors to four-year terms of office. The move to four-year terms was motivated by a desire to spare the governor from perpetual campaigning and to allow for sufficient time to learn the job and to pursue complex policy agendas.

In many states, however, there are limits on the number of terms governors may serve. At the most extreme, the Virginia governor may serve only one four-year term. Such a stringent limit makes it more difficult for a governor to fulfill his or her campaign pledges. The reason is that a one-term governor is quickly deemed a lame duck—an officeholder whose political power is weakened because his or her time in office is coming to an end. Because legislators and other government officials know that the governor cannot run for reelection, they have less incentive to cooperate with the governor's office. Most states sidestep this problem—or at least push it off for a few more years—by adopting a two-term limit. Currently, thirty-five states mimic the Twenty-Second Amendment of the U.S. Constitution and limit their governor to two four-year terms. (A handful of these states do allow a term-limited governor to run for office again after a specified period of time out of office. California instituted its two-term lifetime limit in 1990, thereby allowing Jerry Brown to serve two more terms. His current term is the final one he is allowed to serve.)

No limits on how many terms a governor may serve are found in fourteen states, although among these states, several have an informal norm that limits service to two terms. In recent decades, several Midwestern states have had governors serve for more than two four-year terms. In Iowa, Terry Branstad, a Republican, held the office from 1983 to 1999 and then was elected again by the voters in 2010 and reelected in 2014. In December 2015, he became the longest serving governor in American history.[21] Such lengthy service affords a governor the best chance to leave his or her mark on a state.

The second significant development over the last few decades is that governors have come to sit atop a growing bureaucracy devoted exclusively to serving the governorship.[22] Staff is important, as will be argued again in discussing legislatures and the courts, because it expands an officeholder's reach. In this case, the more people the governor has working for him or her the more information he or she has to use in making policy. In 1980, gubernatorial staffs ranged in size from just four in Texas to eighty-two in California. The mean size of gubernatorial staffs was twenty-eight. By 2016, staff sizes ranged from nine in Nebraska to 277 in Texas, with the mean being fifty-six. These numbers, of course, are often supplemented by additional staff members commandeered by governors from state agencies on whose payrolls the staffers continue to appear.[23] The important point is that governors now have larger numbers of policy experts and other assistants on whom they can rely to help them in making public policy, thereby increasing their policymaking capacity.

Bureaucratic Capacity

Has state bureaucratic capacity kept up with the policy demands being made on it? Over the last half-century, state governments have grown terrifically in size. There are, of course, a number of different ways to document this expansion.

The first and most obvious measure to examine is the number of people employed by state governments. Over the past sixty years, every state government has increased its number of full-time equivalent positions (FTEs). In 1953, the aggregate number of state FTEs was 966,000. By 2013 that number had exploded to 4,312,054.[24]

There are two things driving this growth. The first may be somewhat underappreciated. In 1953, there were about 160 million people resident in the United States. By 2016, the estimate was close to 323 million residents, the population having doubled in roughly sixty years. Obviously, the states were providing governmental services to far more residents, requiring some increase in the number of FTEs.

The second driving force in the growth of state government is, perhaps, more obvious: state government is being asked to do more than it was asked to do in the past. Evidence for this is provided by the dramatic expansion of state bureaucracies over the last half-century, not just in the sheer number of agencies but, more importantly, in the scope of their activities. As noted in chapter 3, in the 1960s, twelve additional agencies were present in thirty-eight or more states that had not been present the decade before. Among the agencies added were ones devoted to then-emerging policy issues, such as air quality, community affairs, highway safety, and natural resources.[25] The next decade witnessed the emergence of twenty-nine more agencies appearing in most of the states, dealing with a series of new problems confronting state governments, including alcohol and drug abuse, historic preservation, Medicaid, occupational health and safety, and women's commissions. The 1980s and 1990s saw fewer new agencies being established across most of the states—sixteen total in the two decades—but again those that were created allowed government to respond to new policy concerns, for instance ground water management, hazardous waste, lotteries, mining reclamation, and crime victim compensation. The most recent decade saw seven more agencies established. In the context of the discussion here, the addition of these new bureaucracies represents a significant increase in the capacity of state governments, giving them the ability to respond to a wide range of new issues.

The real capacity of government agencies, however, rests on the abilities of the people working within them. Importantly, the educational credentials of the top state bureaucrats have improved significantly over the last half-century.[26] In 1964, 14 percent of top state administrators had only a high school degree or less. In 2008, only 1 percent had such limited education. At the other extreme, by 2008, 75 percent had a graduate degree or had done graduate work, substantially above the 40 percent who had done so in 1964. Thus the educational credentials of the people running state agencies have improved dramatically since the 1960s.

Current top administrators are also drawn from a substantially larger pool of potential candidates. In 1964, 98 percent of top state administrators were male and 98 percent were white. By 2008, 29 percent of leaders were female and 10 percent were minorities. Their experience levels have also improved.

In 2008, administrative leaders averaged eighteen years in state government, and 44 percent of them had worked their way up through the ranks of the agency they led. In contrast, forty-four years earlier, top administrators averaged eleven years in state government and only 28 percent had held a subordinate position in their agency. Thus administrators today are drawn from a larger pool of potential candidates and have more agency experience than their predecessors several decades ago.

One capacity issue currently facing state bureaucracies is the so-called silver tsunami, the impending retirement of a large number of their workers. In Virginia, for example, 12 percent of the state workforce is already eligible for retirement and another 25 percent will become eligible over the next five years. In Washington, 31 percent of state workers are age fifty-five or older. Replacing baby boomer workers and their experience and expertise will be a challenge for state governments.[27]

Overall, the evidence shows that state bureaucratic capacity has increased impressively during the last half-century. States today have more people working in a wider array of specialized agencies making policies. Administrative leaders are better educated and more experienced than in the past. All of this suggests that states are well prepared to implement the policies assigned to them. The question then becomes whether states are well equipped to make policy decisions.

Legislative Capacity

State legislatures play a central role in developing state policies. Thus it is important to measure their capacity to make policy. Perhaps even more to the point, it is necessary to assess whether state legislators and the institutions in which they serve have improved their policymaking capacity at a time when the federal government has devolved more policies to state control.

Given the trends that are already evident from the examinations of governors and top state bureaucrats, it should come as no surprise that state legislators today are, on average, better educated than were their predecessors a generation or two ago. Today, 73 percent of state legislators have graduated from college and 40 percent have earned a master's degree or higher. Sixty years ago, far more state legislators had only a high school degree and a few had not even achieved that level of education.[28] State legislators today also are drawn from a much larger pool of potential candidates. In 1971, only 5 percent of the nation's state legislators were women; in 2016, 25 percent were women.[29] Similarly, the number of state legislators from various minority groups has increased substantially in recent decades.[30]

Legislators have also become considerably more experienced over the last century. Legislative experience is typically measured by the turnover rate, the percent of new members coming in to a legislative chamber. A high turnover rate translates into many inexperienced lawmakers and an increased likelihood that the legislature is not a powerful policymaking force. Longer serving legislators gain a better understanding of the complexities and nuances of policymaking. At the institutional level, a legislature with experienced members is better able to compete in policymaking with the governor, the governor's staff, and the state bureaucracy.

There has been a noteworthy decline in the average turnover rate across state legislatures over the last century. In the 1930s, turnover each session averaged over 50 percent in state senates and almost 60 percent in state houses. But over the next five decades, there was a steady decrease in turnover rates. Just prior to the reapportionment revolution in the 1960s, the aggregate figures had declined to 34 percent—admittedly a troubling rate, but clearly not as high as the 1930s. In some states, however, the turnover rate was still extraordinary: 52 percent in Maine, 57 percent in Maryland, 58 percent in Tennessee, 59 percent in Alabama, 61 percent in Utah, and an astounding 67 percent in Kentucky.[31] But by the end of the 1980s, turnover averaged 22 percent in state senates and 24 percent in lower houses. Turnover in some states, notably Arkansas, California, Delaware, Illinois, New York, and Pennsylvania, averaged 15 percent or less for each electoral cycle in the decade, figures comparable to those found in the U.S. Congress.[32]

The implementation of term limits in some states, beginning in the 1990s, has led to two very distinct patterns in turnover. On the whole, the fifteen states that impose legislative term limits have much higher turnover rates than the thirty-five states with term limits. While there is certainly some variation due to other factors and year to year electoral swings, the term-limited states generally experience turnover in the range of 35 percent. In some instances, it is much higher; the Michigan House of Representatives experienced turnover of more than 50 percent in 2010 and it is not unusual to see turnover of 40 percent or more in some term-limited states. Meanwhile, the states without legislative term limits experience turnover that averages around 20 percent, although this figure varies by state and circumstance. For the states that limit legislative service, the benefits experience generates in terms of increased policymaking capacity are largely sacrificed.[33] Furthermore, term limits heighten partisanship in the legislature and suppress collaboration across the aisle. By limiting the time legislators can stay in the institution, the incentive for bipartisan compromise is not as strong, exacerbating polarization.[34]

The effect of term limits is conditioned by several factors. One of the most important is the severity of the term limit law. There is a significant difference between a six-year lifetime term limit, such as exists for the Michigan House of Representatives, and a twelve-year consecutive limit allowing for legislators to return after sitting out for a term like the Louisiana House of Representatives limit.[35] In chambers with more restrictive limits, the effects on the institution may be substantial. The substantial increase in turnover appears to accelerate the heightened partisanship evident in many legislatures and exacerbate the incivility and the inability to compromise.[36] Recent research finds that such behavioral consequences have important fiscal implications; for example, states with strict legislative term limits develop lower bond ratings over time.[37] So while state legislatures as a group are certainly more capable policymaking institutions than they were a few decades ago, not all legislatures have progressed at the same rate, and some may have even regressed a bit.

The evidence presented here shows that state legislators today are better educated, more experienced, and drawn from a larger segment of the population than were their predecessors a generation or two ago. This suggests that they are now better prepared to act as policymakers. The question then turns to whether the institutions in which they serve have also changed. The informational capacity of a legislature is usually measured by its level of professionalization.[38] Professionalization has three components: the salary paid to legislators, the number of days the legislature meets in session each year, and the staff provided. Legislatures that pay members well, meet for extended periods, and have adequate staff resources are more professional, meaning that they have a greater capacity to generate and process the information needed to make policy. More professional legislatures are also better equipped to compete with the governor and bureaucracy in the policymaking process.

How, then, do contemporary state legislatures compare to legislatures several decades ago on the components of professionalization? Table 4.2 compares state legislatures in 2016 with state legislatures in 1979 on each of the three dimensions. It must be pointed out that 1979 was a point in time when the significant advances made in professionalization during the 1960s and 1970s had begun to stall.[39] Perhaps it is a bit surprising that in terms of constant dollars, legislative salaries have lost ground over the last four decades. The mean salary has dropped by $746, while the median salary is lower by $1,976. Both the mean and median salaries for 2016 are modest sums, well under the national median household income of $53,647. These numbers, of course, mask the great range in legislative salaries across the states. California lawmakers, for example, earned $100,113, a sum that actually represented a drop from the $116,098 they were paid until late in 2009. (On December 1, 2016, California legislators had their pay increased to $104,117.) In contrast, New Hampshire legislators were paid the same $100 a year the state has paid

TABLE 4.2
Capacity Indicators for State Legislatures, 1979 and 2016

Indicator	1979	2016	Change from 1979 to 2016
Mean Member Salary	$31,170*	$30,424	–$746
Median Member Salary	$25,760*	$23,784	–$1,976
Mean Days in Session	62.4	74.3	+11.9
Median Days in Session	58.5	61.8	+3.3
Mean Staff per Member	3.7	4.5	+0.8
Median Staff per Member	2.7	3.3	+0.6

*1979 salary calculated in 2016 dollars.
Source: Calculated by authors from data in various editions of *Book of the States* and http://www.ncsl.org/research/about-state-legislatures/staff-change-chart-1979-1988-1996-2003-2009.aspx (included 2015).

since 1889. New Mexico lawmakers are not paid a salary, only a per diem. Overall, in most states legislative compensation does not appear adequate to attract the best policymaking talent.

There has been an increase in the number of days state legislatures meet in session over the last four decades. The mean number of days in session in 2016 was 74.3, while the median was 61.8. The difference between the two numbers reveals that a few state legislatures meet for many days, thereby greatly increasing the overall mean. Indeed, that is the case. The National Conference of State Legislatures considers four state legislatures to be full-time institutions like the U.S. Congress: California, Michigan, New York, and Pennsylvania. On the other end of the spectrum are a handful of legislatures that demand considerably less time from their members: Montana, New Hampshire, North Dakota, South Dakota, Utah, and Wyoming. Most state legislatures fall somewhere in between the two extremes, with sessions that last four or five months each year. Such sessions allow legislatures to play a role in the policymaking process, but it makes it more difficult for them to challenge the governor and the executive branch, both of which are, of course, year-round institutions. Indeed, the challenge to keep up with the rest of the government is even more acute in the four states (Montana, Nevada, North Dakota, and Texas) that allow their legislatures to meet only every other year.

Perhaps the only hopeful sign for the increased policymaking capacity of state legislatures is found in the area of staff support. Both the mean and median number of staff per state legislator have increased since 1979. Again, some legislatures, such as California, afford their legislators considerable staff while others, notably New Hampshire, provide very little. Staff is important because it greatly increases the informational capacity of a legislator to make policy by allowing them to uncover and analyze much more data than they could hope to do on their own. Research shows that more legislatures with more staff are better able to monitor and review the actions of state agencies to ensure the agencies comply with legislative intent. In other words, legislative oversight of the agencies is stronger in more professionalized legislatures, just as we would expect.[40]

One saving grace for less professionalized legislatures may be the resources made available to them through the National Conference of State Legislatures and the Council of State Governments, which provide access to detailed information about policies being developed across the nation. When asked about the American Legislative Exchange Council (ALEC), an organization that offers pro-business and conservative "model legislation" to state legislators to introduce, an Oregon senator said the group was a great resource, noting that "we have such limited staff that this helps us look at things and consider them."[41] Indeed, recent research finds that part-time legislatures with limited staff and information resources are especially likely to adopt "model legislation" offered by outside groups.[42]

Overall, state legislators appear to be increasingly capable to make policy, but the institutions in which they serve may lag a bit in that regard. This is, of course, in contrast to the increased capacities exhibited by the governor and the executive branch, both of which have made significant progress over the last several decades. Any inability of state legislatures to keep up may signal a potential problem with shifting policymaking demands back to the states.

Judicial Capacity

The bulk of the judicial system in the United States is at the state level. While there are about 1,200 judges in the entire federal judicial system, there are more than 30,000 judges in the state systems.[43] More judges are required at the state level because state judicial systems handle far more cases than does the federal court system. In 2013, approximately 1.6 million cases were filed with U.S. District Courts, U.S. Bankruptcy Courts, and U.S. Appellate Courts. In comparison, that same year 94 million cases were filed in state courts. The latter figure actually represents an 11 percent decline in filings since 2008.[44] If someone comes in contact with the judicial system, it is far more likely to be at the state level than at the federal level.

Although controversy occasionally surrounds state courts and their legal decisions, most scholars accept the reality that they are, at least in part, policymaking institutions, particularly at the appellate level. But courts differ from other policymakers in at least one important regard: They cannot act as policy entrepreneurs surveying the political landscape for problems to solve, as legislators and executives can. Instead the courts are inherently reactive, only solving problems that are brought to them. This means that they typically get involved with policies that the other governmental institutions have failed to adequately resolve, leaving some aggrieved party or parties to take their complaints to them.

The courts also differ in that the public has always assumed (if not actually required) that their members have attained a certain level of education. In the nineteenth century, this typically meant that aspiring lawyers had "read" the law and been trained by established attorneys. By the twentieth century, formal law schools had taken over the education of new lawyers.[45] And of course, although it was not always spelled out in early constitutions (including the U.S. Constitution), the expectation was that judges would have the appropriate legal training. So from an educational perspective, state courts have always had the capacity to render legal decisions because judges were expected to have attained a high level of education prior to being put on the bench. Thus, for example, while less than 50 percent of New Hampshire's state legislators have college degrees, all of their state judges have both bachelor's and law degrees. Today almost every current state constitution requires some number of years as a state bar association member before becoming a state judge.[46] So state judges are expected to have both legal training and experience as a lawyer before gaining the bench.

The next question is whether states are willing to offer salaries sufficient to attract top legal talent. Here again the contrast with state legislatures is dramatic. As shown in table 4.3, in 2016, judges on state courts of last resort were paid a mean salary of $164,974 and a median of $165,619. The range of salaries was from Maine's $129,625 to California's $230,750. Even general (or trial) court judicial salaries are high relative to legislative salaries: in 2016 the mean salary was $148,357 and the median was $146,520, with a range from $118,385 to $193,248.[47] Thus the lowest paid state trial court judge is paid more than the highest paid state legislator. States are much more willing to invest in their judges than they are to invest in their state legislators. The most extreme example of this is New Hampshire. As noted earlier, New Hampshire state legislators are paid $100 a year, with no per diems. That means each year the state pays its 424 state lawmakers a total of $42,400 in salary. The five members of the New Hampshire Supreme Court each make $155,907, thereby costing the state $779,535 in salary.[48] This is not to claim, of course, that judicial salaries are necessarily sufficient to attract the top legal minds. State judges are paid less than their federal counterparts and less than what top lawyers in their state make. And there are ongoing battles in many states over judicial pay, with judges decrying stagnant wages. Still, there is evidence that current salaries attract and maintain competent jurists.[49]

TABLE 4.3
Judicial Salaries, 2016

Level	Mean Salary	Median Salary	Highest Salary	Lowest Salary
State Court of Last Resort Justice	$164,974	$165,619	$230,750 (California)	$129,625 (Maine)
State Appellate Court Judge	$159,559	$159,484	$216,330 (California)	$124,616 (New Mexico)
State Trial Court Judge	$148,357	$146,520	$193,248 (Hawaii)	$118,385 (New Mexico)
		Salary		
U.S. Supreme Court Justice		$249,300		
U.S. Appellate Court Judge		$215,400		
U.S. Trial Court Judge		$203,100		

Source: State judge salaries calculated by authors from National Center for State Courts, "Survey of Judicial Salaries," January 2016.

Like governors and bureaucrats—and unlike most state legislators—almost all state judges, and all appellate court judges, work full-time. As argued earlier, this time commitment enhances their policymaking capacity. State appellate judges also benefit from staff assistance, most importantly in the form of law clerks. Typically, clerks are relatively recent law school graduates with distinguished academic records. Their efforts greatly increase the judiciary's capacity. At the state court of last resort level, the number of clerks varies, from less than one clerk per justice in Alabama to more than five clerks per justice in Pennsylvania. Once again, most states are far more willing to invest in assistance for judges than in assistance for lawmakers. In New Hampshire, for example, supreme court justices are each allowed two clerks. In contrast, each of the state's legislators enjoys only half of a staff member (including clerical support). Trial court judges in many states also have law clerks.[50]

As with the other institutions of state government, state courts now draw on a larger pool of potential judges than in the past. Over time, more women and minorities have entered law school. In recent years, this has translated into more of them making it onto the state bench. In 2016, women held 31 percent of state judgeships, with a high of 43 percent in Oregon and a low of 15 percent in Arkansas. They held 35 percent of all state court of last resort positions.[51] Minorities have also increased their numbers. In 2010, a few states, such as New Hampshire, had no minorities on the bench, but other states, notably Florida and Maryland, had large contingents.[52] By 2016, no state had achieved population parity with either women or minority judges: Hawaii, Oregon, and New Mexico came the closest to doing so, while West Virginia, Alaska, and Utah had the farthest to go.[53] But progress continued to be made. With the 2016 appointment of Anne McKeig, a descendant of the White Earth Nation, as a justice, the Minnesota Supreme Court gained a female majority.[54]

Overall, state courts are full-time institutions, populated by well-educated judges who in turn are assisted by capable law clerks. Salaries are sufficient to attract and keep qualified people on the bench. All of this suggests that in terms of judicial capacity, state courts are currently well positioned to handle the tasks given them. There is strong evidence to support this assertion. Over the course of the twentieth century, state courts of last resort have greatly reformed, restructuring to allow them to gain greater control over the cases they decided.[55] When modern state courts of last resort are compared to the U.S. Supreme Court, they stack up well. Indeed, state courts of last resort in California and Pennsylvania are on the same level as the U.S. Supreme Court in terms of salary and the provision of law clerks. Overall, the typical state court of last resort is much more like the U.S. Supreme Court in terms of its capacity than any state legislature is like the U.S. Congress.[56] Consequently, it is not surprising to learn that because of its importance in the corporate world, Delaware has made sure its court of last resort is capable of meeting the unusual demands on it. According to a law professor, "Academics regard [the court's justices] as among the most scholarly bench to be found anywhere. Corporate lawyers know them by name and temperament in much the same way that others know the justices of the U.S. Supreme Court. Their published opinions and academic articles are influential in other states and with the federal judiciary."[57]

This brings us to one final question about state court capacity: Are there enough state judges to meet the demand for their services? Given 1,600,000 federal cases each year—the bulk of which are bankruptcies—each federal judge handles approximately 1,333 cases. The 30,000 state court judges tackle 94,000,000 cases annually—over half of which are traffic violations—or about 3,133 cases per judge. These are, of course, crude calculations. Many of these cases get settled outside the courtroom. But there is little to suggest that state courts are overwhelmed. There is a tendency for smaller population states to enjoy a lower ratio of residents (and therefore likely cases) per judge. This is to be expected because in the American federal system, most legal cases fall under state law, requiring each state to create an extensive judicial system. Consequently, even small population states have to have the same basic court structures that larger states have.[58] In any event, the indications are that state courts are capable institutions.

Conclusions

Much is now demanded of state governments. The pressure on them has come from two directions. First, the public expects them to be involved in a much wider range of policy areas than in the past. Second, the federal government over the last few decades has devolved many policy decisions to the states. The question we have tried to address is whether state governments are up to the tasks given them. By and large, we find that state government capacity has increased as more is being asked of it. Governors are better educated, more experienced, and supplemented with more staff than in the past. State bureaucracies are led by better educated and more experienced people drawn from a wider pool of candidates. State courts also appear to have increased their capacity.

Perhaps the only concerns are with the capacities of state legislatures. Lawmakers are, like their counterparts in the rest of the government, better educated than in the past. Increases in member experience, however, have been forcibly truncated in the fifteen states with term limits. There are also doubts that the salaries offered in many states are sufficient to recruit the best and brightest to service; indeed, they have fallen behind in most states over the last few decades. But the most troubling limitation involves staff support. Legislators are asked to respond to policy questions across a wide range of issues, taxing their own abilities to be competent in developing appropriate responses. Staff support is necessary to allow lawmakers to generate and digest the vast amounts of information they need to consume to make good public policy. Unfortunately, in a number of states, legislators are not provided the assistance they need, leaving them to look to other parts of the government or to people and groups outside of government to give them the information they need. As the eminent legislative scholar Alan Rosenthal said of state legislatures, "They are probably the most unappreciated institutions in the country."[59]

Of course, legislatures and all other state government institutions must have more than policymaking capacity to effectively serve the public. Institutional capacity does not guarantee proper individual behavior. Recently, there have been a few spectacular examples of state officials failing to meet expected standards. Between 2013 and 2016, the Speaker of the House—the highest legislative office in the state house of representatives—resigned amid scandal in at least four states (Missouri, New York, Rhode Island, and South Carolina). In Alabama, the Chief Justice of the state supreme court was suspended, the governor was facing impeachment, and the house speaker was convicted on corruption charges—all at the same time. An Illinois legislator admitted to taking a bribe, a long-time California lawmaker was sent to prison for racketeering and money laundering, and a Michigan member was convicted for shooting his ex-wife's Mercedes. The governor of Oregon resigned over conflict of interest allegations involving his fiancée. Leaders in both houses of the New York legislature were convicted. These are, to say the least, disheartening signs. In chapter 8, we will have more to say about these and similar events, and why it is more important than ever that citizens become knowledgeable about state politics.

In this chapter we have focused on the policymaking capacity of state officials. But we cannot leave this topic without noting that most policies also involve funding. And the funding, or fiscal capacity, of states is another matter entirely. It is clear that the chronic federal budget problems will impact states. This impact will be two-fold. First, a reduction in federal aid to state and local governments (outside health care) is likely. Second, the national government's "policy footprint" may shrink as the national budget is increasingly constrained. If so, then the states will have to decide which programs to fund and how to fund them on their own. Developing the fiscal and analytical capacity to do so is emerging as one of the major challenges for state officials.

Notes

1. See Larry Sabato, *Goodbye to Good-Time Charlie*, 2nd ed. (Washington, DC: CQ Press 1983).

2. James Reston, "Boston: Big Problems and Little Men in State Capital," *New York Times*, October 5, 1962.

3. Martin F. Nolan, "The City Politic: Rocky's Road to Albany," *New York Magazine*, August 31, 1970.

4. Alan Rosenthal, *The Best Job in Politics* (Washington, DC: CQ Press, 2013).

5. Rosenthal, *The Best Job in Politics*, 3.

6. Rosenthal, *The Best Job in Politics*, 5

7. Bryan Lowry, "Kansas Gov. Sam Brownback Cuts Medicaid Reimbursements, Higher-Ed Spending," *Kansas City Star*, May 18, 2016.

8. See Thad Beyle and Margaret Ferguson, "Governors and the Executive Branch," in *Politics in the American States*, ed. Virginia Gray and Russell L. Hanson, 9th ed. (Washington, DC: CQ Press, 2008).

9. Quoted in Louis Jacobson, "Experience Preferred," *State Legislatures Magazine*, January 2016.

10. Bernard Schoenburg, "Former Gov. Jim Edgar Urges Gov. Bruce Rauner to Quit Holding Budget Hostage," *State Register-Journal*, October 16, 2015.

11. Kerry Lester, "Thompson Says State in 'Worst Position Ever,'" Arlington Heights *Daily Herald*, October 20, 2015.

12. Keviun McDermott, "Budget Showdown Looming in Illinois as Rauner's First Session Ticks Down," *St. Louis Post-Dispatch*, June 1, 2015.

13. See John A. Hamman, "Career Experience and Performing Effectively as Governor," *American Review of Public Administration* 34 (2004): 151–63.

14. Margaret Ferguson, "Governors and the Executive Branch," in *Politics in the American States*, ed. Virginia Gray and Russell L. Hanson, 10th ed. (Washington, DC: CQ Press, 2013), 211.

15. Peverill Squire, "Electoral Career Movements and the Flow of Political Power in the American Federal System," *State Politics and Policy Quarterly* 14 (2014): 72–89.

16. These data were calculated by the authors from gubernatorial salary data found in various editions of the *Book of the States*.

17. http://blog.timesunion.com/capitol/archives/245694/payroll-data-1797-state-employees-earned-more-than-the-governor/.

18. Erin Jordan, "University of Iowa Coaches, Surgeons Again Top State Pay List," *Cedar Rapids Gazette*, November 3, 2015.

19. "Another Aide to Illinois Governor Making Nearly $200,000," *St. Louis Post-Dispatch*, May 6, 2015.

20. Peter Holley, "'She's an Amazing Employee': Wife of Maine Governor Takes Waitressing Job to Make Ends Meet," *Washington Post*, June 25, 2016.

21. Amber Phillips, "Terry Branstad Just Became the Longest Serving Governor in American History," *Washington Post*, December 14, 2015.

22. See Ann O'M. Bowman, Neal D. Woods, and Milton R. Stark II, "Governors Turn Pro: Separation of Powers and the Institutionalization of the American Governorship," *Political Research Quarterly* 63 (2010): 304–15.

23. Missouri State Auditor, "Findings in the Audit of the Office of the Governor," April 2015; John O'Connor, "Illinois Agencies Cover Half the Pay for Gov. Rauner's Staff," *St. Louis Post-Dispatch*, August 10, 2015.

24. These data are taken from the *Book of the States* (page 396).

25. These data are taken from Cynthia J. Bowling and Deil S. Wright, "Public Administration in the Fifty States: A Half-Century Administrative Revolution," *State and Local Government Review* 30 (1998): 52–64.

26. These data are taken from the American State Administrators Project, http://www.auburn.edu/outreach/cgs/ASAP/index.htm.

27. Mike Maciag, "The 'Silver Tsunami' Has Arrived in Government," *Governing*, May 31, 2016.

28. Data from 1957 can be found in John C. Wahlke, Heinz Eulau, William Buchanan, and LeRoy C. Ferguson, *The Legislative System* (New York: Wiley, 1962), 489. Data for 2015 are from http://www.ncsl.org/research/about-state-legislatures/who-we-elect.aspx and http://www.pewtrusts.org/en/research-and-analysis/blogs/stateline/2015/12/10/state-legislatures-have-fewer-farmers-lawyers-but-higher-education-level.

29. These data are taken from the Center for American Women in Politics, http://www.cawp.rutgers.edu/women-state-legislature-2016.

30. Data on African American and Hispanic American state legislators over time can be found at http://www.ncsl.org/default.aspx?tabid=14850.

31. These figures are from Duane Lockard, "The State Legislator," in *State Legislatures in American Politics*, ed. Alexander Heard (Englewood Cliffs, NJ: Prentice-Hall, 1966), table 1. The figures are for lower houses. Turnover was often even higher in state senates, but many of the "newcomers" in the senates had come over from the house, so it is difficult to get a good historical measure of true turnover in the upper chambers.

32. On turnover over the several decades, see Gary Moncrief, Richard G. Niemi, and Lynda W. Powell, "Time, Term Limits, and Turnover: Membership Stability in U.S. State Legislatures," *Legislative Studies Quarterly* 29 (2004): 357–81; Richard G. Niemi and Laura R. Winsky, "Membership Turnover in U.S. State Legislatures: Trends and Effects of Districting," *Legislative Studies Quarterly* 12 (1987): 115–23; and Kwang S. Shin and John S. Jackson III, "Membership Turnover in U.S. State Legislatures: 1931–1976," *Legislative Studies Quarterly* 4 (1979): 95–114.

33. On turnover in recent years and the difference between states with term limits and states without term limits, see Peverill Squire and Gary Moncrief, *State Legislatures Today: Politics Under the Domes*, 2nd ed. (Lanham, MD: Rowman & Littlefield, 2015), 50–51.

34. Clint S. Swift and Kathryn A. VanderMolen, "Term Limits and Collaboration Across the Aisle: An Analysis of Bipartisan Cosponsorship in Term Limited and Non-Term Limited State Legislatures," *State Politics and Policy Quarterly* 16 (2016): 198–226.

35. Marjorie Sarbaugh-Thompson, "Measuring 'Term-Limitedness' in U.S. Multi-State Research," *State Politics and Policy Quarterly* 10 (2010): 199–217.

36. See Daniel C. Lewis, "Legislative Term Limits and Fiscal Policy Performance," *Legislative Studies Quarterly* 37 (2012): 307; David R. Berman, "Legislative Climate," in *Institutional Change in American Politics*, ed. Karl Kurtz, Bruce Cain, and Richard Niemi (Ann Arbor: University of Michigan Press, 2007), 107–18; and Thad Kousser, *Term Limits and the Dismantling of State Legislative Professionalism* (New York: Cambridge University Press, 2005).

37. Lewis, "Legislative Term Limits and Fiscal Policy Performance."

38. This discussion of legislative professionalization is derived from Peverill Squire, "Measuring Legislative Professionalism: The Squire Index Revisited," *State Politics and Policy Quarterly* 7 (2007): 211–27.

39. See the discussions in Squire, "Measuring Legislative Professionalism," and Squire, *Evolution of American Legislatures*, chap. 7.

40. Frederick J. Boehmke and Charles R. Shipan, "Oversight Capabilities in the States: Are Professionalized Legislatures Better at Getting What They Want?" *State Politics and Policy Quarterly* 15 (2015): 366–86.

41. Michelle Cole, "ALEC Gains Foothold in Oregon, with One-Fourth of Legislators as Members," May 26, 2012, http://www.oregonlive.com/politics/index.ssf/2012/05/alec_gains_foothold_in_oregon.html.

42. See Alexander Hertel-Fernandez, "Who Passes Businesses 'Model Bills'? Policy Capacity and Corporate Influence in U.S. State Politics," *Perspectives in Politics* 12 (2014): 582–602. For an intriguing look at how interest group model legislation is disseminated as policy innovation, see Kristin Garrett and Joshua Jansa, "Interest Group Influence in Policy Diffusion Networks," *State Politics and Policy Quarterly* 15 (2015): 387–417.

43. Melinda Gann Hall, "State Courts," in *Politics in the American States*, ed. Virginia Gray, Russell Hanson, and Thad Kousser, 10th ed. (Washington, DC: CQ Press 2013), 255.

44. The federal court data were taken from *Federal Judicial Caseload Statistics: March 31, 2013* (Washington, DC: Administrative Office of the United States Courts, 2013). The state court data were taken from R. LaFountain, S. Strickland, R. Schauffler, K. Holt, and K. Lewis, *Examining the Work of State Courts: An Overview of 2013 State Court Caseloads* (National Center for State Courts, 2015).

45. See Lawrence M. Friedman, *A History of American Law* (New York: Touchstone, 1973), 525–38; Robert A. Kagan, Bobby D. Infelise, and Robert R. Detlefsen, "American State Supreme Court Justices, 1900–1970," *American Bar Foundation Research Journal* (1984): 371–408.

46. See the qualifications listed in the *Book of the States* (pages 248–49).

47. These data are taken from National Center for State Courts, "Survey of Judicial Salaries," Vol. 40, No. 2, as of July 1, 2015.

48. The chief justice is actually paid slightly more.

49. See Stephen J. Choi, Mitu Gulati, and Eric A. Posner, "Are Judges Overpaid? A Skeptical Response to the Judicial Salary Debate," *Journal of Legal Analysis* 1 (Winter 2009): 47–117. For examples of controversy, see Michael Cooper, "New York's Top

Judge Threatens Suit to Get Raises for Bench," *New York Times*, April 10, 2007; "On Oklahoma Judicial Pay Issue, Politics Needs to Take a Back Seat," *The Oklahoman*, October 7, 2013; http://blogs.wsj.com/law/2012/07/24/state-courts-concerned-about -losing-judges-after-no-salary-growth/.

50. http://www.ncsc.org/Topics/Human-Resources/HR-Management/Stat -Links.aspx?cat=Judicial%20Clerkship%20in%20State%20Trial%20and%20Appel late%20C.

51. These data are from http://www.nawj.org/us_state_court_statistics_2016.asp.

52. These data are taken from Ciara Torres-Spelliscy, Monique Chase, and Emma Greenman, "Improving Judicial Diversity" (Brennan Center for Justice, 2010).

53. Tracey E. George and Albert H. Yoon, "The Gavel Gap" (American Constitution Society, 2016).

54. Ricardo Lopez, "Dayton Selects McKeig as Next Supreme Court Justice," *Star Tribune*, June 28, 2016.

55. See Robert A. Kagan, Bliss Cartwright, Laurence M. Friedman, and Stanton Wheeler, "The Evolution of State Supreme Courts," *Michigan Law Review* 76 (1977): 961–1005.

56. See Peverill Squire, "Measuring the Professionalization of U.S. State Courts of Last Resort," *State Politics and Policy Quarterly* 8 (2008): 223–38.

57. G. Marcus Cole quoted in Louis Jacobson, "Obscure, Yet Influential, Jobs in State and Local Government," *Governing*, September 30, 2015.

58. Data on judges per state were gathered from National Center for State Courts, Court Statistic Project, "State Court Caseload Statistics: An Analysis of 2008 State Court Caseloads," 2010.

59. Alan Rosenthal, *Engines of Democracy: Politics & Policymaking in State Legis-latures* (Washington, DC: CQ Press, 2009), 8.

5

Public Policy and the Role of the States in a Changing Federal System

---

States matter because

- Significant issues are addressed in state legislative sessions every year
- Innovative policy often begins with a single state and later gets adopted by other states and/or by the national government
- States are the "default" setting of policymaking
- Gridlock at the national level increases the opportunity for state-based policymaking
- Concerns over the federal deficit will increase the opportunity for state-based policymaking

---

THE TITLE OF THIS CHAPTER can be read two ways. It can be read retrospectively, as a comment on the past, as in "because of the centralizing tendencies of the changes in the federal system the role of the states has changed." Or it can be read prospectively, as a prediction of the future, as in "fiscal exigencies at the federal level are going to require a recalibration of the federal relationship." We intend that it be read both ways because federalism is indeed a dynamic relationship, ever changing, and citizens of every state need to be aware of that reality.

There are those who see the states today as mere administrative outposts of the federal government.[1] In some policy areas that may in fact be close to the truth. But in most domestic policy arenas, states retain a fair amount of discretion. And in other areas, they are still the dominant crafters of public policy.

If states were not important actors, why would there be such interest and anticipation at the beginning of each new state legislative session? Every year, in just about every state, one can find a news story about the issues to watch. Take, for example, this sample of headlines from January 2016, as many state legislatures were about to convene (with key issues in parentheses):

- *Tampa Bay Times:* "The Florida Legislature's 2016 Session: 5 Issues to Watch and 5 People to Watch" (tax cuts, health care, Seminole gambling pact, education, the environment).[2]
- *Atlanta Journal-Constitution:* "Top Issues to Watch at the 2016 Georgia General Assembly" (education, budget and taxes, criminal justice, religious liberty, medical marijuana).[3]
- *Wichita Eagle:* "Kansas Legislative Issues to Watch in 2016" (court funding, education, Medicaid expansion, prescription drugs, public safety).[4]
- *South Seattle Emerald:* "Preview of Washington State's 2016 State Legislative Session" (budget adjustments, education funding, taxes, charter schools, carbon tax).[5]

National publications such as *Governing* identified the key state legislative issues for 2016 across the country as worker pay, local government preemption, school choice, prison reform, police accountability, opioid addiction, and Medicaid expansion, among others.[6] None of these issues is trivial. As Martha Derthick noted, absent concerted national action, "the states are the 'default setting' of the American federal system. To the extent that other levels of government lack the resources to act—authority, revenue, will power, political consensus, institutional capacity—the states have the job."[7]

In the previous chapter, we showed how state governmental institutions, which were denigrated for decades, have become much more capable and professional over the past two generations. Today, state policymakers across the country are far more likely to share information and experiences about issues and how each state is addressing specific problems than their counterparts were in the past. But this does not mean that the states follow the same policy paths—far from it. The policy variation across the states may not be as wide as it once was, but it is still considerable. States continue to be the "laboratories of democracy," as Justice Brandeis once characterized them. Different states have taken the lead on a range of policy innovations. These states and policies are as varied as Minnesota (the first state to experiment with charter schools), Oregon (the first to permit doctor-assisted suicide for terminally ill patients), Florida (the first to require drug testing to qualify for public assistance), California (the first to create a carbon trading market), Massachusetts (the first to ban cell phone usage while driving), and Texas (the first to pass an in-state resident tuition policy for undocumented immigrant students). It was a Wisconsin policy requiring welfare recipients to be enrolled in school or training for a job (workfare) that became an integral part of the federal welfare law in 1995 and the Massachusetts health insurance program was the model on which the federal Affordable Care Act law was based in 2010.

States approach policy problems in different ways. Variables such as a state's political culture and economic resources lead to policy variation. Dramatic shifts in policy are often evident when a state changes control from one political party to the other. Examples from recent years include the enactment of policies by Republican-dominated governments to weaken unions in Wisconsin and Michigan, places where labor had traditionally been strong. But partisanship is not always the driver of innovation. In 2016, both Connecticut, under unified Democratic Party control, and South Carolina, under GOP leadership, adopted trial "pay for success" programs. "Pay for success" is a novel approach to funding social programs, one where funding organizations only get promised public monies once their approach has proven successful.[8]

In this chapter, we discuss some of the important ways in which policies vary from state to state. As a team of political scientists recently put it, "Although the states share cultural and historical similarities, the political, economic, and demographic heterogeneity at the state level is enormous."[9] Some of these variables, such as political party control, are obvious. Among other less obvious variables are the level of competition between the two parties; the policymaking capacity of the legislative, executive, and judicial branches of state government; interest group balance and strength within a state; public opinion; and the presence or absence of instruments of direct democracy such as the initiative process.

Public opinion and ideology appear to be especially important in a type of policymaking that has come to be called "morality policy."[10] Morality policy is a type of social policy characterized by an appeal to "core values." Typically, it does not have significant economic impacts. The policy discussion surrounding morality policy is less technical and more about "right" and "wrong" than is the case in most other policy areas. It is often highly salient and emotional. Because at least one side of the policy debate views the issue as about core values, there is little room for negotiation and compromise. Religiosity is often strongly related to public opinion on morality policy.

Physical and socioeconomic characteristics are important because, as Virginia Gray points out, "These factors structure a government's problems and affect a state government's ability to deal with them."[11] State demographics are an example; the size and structure of the population are often important in determining the context in which problems are defined. For instance, in Utah a larger proportion of the population is under eighteen years old than in any other state. This puts a special burden on the public education system. Several states, notably Arizona and California, have significant numbers of K–12 students who are from immigrant families with limited English-speaking skills. This puts a different burden on the state's public education system.

A state's physical characteristics define some policy problems and solutions. Montana is a geographically large state with a small population, which means road and highway expenditures per capita are higher than in most states. The differences in terrain and climate from one state to another help define the role of such diverse economic sectors as agriculture and tourism. The presence of nonrenewable natural resources such as oil, natural gas, or coal and renewable ones such as hydro, solar, and wind affect the nature of economic activity and the types of environmental concerns in a state. Sometimes the economic future and the state budget outlook can change rapidly because of the discovery of oil or some other resource. Just look at recent developments in North Dakota. Between 1930 and 2000 North Dakota had a net population loss of 40,000 people—an extraordinary statistic when one realizes that the overall population of the United States more than doubled during that time period. But over the last fifteen years the state has experienced something of a population boom, adding almost 115,000 residents. Why this sudden change? It was driven by the development of the oil- and shale-rich Bakken Formation in the western part of the state. North Dakota is now the second largest oil producer among the states behind Texas and its per capita income ranking leaped from thirty-eighth to ninth among the states between 2000 and 2015. The financial benefits to the state government were substantial: North Dakota was the only state to enjoy a budget surplus every year during the recent recession and its aftermath.

State economies play an important role in state policymaking. First, the relative wealth or poverty in a state is a major variable in social welfare costs and the ability or inability to finance the service and regulatory activities of the state government. Second, the nature of the economy—agricultural, industrial, service, resource extraction—has a significant effect on the nature of the interest group system in a state and the ability of the state to adjust to changing economic realities. Once the price of a barrel of oil declined dramatically in 2015, for example, North Dakota and other states that rely on revenue from oil extraction faced budget shortfalls.

While many policies vary from state to state, it is also true that states learn from one another. A good contemporary example is cell phone use while driving. In 2001, New York became the first state to ban talking on a cell phone while driving. By 2016, thirteen additional states have done so, but thirty-six states have not followed New York's example. Some states ban texting but not talking; still others ban talking for young drivers (under age eighteen) only.[12] Within the field of comparative state politics, there is a remarkably rich literature on policy innovation and diffusion.[13] Often policies begin in one state and are incrementally adopted by a few other states. A larger group of states then may adopt in rapid succession, while some states may never implement them. In these types of cases, if one were to graph the policy adoption by states over time, an "s-curve" pattern emerges.

At other times, one state develops a policy that then "breaks outs" and experiences "rapid and sudden adoption" across states.[14] "Amber Alert" laws are an example; first adopted in Texas, every state in the United States passed such a law within six years. The pattern of innovation diffusion depends in part on the type of policy being addressed. Some policy problems are highly salient to the public and the media, others are not. Some policy problems (and their potential solutions) are extremely complex, others are simpler. Research shows that the interplay between issue salience and complexity help define the degree and manner to which other states adopt the policy.[15]

There is also evidence that some states are consistently more likely to be innovators (policy leaders) and that innovation often comes in "waves"—periods in which many states are adopting new policies.[16] Among the states that are innovation leaders are California, Colorado, Florida, Illinois, Minnesota, and North Carolina. Furthermore, we have been experiencing an extended "innovation wave" for the past quarter-century just as we might expect, given the growing capacity of state governments. Keeping in mind the political, physical, and socioeconomic factors and how they define the context of policymaking and how policies diffuse across states, we now turn to an examination of some of the most important policy areas for the states.

Public Education and the States

Along with public safety, education has long been considered the primary responsibility of the states and their local governments. Almost all state constitutions contain provisions to this effect, although the specific language varies. Consider, for example, the mandates in the following state constitutions:

- Oklahoma: "The Legislature shall establish and maintain *a system of free public schools* wherein all the children of the State may be educated."

- New York: "The legislature shall provide for the maintenance and support *of a system of free common schools*, wherein all the children of this
state may be educated."
- Minnesota: "It is the duty of the legislature to establish a general and uni-
form system of public schools. The legislature shall make such provisions
by taxation or otherwise as will secure *a thorough and efficient system of
public schools* throughout the state."
- Illinois: "The State shall provide for *an efficient system of high quality
public educational institutions and services.*"[17]

The last two clauses appear to hold those states to a higher standard in the
provision of public education than the first two. This is not a casual observation; most states (especially the state legislatures) have been sued at one time
or another for not maintaining the public school system at state constitutional standards. Whether the state constitution simply requires "a system of
free public schools" or "a thorough and efficient system of high quality public
educational institutions" may determine how these lawsuits are decided by
state courts. There are many ways in which states matter in education policy.
Here we will emphasize four: funding patterns, curriculum content, school
choice, and higher education.

School funding. K–12 education funding is the single largest expenditure
for the states (although health care is challenging that position), accounting
for about one-quarter of a typical state budget. It varies by state depending
on how a particular state divides up the funding responsibility with its local
school districts. (As another example of how states differ, Hawaii does not
have school districts; the state department of education oversees all of its
public schools.) Some states require most of the K–12 school funding to
come from the local level, which means the primary funding source is the
local property tax. Because of its heavy reliance on local school districts, only
31 percent of public school funding in South Dakota comes from the state.
In contrast, in Vermont very little of the K–12 money comes from the local
governments and the state undertakes the primary responsibility through a
state property tax, paying more than 88 percent of the total cost from the state
budget. The consequence, therefore, is that public schools account for a much
larger state expenditure in Vermont (32 percent of the entire state budget)
than in South Dakota (14 percent).[18]

Regardless of how a state divides this revenue and spending function with
its local governments, public education is ultimately the state's responsibility.
The amount of total state and local spending on K–12 per student varies substantially, as shown in table 5.1. Utah spends the lowest amount per student
($6,555), while New York spends three times as much ($19,818).[19] Some of

TABLE 5.1
Spending per Pupil K–12, FY 2013

Alabama	$8,755
Alaska	$18,175
Arizona	$7,208
Arkansas	$9,394
California	$9,220
Colorado	$8,647
Connecticut	$16,631
Delaware	$13,833
Florida	$8,433
Georgia	$9,099
Hawaii	$11,823
Idaho	$6,791
Illinois	$12,288
Indiana	$9,566
Iowa	$10,313
Kansas	$9,828
Kentucky	$9,316
Louisiana	$10,490
Maine	$12,147
Maryland	$13,829
Massachusetts	$14,515
Michigan	$10,948
Minnesota	$11,089
Mississippi	$8,130
Missouri	$9,597
Montana	$10,625
Nebraska	$11,579
Nevada	$8,339
New Hampshire	$13,721
New Jersey	$17,572
New Mexico	$9,012
New York	$19,818
North Carolina	$8,390
North Dakota	$11,980
Ohio	$11,197
Oklahoma	$7,672
Oregon	$9,543
Pennsylvania	$13,864
Rhode Island	$14,415
South Carolina	$9,514
South Dakota	$8,470
Tennessee	$8,208
Texas	$8,299
Utah	$6,555
Vermont	$16,377
Virginia	$10,960
Washington	$9,672
West Virginia	$11,132
Wisconsin	$11,071
Wyoming	$15,700
United States	$10,700

Source: *Governing* calculations of per pupil current spending data published in U.S. Census Bureau Annual Survey of School Systems. Figures shown in FY 2013 dollars. See http://www.governing.com/gov-data/education-data/state-education-spending-per-pupil-data.html.

the variation can be accounted for by differences in state wealth, the cost of living, the magnitude of the school-age population relative to total state population, and average class size. Education is a personnel-intensive endeavor, so most (about 75 percent) of the K–12 funding is spent on personnel—teacher and staff salaries and benefit packages. A recent study finds a "moderately positive correlation between per-pupil spending and education ranking."[20] The correlation is far from perfect; there are numerous variables that are important in determining the overall quality of education from one state to another, including the number of students for whom English is a second language. Nonetheless, of the ten states ranking highest in education quality, eight spent more than the average per child. Of the ten states ranking lowest in education quality, seven were below the average state spending per child. Consequently, lawsuits by citizens to force states to spend more on K–12 education are not uncommon.

The policy consequences of those lawsuits are quite different from one state to another. First, remember that most of these are lawsuits settled at the state supreme court level and not by the federal courts. With certain exceptions, the U.S. Supreme Court has determined that K–12 school funding is a state function. So while both the level and formula used to fund public schools in some states has been upheld, in others the courts have required dramatic changes. One recent analysis finds that since 1989 lawsuits based on "education adequacy liability" have been decided in forty-four states, and in twenty-four of those states the decision went against the state, with mixed results in two others.[21] In most instances, "the funding systems were completely or partially overturned."[22] Kentucky and Michigan are two such cases, and in both significant changes were made to the state education system, including the manner in which they were funded. In Kansas, the state legislature and the state supreme court engaged in a heated battle over K–12 funding for more than three years. In 2016, the court finally forced the state legislature to revise its K–12 funding allocation process. States, therefore, are intimately involved in the funding of K–12 education.

It is also the case that states continue to grapple with the school funding issue—both in terms of how schools are funded and the level at which they are funded. Lawsuits continue to be filed. This remains a key policy issue for states because they are a large funder of public schools. Taking all states together, the source of funding for public schools is equally derived from state and local sources—45 percent from the state government and 46 percent from local school districts. From 1995 until 2013, states were supplying a slightly larger share overall than the local districts (about 47 to 50 percent depending on the year), but many states cut their funding to local schools during the Great Recession. The federal government provides only about 8 to 13 percent of public school funding, depending on the year. These figures vary considerably by state, of course. Wealthier states (Connecticut, New Jersey, and New York) rely very little (4 percent to 5 percent) on federal funds, while poorer states (Louisiana, Mississippi, New Mexico, and South Dakota at 15 percent to 16 percent) are more dependent on federal money.[23]

Curriculum. High school graduation rates diverge by state more than one might imagine. The most recent report of the adjusted cohort graduation rate showed Nevada and New Mexico are on the low end at 70 percent and 69 percent, respectively, while Iowa (91 percent) and Nebraska (90 percent) had the highest rates.[24] There are many reasons for differences in graduation rates, including the percentage of students for whom English is not their native language.

Different states also have different curriculum requirements. While there remains a voluntary but politically controversial effort among the states to develop a "common core" of subjects and classes, there is still considerable variation in what each state requires. For example, there are nine states that do not require students to take at least one course in American government or civics.[25] In 2015, eight states—Arizona, Idaho, Louisiana, North Dakota, South Carolina, Tennessee, Utah, and Wisconsin—adopted laws requiring high school students to pass a citizenship test along the lines of those taken by people seeking to become naturalized citizens in order to graduate.[26] Mapping course content requirements in about a dozen states at several different grade levels, scholars recently found only moderate alignment of curriculum content requirements from one state to another, with minimal alignment between some states' requirements in certain subjects.[27] Meanwhile, controversies erupted in some states over the curricular content of a variety of school subjects. In Texas, there was a heated debate over material covered in high school history textbooks and who has the authority to review such materials.[28] Lawmakers and teachers in Arizona have battled over Mexican American studies courses.[29]

Perhaps the most contentious issue in regard to curriculum is the teaching of evolution and creationism in science classes. Most people are at least vaguely familiar with the "Scopes Monkey Trial," a 1925 case involving a prohibition against teaching evolution in Tennessee public schools. Fewer people know that Tennessee was not the first state to pass "anti-Darwin" legislation. Oklahoma was the first in 1923, followed by Florida. Mississippi and Arkansas also passed such laws soon after Tennessee. The issue reemerged toward the end of the twentieth century. In Kansas, where the state board of education is an elected body, religious conservatives won six seats on the ten-member board in 2005 and the new majority voted to change the way evolution was addressed in the school curriculum. They required evolution be presented as a flawed theory and permitted "intelligent design" to be taught as an alternative theory.[30] By 2007, several of the conservatives on the state board had been defeated, resulting in a more moderate majority. The board subsequently repealed the 2005 policy. That action did not, however, end the controversy. In 2012, Tennessee passed a law that permits teachers to discuss alternatives to evolution in science class, claiming an "academic freedom" right to do so. Louisiana had passed a similar law in 2008.[31] In recent years, a handful of other states legislatures have considered similar measures, while other states have specifically rejected such policies.[32]

The issue of teaching evolution and alternative theories in public schools is interesting because it is tied, in a broad sense, to state political culture and public opinion. Polls find that, while a solid majority of respondents believe evolution should be taught in science classes, a majority also believes that creationism should be taught.[33] The belief that creationism should be part of the curriculum is especially strong among Evangelical Christians, a group that is prevalent in the South. Many (but not all) of the states in which the public school curriculum provides an alternative to evolution in science classes or at least a challenge to evolution are, indeed, southern states. As one report on this topic notes, "State evolution standards are strongly influenced by public opinion, which is itself strongly related to the number of Evangelicals and the number of advanced degree holders in the state."[34]

Another example of political culture influencing curriculum is sex education. As of 2016, twenty-four states require their public schools to teach sex education. Almost all of these states mandate HIV education as well. At the same time, three states (Arizona, Nevada, and Utah) require parental consent before a child can receive sex education instruction and thirty-six states allow parents to opt out of such instruction on behalf of their children. Abstinence must be stressed in sex education instruction in twenty-six states and covered as a topic in eleven other states; thirteen states have no requirements on abstinence.[35] Consequently, the sort of sex education children get varies across the states.

School choice. One of the biggest educational movements in the past two decades has been the effort to allow parents and children more choice in the public schools they attend. By far the largest component of this program is the charter school movement. The first state to authorize charter schools was Minnesota. According to the Minnesota Legislative Reference Library, "The basic charter concept is simple: a group of teachers or other would-be educators apply for permission to open a school. The school operates under a charter, a contract with the local school board or state." A charter school is exempt from most of the regulations required of traditional public school and is authorized to experiment with different types of curriculum or learning techniques. Students must still meet traditional graduation requirements and the school must demonstrate that it has accomplished the learning objectives stipulated in the charter. If the school has not met those objectives, it may lose its charter to operate. The idea is to introduce more innovation into the public school system. The key, and the source of much of the initial resistance to charter schools in many quarters, is that the charter schools receive state tax dollars, generally in the same amount as traditional public schools. In addition, some charter schools are created and managed by private companies—another reason for resistance to them from some quarters.

Since the first charter schools were authorized in 1991, the system has expanded rapidly. Today, there are over six thousand charter schools enrolling more than 2.5 million students in forty states. Even with this rapid growth, however, charter schools remain a small part of the overall public school system, comprising less than 7 percent of all public schools and enrolling just over 5 percent of all public school students, although in a few cities such as Detroit, St. Louis, and Gary, Indiana, more than 30 percent of public school students attend public charter schools.[36] There are ten states in which there are no charter schools.[37]

The success of the charter school movement appears uneven. Research comparing student outcomes among charter school and traditional school students is mixed and inconclusive.[38] Some schools have had their charters revoked for failure to meet state graduation standards or for mismanaging public funds. But others are innovative, popular, and successful, with long waiting lists of prospective students desiring to attend. Over half of the charter schools are in urban areas, and many serve minority communities for whom the public school system has not succeeded. There is evidence that charter schools often outperform traditional public schools in these settings.[39] It is clear that charter schools are not a panacea for the ills of the public school system. But at their best, they offer the potential to experiment with learning strategies that, in the long run, may provide "best practices" that will advance the larger education system in many states.

While the overall assessment of charter schools' success remains open, the concept of them appears to be accepted by a majority of the public. A 2015 poll found that almost two-thirds of the respondents favored the idea of charter schools, with greater support being found among Republicans and independent voters than among Democrats.[40] The public is considerably less enthusiastic about the concept of using publicly funded vouchers to help pay for a student to attend private schools. Vouchers take the idea of school choice further. The idea is that under certain circumstances students may take all or a significant portion of their public education tax dollars with them as they move from public schools to private schools. Because most private schools in the United States are church-affiliated, many people are reluctant to see taxpayer funds used in this way. Less than one-third (31 percent) of the respondents to the poll mentioned earlier favored permitting students to attend private school at public expense. These are not just opinions held about an abstract concept. After the Utah legislature passed a statewide universal school voucher program in 2007, opponents of the measure gathered enough signatures to put the matter on the ballot, where voters rejected it, 62 percent against to 38 percent in favor.

Relatively few states allow such voucher programs. Both Maine (1873) and Vermont (1869) have actually had targeted voucher programs in place for over 140 years. In each state they are granted to students living in towns that do not operate public schools. Other sorts of voucher programs exist in only a handful of states. Currently, eight states offer them to students with certain disabilities to attend private schools. A few other states make them available to students from failing schools or from low-income families, and several states allow both students with disabilities or from low-income families to use them. Even in these states such programs are limited in use. For example, Wisconsin initially permitted students in two cities (Milwaukee and Racine) to use vouchers (up to $7,366 in 2014–2015) to attend a private school. In 2013, it passed the Parental Choice Program, allowing parents living outside of Milwaukee and Racine and who meet certain income qualifications to use a voucher to send their children to private schools. In 2014–2015, only about 2,500 students used the vouchers. Other states, such as Louisiana, only allow students to make use of vouchers if they 1) meet certain income eligibility requirements and 2) attended a public school that was poorly performing on the state school assessment report, which again constrains their use.[41]

Perhaps because of public resistance to the idea that government funds should be transferred to private schools through a voucher system, some states have instead moved toward a "tax credit" program. Such programs allow taxpayers to reduce their tax liability by "donating" money to private schools for scholarships, similar to a tax credit for charitable contributions. But because the taxpayer (that is, the parent) can specify the scholarship recipient (their child) in some states, this program can become a "backdoor voucher" system. Ultimately, tax revenue that would have gone to the state is transferred to a private school as part of the private school tuition. Currently, sixteen states have some sort of tuition tax credit program.[42] The first state to authorize such tax credits was Arizona in 1997. The U.S. Supreme Court upheld Arizona's law in 2011, and several states (most notably Georgia) have adopted an expanded version of it.[43]

Another alternative to traditional K–12 schools is homeschooling, a phenomenon that is growing rapidly; by 2012 almost 1.8 million students were homeschooled.[44] This number constitutes 3.4 percent of all K–12 school-age children in the United States, only slightly fewer students than are enrolled in charter schools. Generally, it is up to the state legislature, the state board of education, or the state department of education to set standards for homeschooling. As one might expect, these standards differ from one state to another. According to the Home School Legal Defense Association, seven states (mostly in the northeast) are "high regulation" states, requiring parents of homeschooled students to supply the state with achievement test scores, an approved curriculum, the teacher qualifications of the parent, and allowing home visits by state officials. At the other extreme are eleven states that have no requirements. In these states, parents neither have to notify the state that they intend to homeschool their child nor show any evidence of the students' academic progress.[45] Another fifteen states, many Midwestern and western states, are categorized as having low requirements.[46] The remaining states, scattered around the country, are classified as "states with moderate regulation" of homeschooling.[47]

The issue of school choice will remain a difficult one, as many states wrestle with issues of underperforming schools, the costs of public education, and the need to adapt to new technologies and circumstances. Like Minnesota (charter schools) and Wisconsin (vouchers), some states will be at the forefront of new, intriguing educational ideas. Different states will likely try different things; some will succeed and others will not. This is the essence of states as "the laboratories of democracy."

Higher education. Unlike many other federal countries, there are no national universities (with the exception of the service academies) in the United States. For public universities in the United States, the direct support of teaching is provided through an appropriation from the state budget and student tuition.[48] Table 5.2 shows the tuition cost for in-state students in 2015–2016 at the flagship public university in each state. The differences are substantial. There are a number of reasons for the variations. An obvious one is labor (faculty and staff) costs. These tend to vary by region, with the costs being higher in the east and lowest in the south. The state appropriation to higher education is another variable. If State A appropriates a larger share of the total higher education budget than State B, then, all other things being equal, tuition should be lower in State A. Of course, all other things are not usually equal from one state to another. Research shows that other variables that affect tuition costs include the amount of state financial aid awarded to students and the number of private colleges and universities in a state.[49]

Public universities are funded by a combination of sources: appropriations from the state budget, student tuition and fees, research grants and contracts, donations (gifts and endowments), and licensing and merchandising fees.

TABLE 5.2

**In-State Tuition and Fees per Year at State Public "Flagship"
University, 2015–2016, and Five-Year Percent Change**

State	2015–2016 Tuition and Fees	Percent Change in Tuition, 2011–2016
AK	$6,804	17
AL	$10,170	18
AR	$8,522	15
AZ	$11,400	26
CA	$13,431	12
CO	$11,091	19
CT	$13,364	17
DE	$12,250	12
FL	$6,381	16
GA	$11,622	45
HI	$11,164	26
IA	$8,104	0
ID	$7,020	19
IL	$15,626	9
IN	$10,388	5
KS	$10,802	13
KY	$10,936	16
LA	$8,827	40
MA	$14,356	10
MD	$9,996	9
ME	$10,610	−4
MI	$13,856	7
MN	$13,790	3
MO	$10,586	14
MS	$7,444	25
MT	$6,158	3
NC	$8,591	18
ND	$7,965	5
NE	$8,279	5
NH	$16,986	13
NJ	$14,131	3
NM	$6,664	11
NV	$6,882	13
NY	$9,461	21
OH	$10,037	−3
OK	$10,090	17
OR	$10,289	15
PA	$17,514	5
RI	$12,862	12
SC	$11,482	7
SD	$8,457	14
TN	$12,436	54
TX	$9,830	−5
UT	$8,197	19
VA	$14,468	24
VT	$16,738	9
WA	$11,839	21
WI	$10,415	6
WV	$7,632	29
WY	$4,891	14

Source: http://trends.collegeboard.org/college-pricing.

The relative importance of these revenue streams to the public higher education system will diverge from state to state, and this makes generalizations difficult.[50] But today most state flagship universities appear to receive between 20 percent and 30 percent of their total budgets from state appropriations, although in some cases it is as low as 6 percent.[51] As a proportion of total funds, this is a sharp decline over the past generation. In 1980, states contributed 46 percent of the public higher education budgets across the United States. By 2000, the figure was 36 percent.[52] Today, it is around 21 percent.[53] For some states, the decline is even more dramatic. According to the University of Michigan, appropriated state support for its academic programs dropped from 87 percent of the university budget in 1960 to a mere 16 percent in 2015.[54] Higher education budgets took a major hit in many states during the 2008 to 2012 period as the effects of the Great Recession caused many lawmakers to cut back on appropriations. During economic downturns, when state finances suffer, higher education budgets are usually among the first casualties because budget writers in the state legislatures know that universities can soften the blow by raising tuition. Thus between 2007 and 2012, tuition and fees doubled in Arizona, California, Florida, and Hawaii.[55] Increases have slowed some since then, but as shown in table 5.2, in some states tuition and fees have still continued to escalate at a dramatic pace.

The cost of a college education is a topic on the agenda of many state officials today, including governors, state legislatures, and university governing boards. States are experimenting with a host of innovative education systems, among them online delivery of instructional materials, the use of massive open online courses (MOOCs), curricular changes, reformation of graduation requirements to squeeze four-year degrees into three years, and performance funding (state appropriations tied to graduate rates, for example).[56] State budget problems are apt to keep public universities and colleges under financial pressure well into the future.

The Police Power of the States: Public Safety, Crime, and Corrections

Despite the role of the federal government in ensuring due process and the rights of the accused, and in interpreting the "cruel and unusual punishment" clause of the Eighth Amendment, states retain substantial police powers. This includes state discretion in determining criminal definitions and penalties. States matter on a wide range of criminal justice issues, from texting while driving laws to capital punishment.

Gun control laws are often a major topic of conversation. As debate over the regulation of firearms continues at the national level, it is worth noting that a few states have adopted much more restrictive gun laws than others. At the beginning of 2016, six states were considered to have comparatively strict gun control laws: California, Connecticut, New Jersey, Maryland, Massachusetts, and New York. In contrast, every southern state save for Virginia and every Mountain West state save for Colorado had the weakest restrictions.[57] In part, this pattern tracks with the political cultures of the states. But it also demonstrates the impact of traumatic events. Following a series of mass shootings in the state, in 2013 Colorado passed a significant array of gun control laws limiting the size of ammunition magazines and requiring universal background checks on all gun purchases. And the 2012 Newtown massacre prompted Connecticut to pass stringent gun control laws the following year.[58] But the responses in those two states were not necessarily representative. One study found that between 1989 and 2014, "A mass shooting increases the number of enacted laws that *loosen* gun restrictions by 75% in states with Republican-controlled legislatures."[59]

Gun laws are far from static in the American federal system. In 2016, for example, voters in California, Nevada, and Washington tightened their states' gun laws. Perhaps the most notable development over the last quarter-century has been the spread of laws allowing people the right to carry a concealed weapon. State government officials were given discretion over the issuance of concealed carry permits ("may issue" laws) in another twenty-six states, essentially allowing them to give permits only to applicants who could demonstrate a need. Officials were compelled to give permits to applicants ("shall issue" laws) in only eight states. Vermont was in its own category, allowing anyone to carry a concealed weapon without any permit or license. Through a sustained campaign spearheaded by the National Rifle Association, over time resistance to concealed carry laws dissipated. In 2013, Illinois became the final state to allow it. But concealed carry law provisions vary. By 2016, Alaska, Arizona, Kansas, Maine, and Wyoming had joined Vermont in allowing anyone to carry a concealed weapon without restriction. Laws in only nine states fell into the "may issue" category, meaning the government retained some discretion over who is issued a permit. The much less restrictive "shall issue" or a "no discretion to deny" mandate applied in the other thirty-five states.[60] A "shall issue" directive really does mean that virtually every permit request is granted. In the first two years following Iowa's switch to "shall issue" rules, 99.6 percent of permit requests were approved.[61] Thus with the recent changes in the law across the states far more people today have the right to carry a concealed weapon than was the case just a few years ago.

One area in which there has been some agreement on gun control involves domestic abusers. Over the last two years, more than a dozen states have passed legislation making it more difficult for those arrested for such violence to have access to guns. Even several states dominated by Republicans, notably South Carolina and Wisconsin, have passed such measures. State laws in this area are generally thought to be stronger than the federal laws.[62]

A related shift in state laws over the last few years has been in so-called castle and stand your ground laws. Castle laws, referred to initially as "make my day" laws, essentially allow a person to do whatever he or she deems necessary, including using deadly force, to protect themselves in and around their home. Stand your ground laws, first passed in Florida in 2005, expand that right to any place a person feels threatened. Between 2000 and 2010, twenty-one states expanded their castle doctrine laws, always by removing a duty to retreat somewhere outside the home and usually by also removing any civil liability attached to one's actions.[63] Almost all of these states also adopted stand your ground provisions. These laws are most common in the South and Mountain West.[64] Consequently, in thirty-two states today people are allowed to legally take actions against another person that they were not allowed to take in the recent past.

Dynamism and differentiation in the American federal system also surface in state laws governing police powers. Take, for example, marijuana laws, which as suggested by chapter 1's opening vignette also vary both across the states and over time. In 2012, two states—Colorado and Washington—legalized possession of marijuana in small amounts. They were the first states to permit the use of marijuana for recreational use, although eighteen states had already legalized use of marijuana for medical reasons.[65] While all of these provisions contradicted current federal law in regard to marijuana use, the Obama administration announced it did not intend to pursue the conflict. Both the Colorado and Washington laws were the product of the initiative process in which the voters approved the measures in a direct vote. In 2014, voters in Alaska and Oregon used the same mechanism to legalize marijuana in their states, as did those in California, Maine, Massachusetts, and Nevada two years later. It is often the case that one of a few states innovate a policy and other states take a "wait-and-see" position. A common pattern is for policy innovations to diffuse slowly across the states, often on a region-by-region basis. Thus, by 2017, medical marijuana was gradually gaining greater acceptance, with twenty-eight states having such laws on their books and several others considering it.[66]

Another example of policy diffusion is a ban on tobacco smoking in public places (worksites, restaurants, and bars). In 1995, only one state banned smoking in restaurants (but not in the workplace). Not surprisingly, that state was Utah. In 2000, Delaware became the first state to pass a comprehensive ban on smoking in all three places (offices, restaurants, and bars). By 2005, four additional states (Massachusetts, New York, Rhode Island, and

Washington) had passed comprehensive bans. A decade later, twenty-four states had such comprehensive laws. None were southern states, where almost all the tobacco in the United States is grown. Indeed, there were fourteen states in which there was no statewide ban on smoking in any of the public sites mentioned earlier.[67] The minimum age at which tobacco products can be purchased may be another emerging example. In 2015, Hawaii raised the legal age to twenty-one, followed the next year by California. The minimum age is nineteen in four states (Alabama, Alaska, New Jersey, and Utah), and eighteen in the rest of the country. But given Hawaii and California's lead, it is likely that other states will consider raising their minimum age.[68]

The Prison Dilemma. One problem faced by all states over the past generation is prison overcrowding. Public concern with the rise in crime rates in the 1960s and 1970s resulted in "get tough" policies being put in place across the states. This was manifested in harsher sentencing laws, including mandatory and determinate sentencing. In particular, tougher mandatory sentences were imposed for nonviolent crimes such as illegal drug possession. A consequence of this policy decision was a dramatic rise in both the number of people incarcerated and the resulting cost of housing prisoners.[69] Today, the United States has the highest incarceration rate of any country in the world and most of those prisoners are in state prisons, not federal prisons, county or city jails, or private correctional facilities. State prisons house 59 percent of all incarcerated individuals in the country, with local jails accounting for most of the rest.[70] Approximately 1.35 million people are currently in state prison systems. Incarceration rates vary considerably by state; Louisiana has an incarceration rate (1,072 per 100,000 residents) six times higher than Maine's (189 per 100,000 residents).[71] Nonetheless, virtually all states experienced a dramatic increase in the number of prisoners they house in the last four decades. Since 1980, state prison populations have more than tripled. By 2008, five states were spending as much or more on their prisons than they were on higher education.[72]

The reasons for this dramatic increase are several. The biggest contributor was a change in penalties for drug convictions. A second reason was the increase in the length of sentences. The consequences of these policy changes are substantial. State corrections budgets grew dramatically, straining state budgets. But states made different decisions on how punitive to be. Although all states became more punitive between 1983 and 2013, some were considerably more punitive than others. Crime was the most severely punished in Mississippi and Idaho and the least severely punished in Washington and Maine.[73]

Since 2010, however, the number of prisoners has declined nationally, in part because of state decisions to supervise some nonviolent offenders in their home communities rather than in prisons.[74] States vary widely in how they choose to supervise their correctional populations. In Rhode Island, 88 percent of the correctional population is under community supervision, usually on probation or parole. At the other end of the spectrum, Oklahoma has only 38 percent of its correctional population under community supervision.[75]

A particularly important case of "policy innovation" in this area over the last two decades was the "Three Strikes and You're Out" (TSAYO) laws passed in the mid-1990s. These measures were adopted by some states in reaction to a particularly heinous crime in California committed by an individual who had been released after serving time for several violent felony crimes. But the first state to adopt such a law was actually Washington in 1993. California quickly followed in 1994, with a law passed by the legislature and subsequently confirmed by the public through the initiative process with over 72 percent of the voters approving it. Significantly, the California law made no distinction between violent and nonviolent felony offenses. A total of twelve states passed TSAYO laws in 1994 and another nine followed suit the next year. In a three-year period, almost half the states passed such laws, but only Arizona (2006) and Massachusetts (2012) have done so since. Nonetheless, TSAYO laws remain quite popular in the states that passed them, and none have been repealed.

The details of these laws diverge. In most of the states that passed TSAYO laws, considerable discretion was left to prosecutors to determine whether or not to pursue penalties under the TSAYO provision. As a result, TSAYO laws did not dramatically alter incarceration rates in most states that adopted them. The case of California, however, was another matter entirely. Its TSAYO law severely limited the discretion available to prosecutors and judges to consider mitigating circumstances, such as the nature of the "third strike" crime. Furthermore, the law allowed some crimes such as shoplifting, which is usually a misdemeanor crime, to be considered a felony if it was the third offense. Thus California's law led to lengthy prison sentences for some "three-time losers" even if their third conviction was for a minor or nonviolent crime. The law also mandated lengthier sentences for "second strike" offenders. Reviewing the impact of the law a decade after its passage, the California Legislative Analyst's Office estimated the additional costs directly attributable to the TSAYO law to be about $0.5 billion per year, which is less than the original projections made when TSAYO passed in 1994.[76] However, one unanticipated consequence of the law is that TSAYO has contributed to an aging of the prison population. In 2012, half of the TSAYO prisoners in California were over fifty years of age.[77] The cost of housing aged prisoners is much higher than for most other prisoners, largely because of increased health care costs. There is also an analysis that suggests that while the deterrent effect of the policy was real and a significant number of career criminals actively sought to avoid committing a third offense, those who did commit them committed more violent acts because they calculated they had little to lose. And California's strict law may have encouraged many of its career criminals to relocate to neighboring states where they did not face any additional sanctions, thus only shifting the problem.[78]

In 2012, again through the initiative process, California amended its TSAYO law to allow consideration of the nature of the third strike offense to be taken into account, a decision that permits minor crimes or nonviolent offenses committed by third-time offenders to be treated less harshly than under the original California TSAYO measure. By 2014, 1,613 inmates sentenced to life for nonviolent crimes under TSAYO had been released. They have had a remarkably low recidivism rate.[79]

States differ considerably on sentencing philosophies, with some states taking stronger "get tough" stances while others emphasize rehabilitation. Based on whether a state has adopted such policies as mandatory sentencing, the abolition of parole, TSAYO laws, and a required minimum prison term for six offender groups, an index of "sentencing policy toughness" has been constructed.[80] By this measure, the states with the toughest sentencing policies are California, Florida, Idaho, and Indiana. The states at the other end of the scale are New Mexico, Massachusetts, Kentucky, and Kansas. Generally speaking, "policy-liberal states tend to have more lenient sentencing practices and lower incarceration rates."[81] But the correlation is far from perfect, and a few states, such as California and New York, which are generally considered to be liberal in policy outlook, have tough sentencing requirements.

Further examples of how states vary in the application of their police powers include the institution of a death penalty and the willingness to turn over some corrections functions to "for-profit" corporations. Capital punishment is not imposed in nineteen states, most in the Midwest and Northeast. The trend in recent years has been to abolish the death penalty.[82] During the current decade, Illinois (2011), Connecticut (2012), Maryland (2013), and Nebraska (2015) have done so. The first three states were under unified Democratic Party control, making their decisions less surprising. In contrast, although Nebraska elects its legislature on a nonpartisan ballot, it has a large Republican majority. Thus, it was politically shocking to see its conservative majority not only pass a bill abolishing the death penalty in that state but also then override the Republican governor's veto of it.[83] But in 2016, Nebraska voters opted to reinstate it, and liberal California voters not only voted to keep it there but also to allow the legal process governing it to be accelerated. Still, there is a growing movement among conservative state lawmakers to reassess the death penalty, if only because of its costs.[84] In 2015 and 2016, bills to end it were introduced by Republican legislators in Kansas, Kentucky, Missouri, Montana, New Hampshire, Ohio, South Dakota, Utah, and Wyoming.

Many states in the South, however, have demonstrated little reluctance to impose and carry out death sentences. Of the ten states with the most executions since 1976, seven are southern states, and two others—Missouri and Oklahoma—border the South. As of May 2016, Texas (537 executions), Oklahoma (112), and Virginia (111) had executed the most prisoners since 1976. Nationally, the number of executions each year has steadily declined over the last decade and a half, from ninety-eight in 1999 to twenty-eight in 2015.[85]

"Prison privatization" also has a distinct regional flavor. While only 8 percent of all state prisoners are currently housed in correctional facilities run by "for-profit" companies such as the Corrections Corporation of America and the Geo Group (by far the two largest such companies), twenty states have no prisoners in such facilities and several others make only minimal use of them. Some states have laws specifically prohibiting such privatization. In contrast, over a quarter of the state prison populations in Montana (39 percent of state prisoners), New Mexico (44 percent), and Oklahoma (26 percent) are incarcerated in for-profit facilities.[86] As private prisons have become big business in many states, particularly in the South and Mountain West, they have become energetic in lobbying state officials and making contributions to candidates for public office.[87] Scandals associated with the way some private prisons have been operated have forced a few states to retake control over them. In 2014, for example, Idaho resumed running one of its major correctional facilities following falsified staffing records by the private company that had been in charge.[88]

The States and Social Issues

The states have traditionally controlled policies lumped together under the label of "social issues" or "morality issues." Currently, the most prominent and controversial of these involve marriage and abortion. Over time, the states have arrived at a number of different policies on these matters, with the federal courts playing a central role in establishing the boundaries of their actions.

Laws regarding marriage have largely been left to the states and there have always been differences across them on who can marry. Today, for example, twenty-five states ban marriages between first cousins and seven more states place some restrictions on it.[89] Well into the twentieth century many states enforced laws banning miscegenation, or marriage between people from different racial or ethnic groups. A handful of states in the Northeast and upper Midwest never had antimiscegenation laws, and several others in those regions repealed the laws they had during the nineteenth century. But the largest movement to overturn antimiscegenation bans was initiated by a California Supreme Court decision, *Perez v. Sharp* (1948), which declared unconstitutional that state's law preventing blacks and whites from marrying.[90] Over the following two decades, other states in the West followed California's lead and swept aside their antimiscegenation laws. But it took the U.S. Supreme Court's decision in *Loving v. Virginia* (1967) declaring such laws to be unconstitutional to force southern and border states to allow such marriages.[91]

In recent years, controversy surrounded the question of state laws governing same-sex marriage. Serious political debate on the question first surfaced in 1993 when the Hawaii Supreme Court ruled that unless the state demonstrated that it had a compelling reason for denying same-sex couples the right to marry, the practice would be held to violate the state constitution. This led to a protracted political struggle over the issue. In 1998, Hawaii voters overwhelmingly passed Constitutional Amendment 2, granting the state legislature the power to limit marriage to only opposite-sex couples. The Hawaii Supreme Court subsequently dismissed the original lawsuit as being moot because of the voter-approved state constitutional amendment.

The decision reached by Hawaii mattered for the rest of the states because had that state recognized a right for gays and lesbians to marry in the mid-1990s, those marriages might have had to be recognized in the other forty-nine states because the U.S. Constitution (Article IV, Section 1) requires that "full faith and credit shall be given in each state to the public acts, records and judicial proceedings of every other state." This clause can be read to mean that marriages performed in one state must be recognized as legal in other states. In response to the possibility of same-sex marriages being allowed in Hawaii, Utah passed a law in 1995 that denied recognition to all out-of-state marriages that did not conform to Utah law. This approach was essentially taken national in 1996 when Congress passed the Defense of Marriage Act (DOMA). The measure, which was signed into law by President Bill Clinton, barred federal recognition of same-sex marriages and permitted states to take no legal notice of same-sex marriages performed in other states where they might be allowed. How DOMA squared with the U.S. Constitution's full faith and credit clause was left for the courts to decide.

Although Hawaii did not pursue same-sex marriage, debate on the issue percolated across the states. Hawaii created domestic partnerships in 1997, a policy that gave same-sex couples limited rights. A few years later Vermont became the first state to pass legislation allowing same-sex partners to establish a civil union, providing them many of the same legal rights granted to married couples under state (but not federal) law. The prospect of legislation creating civil unions led the Massachusetts state senate in 2003 to seek an advisory opinion from the state's Supreme Judicial Court as to whether such unions would be legal under the Massachusetts constitution. The court's advisory opinion, handed down in February 2004, held that any law that fell short of allowing same-sex marriage would be unconstitutional because it would be discriminatory. The advisory opinion set the stage for allowing same-sex marriage in Massachusetts. The decision in Massachusetts pushed the issue of same-sex marriage back onto center stage in national politics.

The same day the Massachusetts opinion was handed down, President George W. Bush asked Congress to "promptly pass, and to send to the states for ratification, an amendment to our Constitution defining and protecting marriage as a union of man and woman as husband and wife." Although he was unequivocally opposed to same-sex marriage, the president recognized the federal dimension of American government by leaving open the possibility of accepting civil unions, saying that state legislatures should be left "free to make their own choices in defining legal arrangements other than marriage."[92] Although President Bush and many members of Congress backed the Federal Marriage Amendment, it never came close to passing. Same-sex marriage opponents enjoyed much greater success at the state level, with bans passing in all thirteen states where they appeared on the ballot in 2004, and two more states in 2005. But while bans passed in another seven additional states in 2006, the first cracks in opposition to same-sex marriage appeared that year when voters in Arizona rejected such a measure.

By 2008, forty-four states had either constitutional provisions or statutory laws on the books that prevented same-sex marriages. Only in Massachusetts and California were such marriages legal, and voters in the latter passed a state constitutional amendment to ban them that November. But public views about same-sex relationships had begun to shift and that change started to show up in state laws. Civil unions had become more accepted after encountering some initial resistance. Connecticut had established them in 2005, followed by New Jersey in 2007, and Oregon and New Hampshire in 2008. Another five states adopted them by 2013.

The biggest change, however, came in same-sex marriage laws. State court decisions forced their acceptance in Connecticut and Iowa. Starting in 2009, state legislatures passed laws allowing same-sex marriage on their own initiative, with such measures being adopted in Vermont, Maine, and New Hampshire. But in a referendum Maine voters soon repealed the law passed by the legislature. Legislatures in Maryland, New York, and Washington, however, soon passed measures allowing same-sex marriage. In 2012, Maryland and Washington voters upheld their measures in referendums, while voters in Maine reversed their earlier decision by passing a ballot proposition allowing same-sex marriage. The political tide that initially rolled so heavily against government recognition of same-sex relationships had clearly begun to recede.

By June 2015, the nation was living under a mishmash of marriage laws, as shown in table 5.3. State legislatures had passed statutes allowing same-sex marriage in eleven states and voters had done likewise in Maine. State courts had established same-sex marriage in five states, while federal courts had done so in nineteen states. There were no provisions allowing same-sex marriage in fourteen states. At that point the U.S. Supreme Court handed down its decision in *Obergefell v. Hodges*, declaring laws prohibiting same-sex marriage to be unconstitutional because they violated the Fourteenth Amendment's due process and equal protection clauses.[93] Thus rights guaranteed by the federal constitution as interpreted by the U.S. Supreme Court trumped state laws.

The decision legalizing same-sex marriage met resistance in some states. Alabama's state supreme court, for example, only ended the battle over the matter in that state in 2016.[94] Even after that decision, the court's chief justice had to be suspended from his position for ordering state probate judges to ignore the U.S. Supreme Court's decision and to refuse to issue marriage licenses to same-sex couples.[95] Most of the defiance in other states has been less overt and has emerged in the form of "religious freedom" bills.[96] In 2015, even before the U.S. Supreme Court decision, Indiana adopted a measure that opponents decried as legalizing discrimination against gays and lesbians. A broad public outcry against the measure forced the legislature to quickly amend the new law, assuring that commercial businesses could not discriminate.[97] The most significant religious freedom bill passed in 2016 was in Mississippi. According to the senator who offered the measure to her chamber, "This is presenting a solution to the crossroads we find ourselves in today as a result of Obergefell v. Hodges. . . . Ministers, florists, photographers, people along those lines—this bill would allow them to refuse to provide marriage-related business services without fear of government discrimination."[98] A similar measure was vetoed by Georgia's governor, while a number of like bills foundered in other state legislatures.[99] Mississippi's law was quickly challenged in federal court and a judge struck it down.[100] So once more the question is whether a state law runs afoul of federal constitutional protections, with appellate court still to weigh in on it.

The second contentious social issue vexing state politics is abortion. Since the U.S. Supreme Court handed down its decision in *Roe v. Wade* (1973), the landmark ruling that made abortion legal during the first trimester of pregnancy but recognized the "legitimate" right of the government to impose restrictions beyond that point, initially to protect the mother's health and later at viability to protect the life of the unborn child, controversy and passion have driven the debate over abortion policies at the state level.[101] Through a

TABLE 5.3

Status of State Same-Sex Marriage Laws at Time of 2015 U.S. Supreme Court Ruling

State Legislature Passed Law Allowing Same-Sex Marriage	Voter Ballot Measure Passed Allowing Same-Sex Marriage	State Court Decision Establishing Same-Sex Marriage	Federal Court Decision Establishing Same-Sex Marriage	No State Provision Allowing Same-Sex Marriage
11 States	1 State	5 States	19 States	14 States
Connecticut	Maine	California	Alabama	Arkansas
Delaware		Iowa	Alaska	Georgia
Hawaii		Massachusetts	Arizona	Kentucky
Illinois		New Jersey	Colorado	Louisiana
Maryland		New Mexico	Florida	Michigan
Minnesota			Idaho	Mississippi
New Hampshire			Indiana	Missouri
New York			Kansas	Nebraska
Rhode Island			Montana	Nevada
Vermont			Nevada	North Dakota
Washington			North Carolina	Ohio
			Oklahoma	South Dakota
			Pennsylvania	Tennessee
			South Carolina	Texas
			Utah	
			Virginia	
			West Virginia	
			Wisconsin	
			Wyoming	

Source: Derived by authors from http://www.ncsl.org/research/human-services/same-sex-marriage-laws.aspx.

seemingly endless series of legislative and legal battles, the states have greatly reconfigured their approaches to regulating abortions. What is less appreciated is that even before the Court's decision in *Roe*, the states had already begun to diverge in the ways they handled the issue.

During the course of the nineteenth century, states passed laws that outlawed abortions. Those laws largely carried over until the 1960s. In 1962, the American Law Institute's Model Penal Code recommended allowing abortions to protect the mental and physical health of the mother and when there was a risk of birth defects. Colorado became the first state to liberalize its abortion laws along the lines of the American Law Institute model in 1967, followed shortly thereafter by California, North Carolina, and Oregon. By 1970, several other states pushed abortion rights even farther, with Hawaii allowing the abortion of nonviable fetuses as long as the procedure was done in a hospital. That same year, New York adopted a law allowing all abortions during the first twenty-four weeks of pregnancy. Similar laws were passed in Alaska and Washington.[102]

By the time the Court decided *Roe*, abortion laws actually varied a great deal across the states. Abortions for any reason were allowed in four states, thirteen states permitted them to protect the physical and mental health of the mother, and twenty-nine states to preserve the life of the mother. Women in Mississippi could get an abortion to preserve their life or if they had been raped. All abortions were banned in Louisiana, New Hampshire, and Pennsylvania.[103] Thus the Court's decision in *Roe* only forced most, not all, of the states to revise their laws.

In the more than forty years since abortion was largely legalized, a number of states have pursued policies that have narrowed the conditions under which one can be obtained. For the most part, these states have operated in the space granted by *Roe* and later decisions, notably in *Planned Parenthood v. Casey* (1992), to limit abortions toward the end of pregnancy.[104] By 2016, forty-three states had passed legislation to prohibit abortions in the latter stages except to protect the life or health of the mother. And the "latter stage" has been interpreted differently across these states. Some set it at after twenty weeks, others at twenty-four weeks, and a few at the start of the third trimester. Over half chose to set it at "viability," an ambiguous standard that has entangled these states in drawn-out legal battles.

A few states have opted to push even harder on when abortions can be prohibited. In 2013, Arkansas passed a law to prohibit abortion after twelve weeks and North Dakota followed by adopting a measure to outlaw the procedure after six weeks, the point at which a fetal heartbeat can usually be detected. The federal courts have had to sort out whether these sorts of restrictions go too far. When he signed the North Dakota six-week bill into law, the governor admitted as much, saying, "Although the likelihood of this measure surviving a court challenge remains in question, this bill is neverthe-less a legitimate attempt by a state legislature to discover the boundaries of Roe v. Wade."[105] His trepidations proved correct; the North Dakota law, along with the Arkansas law, was struck down by the federal courts.[106]

The courts have also been heavily involved in determining whether the nineteen states that have forbidden so-called partial birth abortions have gone too far; the laws in a majority of these states have been enjoined by the courts, preventing them from going into effect. And there have been other ef-forts to restrict abortion. North Dakota tried to outlaw abortion altogether by putting a "personhood measure" on the 2014 ballot. Among other things, the proposal would have banned abortions under any circumstances. The voters rejected the measure with 64 percent voting no. In 2016, lawmakers in nine states introduced bills to effectively outlaw abortion, with Oklahoma's actu-ally making it to the governor's desk. She vetoed it.[107]

Beyond outright bans, a number of regulations have been imposed on abortions. Counseling is mandated before the procedure can be performed in seventeen states. In five of those states, those seeking abortions must be told of a possible link between the procedure and breast cancer, twelve states require that they must be told that the fetus could feel pain, and nine states mandate that negative psychological effects must be discussed. Over half the states require a waiting period before an abortion can be performed, most setting it at twenty-four hours, but Missouri, North Carolina, Oklahoma, and Utah impose a seventy-two-hour wait in most cases. Parental involvement is required for minors getting an abortion in thirty-eight states, with roughly a third of them demanding that only notice be given and the rest mandating that a parent, or in some states both parents, give consent. Another political flashpoint has been over public funding. Public funds can be used for medi-cally necessary abortions in seventeen states, while such funds are limited to situations in which the mother's life is endangered or the pregnancy is the result of rape or incest in thirty-two states. Private health insurance coverage of abortions is limited by law in eleven states.[108] Another route a number of states took to limit access to abortions was the imposition of laws requiring doctors performing abortions to obtain admitting privileges at a local hospital (ten states) and abortion clinics to meet the standards expected of ambulatory surgical centers (six states). But a 2016 U.S. Supreme Court decision struck down those laws in Texas and it was expected to lead to similar laws also being declared an unconstitutional burden on the right of women to have access to abortions.[109]

Thus the obstacles a woman must overcome to secure a legal abortion vary significantly across the states. In North Carolina, for example, an abortion must be performed by a licensed physician and, after twenty weeks, the procedure must be done at a hospital and not a clinic. More important, any abortion after twenty weeks is only allowed if necessary to save the life or health of the mother. Additionally, any woman wishing to have an abortion in North Carolina is required to wait for twenty-four hours following required counseling and she must be told of possible negative psychological effects. In contrast, a woman in New Hampshire seeking an abortion faces few hurdles. She would not be required to have counseling or to wait for twenty-four hours and the procedure could be performed at a clinic by a clinician. These two cases not only highlight the substantial differences in an important social policy across the states, but they also reveal the dynamism of state politics and policies. When *Roe* became the law of the land four decades ago, New Hampshire was one of the few states where all abortions were outlawed. In contrast, North Carolina had been one of the states that had pioneered liberalizing abortion laws. Now, their relative positions are reversed.

Health and Public Welfare Policies in the States

Traditionally, states have also controlled health and public welfare policies. But as noted in earlier chapters, over time the federal government has come to play a larger role in these areas. This is perhaps most obvious in the way government provides health care.

Currently, questions about government's role in health care are centered on the implications of the Patient Protection and Affordable Care Act, a measure signed into law by President Obama in 2010 and more commonly referred to as "Obamacare." Among the many provisions in this law are requirements that businesses with more than fifty employees provide them with health care coverage or pay a penalty, that individuals have health care coverage or again pay a penalty—the so-called individual mandate—and that the states either set up and operate their own health care exchanges or have the federal government operate one on their behalf or jointly with them.

Each of these provisions is controversial and there is a widespread perception that they represent radical change. But each policy is rooted in programs that were already employed in some states. Indeed, people fail to appreciate the diversity of health care laws that were in place across the country prior to the adoption of the Affordable Care Act. For instance, under a 1974 state law employers in Hawaii have to provide health care coverage for all employees who work at least twenty hours a week, a requirement that has greatly lowered the number of uninsured people over the years.[110] Health care exchanges already operated in Massachusetts and Utah; in both states they had been pushed into law by Republican governors.[111] And of course, the Affordable Care Act's individual mandate was modeled on a similar provision in the health care law adopted by Massachusetts in 2006. As a consequence of its mandate and health care exchange, Massachusetts had the lowest percentage of uninsured people among the fifty states.[112]

Another state-level health care policy innovation passed at the same time the federal government adopted the Affordable Care Act. In 2010, Vermont established Green Mountain Care, a system that would eventually lead to the first statewide single-payer health care system. The program, which was intended to provide universal coverage for people in the state, was scheduled to be rolled out over the rest of this decade. But in late 2014, the state abandoned the effort, citing its projected cost.[113]

The federal government's involvement with health care did not begin with the Affordable Care Act. It actually became prominent with the passage of the law creating Medicaid in 1965. Medicaid was designed to allow the federal government to assist the states in providing care for eligible needy people. It is a complicated program; the federal government establishes national guidelines, but eligibility and service standards are set by the states. Costs are split. Overall, the federal government covers at least half of the expense for Medicaid in each state, but the amount of money it contributes varies based on a state's per capita income. The wealthiest states receive the statutory minimum of 50 percent, leaving the other 50 percent of the program's cost for the state to cover. The federal government covers a greater share of the cost of the program for poorer states. In fiscal year 2017, fourteen states received the minimum 50 percent federal match, while Mississippi, the poorest state, received a match of 75 percent, leaving it to pay for only 25 percent of the program's cost.[114]

The Affordable Care Act provides financial incentives for the states to expand their Medicaid programs. The U.S. Supreme Court's decision that found the Affordable Care Act to be constitutional allowed the states the option of whether or not to accept the incentives. The expansion decision has proven to be contentious and different states have arrived at different conclusions. As of June 2016, thirty-one states had expanded their Medicaid programs, while the other nineteen had not yet decided to do so.[115] That outcome means residents in some states are much more likely to have health care insurance coverage than are residents of other states.

Given their control over Medicaid eligibility and service standards and whether to expand the program or not, it should come as no surprise that the program's details vary considerably across the states. As of 2016, twenty-nine states have Medicaid eligibility levels for parents and other adults set at 138 percent of the federal poverty level (FPL), as required by the Affordable

Healthcare Act's Medicaid expansion provision. Another two states, Alaska (143 percent of FPL) and Connecticut (155 percent), have adopted even higher thresholds. Among states that have not expanded their Medicaid coverage, three have thresholds below 25 percent FPL: Missouri (22 percent), Alabama (18 percent), and Texas (18 percent). Thus parents in a family of three in Connecticut with an annual income under $31,248 qualify for Medicaid, while in Alabama and Texas that same family of three would only qualify with an income of less than $3,628. Childless adults in eighteen states do not get any Medicaid coverage at all.[116]

Medicaid and Children's Health Insurance Program (CHIP) coverage for children is uniformly more generous. As of 2016, forty-seven states cover children with family incomes above 200 percent FPL, with the median being 255 percent FPL. The three states below the 200 percent FPL are Arizona (152 percent of FPL), Idaho (190 percent), and North Dakota (175 percent). The highest coverage is extended in New York at 405 percent FPL, or incomes up to $81,648. Coverage for pregnant women is also extended in most states, with thirty-five states covering women at levels at or above 200 percent FPL.[117]

States have also arrived at different decisions in regard to whether they wish to establish their own state health care exchange under the Affordable Care Act, partner with the federal government in creating one, or rely entirely on using an exchange built and run by the federal government. The question revolves around state control versus federal control. Michigan governor Rick Snyder, a Republican, calculated it this way: "The state exchange is something I'd ultimately prefer because, otherwise, if you have a federal exchange, you're going to have people at the federal government taking care of Michigan citizens and my preference is to have Michiganders helping Michiganders in terms of customer service."[118] Despite the governor's clear preference, the GOP-dominated state legislature initially refused to allow the state to partner with the federal government, leaving Michigan to use the federal facilitated exchange. Ultimately, the state implemented a state partnership marketplace, allowing the state to take over some consumer assistance functions, while leaving the rest to the federal government. The same trend was found across much of the rest of the country; generally states controlled by the Republicans opted to have the federal government run their exchanges, while states under Democratic control either chose to partner with the federal government or to create their own exchanges. As of June 2016, in addition to Michigan, another six states have state partnership marketplaces. There are twelve states that operate their own state-run marketplaces and four states that have federally supported state-based marketplaces, in which the federal government supplies the site's information technology and the state does the rest. The remaining twenty-seven states direct their residents to the federal facilitated exchange where consumers enroll through the healthcare.gov website.[119] But these decisions are subject to change. Following his election in 2015, Kentucky governor Matt Bevin, a Republican, informed the federal government that his state would close its state-run marketplace, kynect, and transition consumers to the federally run marketplace.[120]

Perhaps the most significant instance of decentralization of power to the states from the federal government occurred in 1996, when Congress passed the Personal Responsibility and Work Opportunity Reconciliation Act. This legislation reformed welfare and created the Temporary Assistance for Needy Families (TANF) program, over which the states gained primary responsibility. Like Medicaid, TANF is funded jointly by the federal government and the states have considerable leeway over eligibility standards for receiving benefits from the program. As a result, the stringency of eligibility standards varies. In 2014, for example, a family with one parent and two dependent children could make, at most, $269 a month to be eligible in Alabama, while in Hawaii that same family could earn $1,740 a month and still be eligible. Benefits also vary. A family of three with no income would receive $215 a month in TANF benefits in Alabama, but $923 a month in Alaska. The median monthly benefit was $428.[121]

There are, of course, other important differences in TANF programs across the states. A central component of the program is an effort to move recipients into jobs. Indeed, most of those who receive TANF must participate in "work activities." States have devised a number of different approaches to fulfilling this requirement.[122] Occasionally, states adopt TANF policies that risk running afoul of federal regulations. Since 2011, at least fifteen states have passed laws requiring drug testing or screening of public assistance applicants or recipients. As mentioned at the beginning of the chapter, Florida adopted a measure requiring all TANF applicants to submit to a drug test. Under the law the applicant is required to pay for the test. If the test turns out to be negative, the applicant is reimbursed through a higher TANF benefit. A positive drug result makes the applicant ineligible for benefits for one year or for six months after the completion of a substance abuse treatment program. An injunction permanently preventing the program from going into effect was granted by a federal judge and upheld by a federal appeals court. The program adopted in Missouri requires a drug test only of those applicants about whom there is reasonable suspicion of drug use. That approach appears to pass judicial scrutiny.[123]

Health and welfare benefits vary across the states. But they do not always do so in the ways we might predict. A few decades ago, health and welfare benefits largely tracked each other, with states that were generous on one policy also being generous on the other policy. Today, that relationship has broken down. Wisconsin, for example, ranks high on the amount of money it spends per TANF recipient but low on money per Medicaid recipient. Additionally, there are no real regional differences in benefits. The only apparent relationship between health and welfare benefits and state characteristics is with state wealth: wealthier states tend to provide better benefits. Surprisingly, wealth is a much stronger predictor of benefits than is the prevailing political ideology of a state.[124]

The Responsiveness of State Policy Making

One of the underappreciated aspects of the American federal system is that states can, on their own initiative, respond to emerging issues. Indeed, with the federal government's policymaking capacity appearing in recent years to be paralyzed, states have had to fill the governing vacuum. Take, for example, paid family leave insurance laws to allow people to take care of new children or sick family members. There are now five states—California (originally adopted in 2002), Washington (2007 but has not gone into effect for lack of a funding mechanism), New Jersey (2008), Rhode Island (2013), and New York (2016)—that have put in place such measures.[125] Because nearly half of all working Americans do not have an employment-based retirement plan, several states have created automatic individual retirement accounts for those workers who are not offered such a plan by their employer. The first such law was adopted by California in 2012, and since then variations on it have been passed by Connecticut, Illinois, Maryland, Oregon, and Washington.[126] In the area of environmental regulations, in recent years twenty-nine states have adopted renewable energy standards, forcing their utilities to secure more power from wind, solar, and other renewable sources.[127] All of these actions have come largely in advance of federal laws or regulations.

Indeed, the states have been proactive on a wide range of emerging issues. Since Georgia passed an antibullying law in 1999, every state has followed suit, with Montana being the last to do so in 2015. The laws passed have differed; some focused on cyberbullying, while other have centered on behavior in school.[128] But as bullying rose on the national agenda, the states responded. As Congress fumbled its way toward passing legislation to deal with the opioid abuse crises sweeping parts of the country, states again took the initiative. In 2016, Massachusetts, for example, passed what was hailed as the most comprehensive legislation on the problem.[129] Technological innovations often force states to make policies in the absence of congressional leadership. As the prospects for autonomous or self-driving cars move closer to reality, several states have passed legislation covering it. Nevada was the first to move, passing a law authorizing their operation. Legislatures in California, Florida,

Michigan, North Dakota, and Tennessee have also passed laws governing self-driving vehicles, while Arizona's governor signed an executive order allowing state agencies to support testing programs.[130] As drones have gained popularity, state governments have responded. In 2016, at least forty-one state legislatures considered bills dealing with drones. Laws governing their use have been passed in ten states. Idaho, for example, now "prohibits the use of UAS [unmanned aircraft systems] for hunting, molesting or locating game animals, game birds and furbearing animals," while Kansas expanded its law prohibiting stalking to include the use of drones in such illegal behavior.[131] In 2016, Virginia became the first state to pass legislation regulating the online fantasy sports industry.[132]

Legislative action does not always mean that the states are moving in the same direction on an issue. Following a series of horrific mass shootings in 2012, governments at all levels began to mull over changes to their gun laws. As noted earlier, within a few months Colorado and Connecticut passed several strict gun control measures, something that New York had actually done first. A number of other states, however, pursued a diametrically different approach to the problem, with legislative efforts not to control guns, but to allow the arming of teachers and others who might be in a position to possibly intervene during a shooting. South Dakota was the first state to pass such a measure in 2013.[133] Indeed, more measures to weaken gun control laws passed in 2013 than measures to tighten them. Similarly, when that same year Arkansas and North Dakota were pushing to see how far they could go to limit abortions by passing pro-life legislation, lawmakers in Washington were pushing to become the first state to require insurers to cover abortion costs. Commenting on all the action on abortion legislation in 2013, one lobbyist commented, "In the states things can happen very quickly."[134]

Government does not always move quickly, but in many cases the states are able to address policy problems faster than can the federal government. The states' policy responses are, however, apt to be varied. Indeed, occasionally the measures they pursue can seem extreme. Following Arizona's passage of several controversial bills during a one-week span in April 2010, comedian Jon Stewart jokingly referred to that state as "the meth lab of democracy."[135] But through the passage of a variety of different approaches to solving problems, states can begin to identify which among them are successful and which are not.

Conclusion

Although we tend to think that all policies flow from Washington, DC, the reality is that there is vast space in the American federal system for the states to adopt different and distinctive approaches to solving problems. More-over, policies often flow from the states to Washington. During the summer of 2016, for example, Congress frantically worked on a bill requiring food manufacturers to label products containing genetically modified organisms (GMOs). The reason Congress spent time on the issue was because in 2014 Vermont had passed a stringent labeling law that went into effect in July 2016. Many members of Congress and the food industry wanted a less demand-ing law that would apply nationally rather than having to meet Vermont's tougher standard.[136] The importance of this story for our purposes here is to point out that Congress (and food manufacturers) had to respond to an in-novative policy developed by a state, in this case the state with the smallest state economy.

A major theme that runs through this book is that where you live makes a difference. Our attention in this chapter has been on large policy questions. But keep in mind that these differences also appear on small matters. Take state laws on noodling. Noodling, or hand fishing, is an activity largely pur-sued in the rural South, where people use their hands to explore nooks and crannies in and around river banks to extract fish—usually catfish—from their hiding places. In recent years, a few states, among them Georgia and Texas, have opted to make noodling legal. Other states, notably Missouri, have decided to keep noodling illegal in order to protect catfish populations from being overharvested.[137] These decisions matter because states that pro-hibit noodling enforce the law, as some noodlers have discovered.[138] So which state you live in will not only determine what sort of educational and health care options you enjoy or the conditions under which you can get an abortion or carry a gun, but it will also dictate whether you can legally noodle.

Notes

1. Pamela Prah attributes this assessment to an analyst at the Cato Institute. See Pamela M. Prah, "Uncertainty from Washington Continues for States," Stateline.org, January 4, 2013, http://www.pewstates.org/projects/stateline/headlines/uncertainty -from-washington-continues-for-states-85899440207.

2. http://www.tampabay.com/news/politics/stateroundup/the-florida-legislatures -2016-session-5-issues-to-watch-and-5-people-to/2260858.

3. http://www.myajc.com/news/news/state-regional-govt-politics/top-issues-to -watch-at-the-2016-georgia-general-as/npyWq/.

4. http://www.kansas.com/news/politics-government/article53916975.html.

5. https://southseattleemerald.com/2016/01/09/preview-of-washington-states -2016-state-legislative-session/.

6. *Governing*, "2016's Top Legislative Issues to Watch," January 2016.

7. Martha Derthick, *Keeping the Compound Republic* (Washington, DC: Brookings Institute Press, 2001), 28.

8. Chris Chieppo, "'Pay for Success': An Idea with Bipartisan Appeal," *Governing*, March 1, 2016.

9. Luke Keele, Neil Malhotra, and Colin McCubbins, "Do Term Limits Restrain State Fiscal Policy?" *Legislative Studies Quarterly* 38 (2013): 292.

10. This discussion is based in part on Todd Donovan, Christopher Mooney, and Daniel Smith, "Morality Policy," in *State and Local Politics: Institutions and Reform*, 3rd ed. (Boston, MA: Wadsworth/Cengage, 2013), chap. 13, and Justin Phillips, "Public Opinion and Morality," in *Politics in the American States*, ed. Virginia Gray, Russell Hanson and Thad Kousser, 10th ed. (Thousand Oaks, CA: CQ Press, 2013), 440–58.

11. Virginia Gray, "The Socioeconomic and Political Context of States," in *Politics in the American States*, ed. Virginia Gray, Russell Hanson and Thad Kousser, 10th ed. (Thousand Oaks, CA: CQ Press, 2013), 6.

12. http://www.ghsa.org/html/stateinfo/laws/cellphone_laws.html.

13. The policy diffusion literature is far too extensive to review here, but one must begin with Jack Walker, "The Diffusion of Innovation in the American States," *American Political Science Review* 63 (1969): 830–99 and Virginia Gray, "Innovation in the American States: A Diffusion Study," *American Political Science Review* 67 (1973): 1174–85. For recent treatments, see Andrew Karch, *Democratic Laboratories: Policy Diffusion Among the States* (Ann Arbor: University of Michigan Press, 2007); Sean Nicholson-Crotty, "The Politics of Diffusion: Public Policy in the American States," *Journal of Politics* 71 (2009): 192–205; Frederick J. Boehmke and Paul Skinner, "State Policy Innovativeness Revisited," *State Politics and Policy Quarterly* 12 (2012): 304–30; and the special issue on policy diffusion, edited by Frederick Boehmke and Juliana Pachecho, *State Politics and Policy Quarterly* (March 2016).

14. Graeme Boushey, *Policy Diffusion Dynamics in America* (New York: Cambridge University Press, 2010), 5.

15. Nicholson-Crotty, "The Politics of Diffusion," 199–200.

16. See Boehmke and Skinner, "State Policy Innovativeness Revisited," and Melissa Maynard, "Which States Are Most Innovative?" The Pew Center on the States, Stateline.org, http://www.pewstates.org/projects/stateline/headlines/which-states-are-most-innovative-858994.

17. Italics added by authors to emphasize relevant phrases.

18. National Association of State Budget Officers, *State Expenditure Report*, 2015, 13; U.S. Census Bureau, 2013 Annual Survey of School System Finances, Table 5.

19. http://www.governing.com/gov-data/education-data/state-education-spending-per-pupil-data.html.

20. Doris Nhan, "Analysis: How Much States Spend on Their Kids Really Does Matter," *National Journal*, October 23, 2012.

21. National Education Access Network, accessed June 1, 2016, http://www.schoolfunding.info/.

22. Michael Berkman and Eric Plutzer, "The Politics of Education," in *Politics in the American States*, ed. Virginia Gray, Russell Hanson, and Thad Kousser, 10th ed. (Thousand Oaks, CA: CQ Press, 2013), 388.

23. These figures are from 2012–2013 and are taken from http://nces.ed.gov/programs/coe/indicator_cma.asp, "Public School Revenue Sources," updated April 2016.

24. http://nces.ed.gov/programs/coe/indicator_coi.asp, "Public High School Graduation Rates," updated May 2016.

25. Tufts University, The Center for Information on Civic Learning and Engagement, "Fact Sheet" October 19, 2012, www.civicyouth.org.

26. http://blogs.edweek.org/edweek/state_edwatch/2015/08/eight_states_add_citizenship_test_requirement_for_grads.html.

27. University of Pennsylvania Graduate School of Education, "Is There an NCLB Curriculum?" http://www.gse.upenn.edu/features/research/de_facto. The article cites work by Andy Porter, Morgan Polikoff, and John Smithson in mapping curriculum content from state to state.

28. ww.csmonitor.com/USA/Education/2015/1120/Texas-textbook-vote-highlights-disputes-over-US-history-and-how-to-teach-it.

29. http://www.theatlantic.com/education/archive/2015/07/how-one-law-banning-ethnic-studies-led-to-rise/398885/.

30. *Oklahoma Historical Society's Encyclopedia of Oklahoma History and Culture*, "Anti-Evolution Movement," http://digital.library.okstate.edu/encyclopedia/entries/A/AN011.html.

31. Elizabeth Flock, "Law Allows Creationism to be Taught in Tenn. Public Schools," *Washington Post*, April 11, 2012.

32. See the 2014 updated discussion at http://www.pewforum.org/2009/02/04/fighting-over-darwin-state-by-state/; https://ncse.com/library-resource/chronology-academic-freedom-bills; http://www.slate.com/blogs/schooled/2016/01/25/oklahoma_evolution_controversy_two_new_bills_present_alternatives_to_evolution.html.

33. Pew Research Center for the People and the Press, "Reading the Polls on Evolution and Creationism," September 28, 2005; http://www.gallup.com/poll/21814/evolution-creationism-intelligent-design.aspx.

34. Michael Berkman, Eric Plutzer, and Nicholas Stark, "Teaching Evolution: State Institutions, Public Opinion and Science Curriculums," paper presented at the 2006 State Politics and Public Conference, Texas Tech University, May 2006.

35. Guttmacher Institution, "State Policies in Brief: Sex and HIV Education," March 1, 2016.

36. http://www.publiccharters.org/press/students-32-school-districts-attend-public-charter-schools-market-share-report/.

37. http://nces.ed.gov/programs/digest/d15/tables/dt15_216.90.asp.

38. Mark Berends, "Sociology and School Choice: What We Know After Two Decades of Charter Schools," *Annual Review of Sociology* 41 (2015): 159–80.

39. Susan Dynarski, "Where Charter Schools Outperform," *New York Times*, November 22, 2015, http://www.nytimes.com/2015/11/22/upshot/a-suburban-urban-divide-in-charter-school-success-rates.html?_r=0.

40. http://pdkpoll2015.pdkintl.org/219.

41. On state school choice programs, see http://www.edchoice.org/school-choice/school-choice-in-america/ and http://www.ncsl.org/research/education/voucher-law-comparison.aspx.

42. http://www.ncsl.org/research/education/school-choice-scholarship-tax -credits.aspx.

43. Stephanie Saul, "Public Money Finds Backdoor to Private Schools," *New York Times*, May 21, 2012.

44. https://nces.ed.gov/programs/digest/d13/tables/dt13_206.10.asp?current=yes.

45. Berkman and Plutzer, "The Politics of Education," 396.

46. https://www.hslda.org/laws/default.asp?.

47. https://www.hslda.org/laws/default.asp?.

48. On the other hand, more than half the research funds for universities in the United States are from the national government. Congressional Research Service, "Federal Support for Academic Research," report 7-5700, October 18, 2012.

49. Jung-cheol Shin and Sande Milton, "Rethinking Tuition Effects on Enrollment in Public Four-Year Colleges and Universities," *The Review of Higher Education* 29 (2006): 213–37 and James Hearn, Carolyn Griswold, and Ginger Marine, "Region, Resource, and Reason: A Contextual Analysis of State Tuition and Student Aid Policies," *Research in Higher Education* 37 (1996): 241–78.

50. The relative importance of these revenue streams varies within states as well. For example, North Carolina State University recently reported that almost 40 percent of its budget was from state-appropriated funds, while the University of North Carolina reported that 20 percent of its budget was from the same source. See http://www.ncsu.edu/budget/faq/ and http://universityrelations.unc.edu/budget/content/FAQ.php#statefundingfactor.

51. College Board Advocacy and Policy Center, "Trends in Tuition and Fees, Enrollment, and State Appropriations for Higher Education By State," July 2012. See 4–6.

52. Kevin Dougherty, "Financing Higher Education in the United States," Address to the Institute for Economics of Education, Peking University, Peking, China, 2004, 10.

53. http://www.pewtrusts.org/en/research-and-analysis/issue-briefs/2015/06/federal-and-state-funding-of-higher-education. See figure 8.

54. http://vpcomm.umich.edu/budget/fundingsnapshot/3.html.

55. College Board Advocacy Center, "Trends in Tuition and Fees," Table 2-9.

56. See Katherine Barrett and Richard Greene, "State Start Making Colleges Work for Funding," *Governing*, April 2016.

57. http://gunlawscorecard.org.

58. Lynn Bartels and Kurtis Lee, "3 New Gun Bills on the Books in Colorado Despite Its Wild West Image," *Denver Post*, March 21, 2013; Ron Scherer, "Connecticut Responds to Newtown with Groundbreaking Gun Control Laws," *Christian Science Monitor*, April 2, 2013.

59. Michael Luca, Deepak Malhotra, and Christopher Poliquin, "The Impact of Mass Shootings on Gun Policy," Harvard Business School Working Paper 16-126, May 2016.

60. See the list provided in http://www.slate.com/blogs/the_slatest/2015/10/07/gun_control_laws_by_state_oregon_new_york_texas_california.html.

61. Jason Clayworth, "Register Investigation: 99.6% of Iowa Gun Permits Approved," *Des Moines Register*, March 10, 2013.

62. Ryan Foley, "States Taking Action to Keep Guns Out of Abusers' Hands," *The Tennessean*, February 5, 2016.

63. See Cheng Cheng and Mark Hoekstra, "Does Strengthening Self Defense Law Deter Crime or Escalate Violence? Evidence from the Expansions to Castle Doctrine," *Journal of Human Resources* 48 (2013): 821–54.

64. https://www.nraila.org/gun-laws/. See Castle Doctrine.

65. Adam Cohen, "Will States Lead the Way to Legalizing Marijuana Nationwide?" *Time Magazine*, January 28, 2013, http://ideas.time.com/2013/01/28/will-states-lead-the-way-to-legalizing-marijuana-nationwide/.

66. http://www.governing.com/gov-data/state-marijuana-laws-map-medical-recreational.html; Anthony Shoemaker, "Ohioans Can Start Using Medical Marijuana Legally in September," *Dayton Daily News*, June 8, 2016.

67. http://www.no-smoke.org/goingsmokefree.php?id=519#maps.

68. Patrick McGreevy, "California's Smoking Age Raised from 18 to 21 Under Bills Signed by Gov. Brown," *Los Angeles Times*, May 4, 2016.

69. See Pew Charitable Trusts, "The Punishment Rate," March 2016.

70. Calculated by authors from data in E. Ann Carson, "Prisoners in 2014," U.S. Department of Justice, Office of Justice Programs, Bureau of Justice Statistics, September 2015; and Danielle Kaeble, Lauren Glaze, Anastasios Tsoutis, and Todd Minton, "Correctional Populations in the United States, 2014," U.S. Department of Justice, Office of Justice Programs, Bureau of Justice Statistics, December 2015.

71. Carson, "Prisoners in 2014."

72. http://www.washingtonpost.com/wp-dyn/content/story/2008/02/28/ST2008022803016.html.

73. Pew Charitable Trusts, "The Punishment Rate."

74. Carson, "Prisoners in 2014."

75. Glaze, Tsoutis, and Minton, "Correctional Populations in the United States, 2014."

76. Legislative Analyst's Office, "A Primer: Three Strikes—The Impact After More Than a Decade," October 7, 2005, http://www.lao.ca.gov/2005/3_strikes/3_strikes_102005.htm.

77. Calculated by the authors from data in Erica E. Phillips, "'Three-Strikes' Prisoners Drawing a Walk," *Wall Street Journal*, March 30–31, 2013.

78. Radha Iyengar, "I'd Rather Be Hanged for a Sheep than a Lamb: The Unintended Consequences of "Three-Strikes' Laws," National Bureau of Economic Research, Working Paper 13784, February 2008.

79. Stanford Law School, Three Strikes Project, "Proposition 36 Progress Report: Over 1,500 Prisoners Released Historically Low Recidivism Rate," April 2014.

80. John Wooldredge, "State Corrections Policy," in *Politics in the American States*, ed. Virginia Gray, Russell Hanson, and Thad Kousser, 10th ed. (Thousand Oaks, CA: CQ Press, 2013), Table 9-1.

81. Wooldredge, "State Corrections Policy," 283.

82. See the timeline at http://deathpenalty.procon.org/view.resource.php?resourceID=001172#timeline.

83. Joe Duggan, Paul Hammel, and Martha Stoddard, "Hours of Suspense, Emotion Lead Up to a Landmark Vote for Legislators on Repealing Death Penalty," *Omaha World-Herald*, May 28, 2016.

84. Marin Cogan, "Meet the Red-State Conservatives Fighting to Abolish the Death Penalty," *Washington Post*, June 3, 2016; Alan Greenblat, "The Death Penalty's New Skeptics," *Governing*, June 2016.

85. Statistics are from the Death Penalty Information Center, "Facts About the Death Penalty," May 12, 2016.

86. Carson, "Prisoners in 2014."

87. Michael Cohen, "How For-Profit Prisons Have Become the Biggest Lobby No One is Talking About," *Washington Post*, April 28, 2015.

88. Rebecca Boone, "Private Prison Company Escapes Idaho Following Scandal, Lawsuits," *Idaho State Journal*, October 3, 2013.

89. http://fivethirtyeight.com/features/how-many-americans-are-married-to-their-cousins/.

90. 32 Cal. 2d 711 (1948). See the discussion in R. A. Lenhardt, "Beyond Analogy: Perez V. Sharp, Antimiscegenation Law, and the Fight for Same-Sex Marriage," *California Law Review* 96 (2008): 839–900.

91. 388 U.S. 1 (1967).

92. "President Bush's Remarks on Same-Sex Marriage," *New York Times*, February 24, 2004.

93. 576 U.S. ___ (2015).

94. http://www.al.com/news/birmingham/index.ssf/2016/03/alabama_supreme_court_dismisse.html.

95. http://www.al.com/news/index.ssf/2016/05/alabama_chief_justice_roy_moor_10.html.

96. Everdeen Mason, Aaron Williams, and Kennedy Elliott, "The Dramatic Rise in State Efforts to Limit LGBT Rights," *Washington Post*, June 10, 2016.

97. Tony Cook, Tom LoBianco, Brian Eason, "Gov. Mike Pence Signs RFRA Fix," *Indianapolis Star*, April 2, 2015.

98. Kate Royals, "Senate Passes 'Religious Freedom' Bill," *Clarion-Ledger*, April 15, 2016.

99. See the list provided in https://www.aclu.org/anti-lgbt-religious-exemption-legislation-across-country.

100. Jimmie E. Gates, "ACLU Files Lawsuit to Declare HB 1523 Unconstitutional," *Clarion-Ledger*, May 9, 2016; Neely Tucker, "U.S. District Judge Strike Down Mississippi's 'Religious Freedom' Law," *Washington Post*, July 1, 2016.

101. 410 US 113 (1973).

102. See Barbara Hinkson Craig and David M. O'Brien, *Abortion and American Politics* (Chatham: Chatham House, 1996), 74–75; Roy Lucas, "Federal Constitutional Limitations on the Enforcement and Administration of State Abortion Statutes," *North Carolina Law Review* 46 (1967–1968): 730–78; Karen O'Connor, *No Neutral Ground?* (Boulder, CO: Westview Press, 1996), 46–47; A. A. Smyser, "Hawaii's Abortion Law 30 Years Old," *Hawaii Star-Bulletin*, March 21, 2000.

103. Craig and O'Brien, *Abortion and American Politics*, 75.

104. Planned Parenthood of Southeastern Pennsylvania v. Casey, 505 U.S. 833 (1992).

105. "North Dakota Governor Approves 6-Week Abortion Ban," *St Louis Post Dispatch*, March 26, 2013.

106. Nina Liss-Schultz, "The Supreme Court Just Rejected the Country's Most Extreme Abortion Ban," *Mother Jones*, January 25, 2016.

107. Amber Phillips, "14 States Have Passed Laws This Year Making it Harder to Get an Abortion," *Washington Post*, June 1, 2016.

108. The Guttmacher Institute provides a useful compendium of state abortion laws: https://www.guttmacher.org/state-policy/explore/overview-abortion-laws.

109. See the discussion in http://www.governing.com/topics/health-human-services/tns-planned-parenthood-abortion-ruling.html?utm_term=Abortion%20Ruling%20Spurs%20Planned%20Parenthood%20to%20Target%208%20States&utm_campaign=The%20City%20Where%20Mayors%20Still%20Run%20the%20Show&utm_content=email&utm_source=Act-On+Software&utm_medium=email.

110. Gardiner Harris, "In Hawaii's Heath System, Lessons for Lawmakers," *New York Times*, October 16, 2009.

111. Christine Vestal, "Utah's Health Insurance Exchange in Limbo," *Stateline*, January 11, 2013.

112. See the data presented at statehealthfacts.org: http://www.statehealthfacts.org/comparecat.jsp?cat=3.

113. http://www.salon.com/2014/12/18/vermont_abandons_plan_for_single_payer_health_care/.

114. http://kff.org/medicaid/state-indicator/federal-matching-rate-and-multiplier/.

115. http://kff.org/health-reform/state-indicator/state-activity-around-expanding-medicaid-under-the-affordable-care-act/.

116. These figures were taken from the Kaiser Commission on Key Facts, "Where Are the States Today? Medicaid and CHIP Eligibility Levels for Adults, Children and Pregnant Women," March 2, 2016.

117. Kaiser Commission on Key Facts, "Where Are the States Today".

118. Rick Pluta, "A Michigan State-Federal Health Care Exchange Killed by Senate Republicans," March 22, 2013, http://www.michiganradio.org/post/michigan-state-federal-health-care-exchange-killed-senate-republicans.

119. http://kff.org/health-reform/state-indicator/state-health-insurance-marketplace-types/.

120. Deborah Yetter, "Bevin Notifies Feds He'll Dismantle kynect," *Courier-Journal*, January 11, 2016.

121. These data were taken from Erika Huber, Elissa Cohen, Amanda Briggs, and David Kassabian, *Welfare Rules Databook: State TANF Policies as of July 2014*, OPRE Report #2015-81, Washington, DC: Urban Institution, August 2015, 90–91, 112–13.

122. See Heather Hahn, David Kassabian, and Sheila Zedlewski, *TANF Work Requirements and State Strategies to Fulfill Them*, Urban Institute, Brief #05, March 2012.

123. See the NCSL compilation of these laws: http://www.ncsl.org/research/human-services/drug-testing-and-public-assistance.aspx.

124. Mark Carl Rom, "State Health and Welfare Programs," in *Politics in the American States*, ed. Virginia Gray, Russell L. Hanson, and Thad Kousser, 10th ed. (Los Angeles: CQ Press, 2013).

125. National Partnership for Women and Families, "State Paid Family Leave Insurance Laws," April 2016.

126. Liz Farmer, "States Forge Ahead of Feds to Address Retirement Crisis," *Governing*, July 16, 2015; Liz Farmer, "States Step In for Retirees," *Wall Street Journal*, September 8, 2015; http://www.pensionrights.org/issues/legislation/state-based-retirement-plans-private-sector.

127. http://www.ncsl.org/research/energy/renewable-portfolio-standards.aspx.

128. http://www.bullypolice.org/; Lisa Baumann, "Gov. Bullock Signs Montana Anti-Bullying Bill into Law," *Great Falls Tribune*, April 21, 2015.

129. Marie Szanizslo, "'Most Comprehensive' Opioid Bill Becomes Law," *Boston Herald*, March 15, 2016.

130. http://www.ncsl.org/research/transportation/autonomous-vehicles-legislation.aspx.

131. http://www.ncsl.org/research/transportation/current-unmanned-aircraft-state-law-landscape.aspx.

132. Jenna Portnoy, "Virginia Becomes the First State to Regulate Fantasy Sports Industry," *Washington Post*, March 8, 2016.

133. Jack Nicas and Joe Palazzolo, "Pro-Gun Laws Gain Ground," *Wall Street Journal*, April 4, 2013; http://www.governing.com/blogs/view/gov-advancing-the-debate-guns-teachers-and-classrooms-in-south-dakota.html.

134. Louise Radnofsky, "States Harden Views Over Laws Governing Abortion," *Wall Street Journal*, April 1, 2013.

135. See http://www.cc.com/video-clips/zpomqm/the-daily-show-with-jon-stewart-law---border. The comment comes at 1:14.

136. http://www.theatlantic.com/business/archive/2016/07/vermont-gmo-food-companies/490553/.

137. Malcolm Gay, "The Catfish Are Biting (and It Hurts)," *New York Times*, July 28, 2007; Missouri Department of Conservation, "Why 'No' to Noodling," http://mdc.mo.gov/fishing/regulations/why-no-noodling.

138. See "Charges Filed Against Men for 'Noodling' Catfish," http://www.wowt.com/news/headlines/160367085.html.

6

Elections and Political Parties

States matter because

- All elections in the United States, including the presidential election, are conducted at the *state* or local level
- Almost all electoral rules of candidacy, qualifications, timing, etc., are *state* rules
- Congressional districts are drawn by *state* officials
- Candidates for federal (national) office often are former *state* elected officials
- Most *state* judges are elected, whereas no federal judge is elected
- Instruments of direct democracy—the initiative, the referendum, and the recall—exist in many *states* but not at the national level, and these instruments have an important effect on public policy
- The presidential nominees are chosen by delegates in a series of fifty separate *state* events
- The mechanism by which we choose the president is the Electoral College, which is a *state*-based system
- Political parties build their base at the *state* electoral level

ONE OF THE ODDEST THINGS ABOUT the American electoral system is that there are no truly nationwide elections; none at all. In the United States, all elections are filtered through the states. For example, the president is not elected in a nationwide popular vote but in a series of fifty-one elections (the fifty *states* plus the District of Columbia), all of which happen to be held on the same day. The purpose of these fifty-one separate elections is to choose a total of 538 individuals (called "electors") who, a month later, cast the actual votes for president. This is the procedure known as the Electoral College. The manner in which these "electors" are chosen is a matter for each state to decide. To reiterate: the president is not selected through a national popular vote but by a group of intermediaries who in turn are chosen through a series of state elections.

What about the U.S. Congress—the legislative branch? The 435 members of the U.S. House of Representatives are elected in 435 separate districts distributed throughout the *states*. And surprisingly, the rules for election are not the same in all 435 districts. This is because most of the rules are determined by each state, not the national government. And of course, each *state* elects two individuals to represent it in the U.S. Senate. And again, the rules by which each state chooses its two U.S. senators are not necessarily the same.

To illustrate this point, consider the 2016 U.S. Senate election in California. Since 2010 California has employed a "top-two" primary system in which all candidates, regardless of party affiliation, run in the same primary election. The top two vote-getters, again regardless of party affiliation, face one another in the November general election. The top-two primary was held in June 2016, and on the eve of the event, the Reuters news agency ran the following headline: "California Poised to Shutout Republicans from the U.S. Senate Race."[1] And that is exactly what happened. A total of thirty-four candidates entered the contest (seven Democrats, twelve Republicans, eleven Independents, two Libertarians, and one each from the Peace and Freedom Party and the Green Party). The top two vote-getters were Democrat Kamala Harris, with 40 percent of the vote, and Democrat Loretta Sanchez, with 18 percent of the vote. Thus the November 2016 U.S. Senate race in California was between two Democrats; Republicans were indeed shut out. The larger point is that the electoral rules of California (a state) defined the vote choice for a U.S. Senate (national) office. In fact, the same phenomenon happened in seven more races for federal office in California in 2016. Because of the top-two primary rules in California, five U.S. House races in that state featured a Democrat against a Democrat in the November general election, while another two U.S. House races pitted a Republican against another Republican.

While the California example shows how the state rules can affect a general election, state rules also affect party primary nomination races. In Texas, candidates seeking the party nomination for U.S. Senate, U.S. House, statewide races, and state legislative races must win a majority of the votes cast. If there is no majority winner in the primary, the top two vote-getters face each other in a runoff election. In the 2012 Republican primary for U.S. Senator, this rule became crucial.

The primary was held in May. The main candidates in the race were Texas Lieutenant Governor David Dewhurst and Tea Party favorite Ted Cruz, making his first run for office.[2] A well-known and longtime elected official in Texas, Dewhurst was the overwhelming favorite and he received 145,000 more votes than the second-place finisher Cruz, as shown in table 6.1. Dewhurst won over 44 percent of the vote compared to Cruz's 34 percent, with the rest of the vote being split among seven other candidates.

But the electoral rule in Texas primaries is that the candidate must receive a majority of the total vote to win the nomination—and 44 percent is not a majority. In the runoff election held nine weeks later, Cruz turned the tables and won by a substantial margin. He went on to defeat his Democratic opponent in the general election, and a few years later became a player in the Republican presidential campaign in 2016. If Texas did not have a majoritarian rule for its state primaries, Ted Cruz would not have been elected to the U.S. Senate in 2012. Clearly, state electoral rules do indeed matter.

National Political Figures Often Come from the States

After the Democratic sweep in the 2008 national elections, one of the first topics for Republicans was where to look for leadership and potential presidential nominees for 2012. Some of the names most commonly mentioned were Haley Barbour, Charlie Crist, Mitch Daniels, Bobby Jindal, Sarah Palin, Tim Pawlenty, and Mark Sanford—the governors of Mississippi, Florida, Indiana, Louisiana, Alaska, Minnesota, and South Carolina, respectively. The eventual GOP presidential nominee was Mitt Romney, a former governor of Massachusetts. In the 2016 presidential race, there were seventeen candidates and nine of

TABLE 6.1
How Electoral Rules Affect Outcomes, the 2012 GOP Texas Primary for U.S. Senate

Candidate	Primary Vote	PrimaryPercent	Runoff Vote	Runoff Percent
D. Dewhurst	624,170	44.6	480,165	43.2
T. Cruz	479,079	34.2	631,316	**56.8**
T. Leppert	186,675	13.3		
C. James	50,211	3.6		
G. Addison	22,888	1.6		
L. Pittenger	18,028	1.3		
3 others	18,400	1.3		
TOTAL:	1,399,451		1,111,481	

them had gubernatorial experience (although only one governor, John Kasich of Ohio, was among the final group). It is no surprise that the "out" party—the party out of power at the national level—almost immediately turns its attention to the states in search of new leadership. Elected officials at the state level are sometimes characterized as the "farm teams" for national office. After all, about half of all members of Congress are former state legislators. Between 1975 and 2016, four of the six presidents (Carter, Reagan, Clinton, and George W. Bush) were former governors and another (Obama) had been a state senator. In other words, the president of the United States was a former state elected official in all but four years. Over American history, more former governors (eighteen) than U.S. senators (sixteen) have served as president.[3]

Despite the anomalous 2016 presidential race—the major party candidates had never served in state government, although for many years Hillary Clinton was Arkansas' first lady—the United States has a long history of choosing candidates for national office who have state political experience. This is not the case in all federal systems. In Canada, for example, provincial and national political careers are largely separate tracks; only a small proportion of the Canadian Parliament previously served in the provincial legislative assemblies.[4] And in Germany, the flow of personnel often runs the other direction; state parliamentary leaders are drawn from the ranks of the national parliament.[5] But in the United States, states provide both a "farm system" and a place for the out party to rebuild its strength. And sometimes, as in 2010, the out party can rebuild very quickly. The Republican Party lost its congressional majority in 2006, the presidency in 2008, and over five hundred state legislative seats in 2006 and 2008 combined. But in 2010, they gained some seven hundred state legislative seats nationally, as well as regaining control of the U.S. House of Representatives. The point here is that these gains were made through elections at the state level.

But the flow of talent in the United States is not just in one direction. Prior to the 2016 election, nine of the fifty governors were former members of the U.S. Congress. As noted in chapter 4, the proportion of governors with congressional experience is higher now than it used to be. This is an important point because it highlights the significance of the states. Strategic politicians do not voluntarily give up a seat in Congress to run for governor "back home" unless they perceive that being governor is a meaningful position.[6] In other words, they recognize that states matter.

State Party and Electoral Systems

In this chapter, we discuss state electoral structures and state political party systems and how they influence federal politics. Electoral laws and party systems are separate but related topics. The electoral structure affects the nature of the party system.

Because both the media and education establishments in the United States place heavy emphasis on the role of the national government, many people are unaware of the variation in electoral laws and political party strength across the states. Far more than most people realize, state electoral laws vary. Here we will focus on four of these differences: electoral rules, redistricting, direct democracy, and term limits.

We will also take a look at political party systems at the state level and note how the state party systems interface with the national parties. Political parties are not equally competitive in all states. We will explore the consequences of this fact, from recruitment to policy impacts.

Finally, we discuss the ways in which national elective office in the United States is heavily influenced by state-based politics. This is clearly true in Congress, by virtue of the fact that its members are chosen from the states. It is also true because of that unique American mechanism known as the Electoral College. Born of a new federal system of government more than two centuries ago, the Electoral College is an important illustration that even national offices are heavily influenced by state politics—as was intended by the Founders. Indeed, an Electoral College–type mechanism was first devised by Maryland to elect members of its state senate.

To emphasize the state-based nature of the national electoral system, we can point to the recent movement to repeal the Seventeenth Amendment to the Constitution—a movement especially favored by "Tea Party" enthusiasts. As we discussed in chapter 2, originally the Constitution stipulated that U.S. senators were to be chosen by their own states' legislature. Obviously, this provision gave important power to state legislatures and it remained in effect for 125 years. But corruption in some state legislatures in the late nineteenth century, coupled with the drive toward greater participatory democracy as embodied in the Progressive reform era, led to a widespread movement to have senators elected by the voters rather than chosen by state legislatures. This was achieved with the ratification of the Seventeenth Amendment in 1913.

Today, some political activists contend that the states would be better served by repealing the Seventeenth Amendment and reverting to the system whereby state legislatures would choose senators. Their argument centers on the notion that senators would be more sensitive to state rather than national interests if they were selected by state legislators. It is unlikely that such a movement will succeed for many reasons. In any event, our point remains that U.S. senators are chosen through mechanisms that are located in the states. Again, there are no real national elections.

State Electoral Rules

Sometimes it takes an outside perspective to truly grasp how different the American system is and how important the states are. The venerable British newsmagazine *The Economist*, with proper British spelling and syntax, recently reported, "America organises its democracy differently from other rich countries. Each state writes its own voting laws, there is no national register of eligible voters and no form of ID that is both acceptable in all polling booths and held by everyone."[7] It is, in other words, a unique crazy quilt system of electoral laws, a quilt largely constructed by the states but with substantial influence on elections for the national offices—the president and vice president, the U.S. House of Representatives, and the U.S. Senate.

As improbable as it may seem, there are more than 500,000 elected government officials in the United States.[8] And 99.9 percent of them are officials elected by rules established in the states. As noted above, even the 537 elected federal offices are influenced by state electoral laws—laws that define the way primary elections operate, for example. And the state electoral laws vary in many ways, among them voter eligibility, ballot structure, district magnitude, and timing of elections. Here we focus on five important ways that states matter when it comes to electoral rules.

1. The prevalence of single member districts using plurality rules

For legislative bodies in a representative democracy, there are many ways to translate votes into seats. While there are a number of important decisions that go into creating an electoral system for translating votes to seats, two are paramount. The first is district magnitude: How many officials will be elected from each district? The choice ranges from one (a single-member district) to two or more representatives being elected in each district (multimember district) to the entire legislature being elected at large.

The second key decision is the allocation formula: On what basis do we decide who wins a seat? The choices are plurality, majority, and proportional (seats are allocated proportionate to the total votes received) or some combination thereof. This is not the place for a lengthy discussion of the fascinating variety of electoral systems that have evolved around the world based on these two key decisions.[9] But it is important to recognize there are consequences to the way an electoral system is structured—consequences for the party system, for the nature of campaigning, and even for the way we think about the job of the representative.

In the United States, the most common current method is single-member, plurality (SMP) elections—known in many places as "first past the post."

Under this system, one person is elected per district. The person elected is the one who received more votes than any other candidate. Like all electoral systems, SMP has certain characteristics. It is generally thought to be a system that reinforces a two-party political system, creates a substantial degree of incumbent stability, and fosters a direct link between constituents and their elected legislator. All of these features have implications for politics.

The SMP system is so prevalent in the modern United States that we might mistakenly think it is the only one used. But there are a few American states that use other systems, at least for some offices. Several southern states, such as Alabama and Georgia, use a single-member district majority rule (also known as a double-ballot system) for primary elections. If no candidate receives a majority in the first election, a runoff between the two top vote-getters is held several weeks later. It is important to note that this majority requirement applies to primaries for congressional seats in these states as well.

Some states use multimember districts (MMDs) for state legislative seats.[10] Fifty years ago, over forty states used MMDs for at least some of their legislative seats.[11] That number has declined dramatically over the years. Currently, ten states use MMDs for all or some house legislative districts, while two states (Vermont and West Virginia) use them for their state senate.[12] The most common form is a two-member plurality district. Each voter casts two votes, and the two candidates with the most votes win. In New Hampshire, as many as eleven members are chosen from a single district, and in Vermont, as many as six state senators are chosen from a single district. At one time, some states used multimember districts to choose their members of Congress, but that practice ended by 1967.[13]

Single-member districts are usually smaller geographic units with fewer constituents per district. Multimember districts are typically larger with more people contained in each district, especially if we are talking about districts that elect four or more officials per district. In terms of representational theory, there are advantages and disadvantages to each. Single-member districts are smaller and easier to gerrymander (discussed shortly). Consequently, some argue, they are likely to lead to more safe seats in which one party dominates. This in turn can accentuate polarization in the sense that many legislators will represent districts that are overwhelmingly Republican, while others will represent safe Democratic districts.[14] There is an appealing logic to the argument that single-member districts facilitate safe seats and therefore encourage polarization. But there is little evidence that multimember districts would eliminate polarization by themselves.[15]

In a few states there is some interest in considering changes to the dominant allocation rule of plurality wins. We already mentioned that a few states require a majoritarian rule, either in primaries or, in the case of Louisiana and Georgia, in general elections. These apply to the congressional seats in these states as well as the state offices. And the "top-two" primary system now being used in California and Washington forces a majoritarian requirement in the general election (because there can only be two contestants in the general election).

A few states have considered another version of a majoritarian requirement variously known as the instant runoff vote (IRV) or the ranked-choice vote (RCV). This system allows voters to rank order the various candidates. If no one candidate receives a majority of first-place votes, second-choice votes are added. If still no one has a majority, third-choice votes are added, and so on. Some people favor this system because it allows voters' preferences to continue to be considered even if no one candidate receives a majority on the first ballot. Some think this system discourages the election of ideologically extreme candidates and therefore may help dampen polarization.[16]

A statewide vote was held in Maine in November 2016 to determine if the state wished to move to RCV for all state elections—including the election of U.S. senators and members of the U.S. House of Representatives from Maine. The referendum passed, and the RCV system could potentially be in place for the 2018 election.

State law also applies to local governments, of course. And some states allow their local units considerable latitude in electoral design. Exotic (by American standards) voting systems such as the cumulative vote, limited vote, and instant runoff vote are used in some local jurisdictions in the United States. But again, it is important to emphasize that this is all a matter of *state* law and local governments cannot establish electoral systems that are not permissible in state law, as the cities of Austin, Texas, and Vancouver, Washington, discovered. Both cities established IRV for municipal elections but were denied implementation because state law in both Texas and Washington prohibited rank-choice systems.[17] The system is allowed for municipal elections in some states, notably in California (used in Berkeley, Oakland, San Francisco, and San Leandro), Maine (Portland), and Minnesota (Minneapolis and Saint Paul).

2. The election schedule

Not all elections are held concurrent with the presidential contest. In fact, most states hold elections for their governors and other statewide officials (such as attorney general) in a year other than the presidential election year. The reason is obvious; the presidential contest commands much time, media focus, and campaign resources. Within the last fifty years or so, most states moved the election for their own chief executives (the governors) to what is known as the "off-year"—the even numbered years in which the presidency is not on the ballot. Thus while the presidential elections are 2016, 2020, 2024, and so on, thirty-four states hold gubernatorial and other statewide elections in 2018, 2022, etc. Granted, there are still congressional races in those years, but these are really state elections, even though taken collectively they have national implications. A few states like New Jersey, Virginia, Kentucky, Louisiana, and Mississippi go even further and hold their state elections in odd-numbered years, when there are no presidential *or* congressional races at all. Perhaps the strangest arrangement of all is Kentucky's; the Bluegrass State holds its election for governor and other executive officers (secretary of state, etc.) in an odd-numbered year but the state legislative races in an even-numbered year. Focusing on statewide elections for governor, then, we find the following arrangements: two states (New Hampshire and Vermont) elect their governor every two years in even numbered years, thirty-four states hold their governor's election every four years in the even-numbered non-presidential years, and five states hold governor's elections in odd-numbered years.[18] Only nine states are on the same gubernatorial electoral cycle as the presidential electoral cycle.[19]

3. Judicial elections

A major difference between the states and the federal government, as noted in chapter 3, is that while no federal judge is elected, *most* state judges must win election in some way or another.[20] This includes state courts of last resort judges in over forty states.

Most state judges are chosen through one of three types of elections: partisan, nonpartisan, or retention. The most common is a retention election, a procedure whereby judges who are initially selected by the governor for an initial term of office must eventually stand for election for a full term, with the question being whether they should be retained on the bench or not.

The financing of judicial campaigns is currently a major topic of discussion in a number of states. A recent example that garnered considerable attention nationally was the 2011 election for the Wisconsin Supreme Court. Coming on the heels of the bitterly contested legislation to end public employee collective bargaining rights in Wisconsin, the supreme court election was viewed as a referendum on Governor Walker's controversial policies. Over $3 million was spent on the judicial campaign.[21] It was not an isolated episode. In 2016, over $3 million was spent on another Wisconsin supreme court race. Most of that money was not spent by the candidates but by independent groups.[22]

Such spending in court contests is increasingly common. In 2000, two successful candidates running for the Ohio Supreme Court spent $2 million *each*.[23] Even more dramatic was the level of independent spending outside the candidates' control; the Ohio Chamber of Commerce spent over $5 million in support of one of the candidates.[24] In 2008, two candidates for the Michigan Supreme Court spent $2.5 million between them, and interest groups allied with one or the other candidates spent another $3.8 million.[25] In Alabama, a 2008 supreme court race cost over $4 million.[26] Even retention races have become expensive. As mentioned in chapter 3, in Iowa in 2010, three Supreme Court justices were voted out because of their decision in support of gay marriage. Interestingly, most of the money spent on the campaign to oust the justices came from out of state.[27] This too has become commonplace. A 2014 campaign to oust three Tennessee supreme court justices up for retention was organized by several Republican state legislators and funded by conservatives, some of whom were not Tennesseans. One retired judge, a former member of the State Court of Appeals, was offended by the out-of-state money, "I kind of look at it like they're carpetbaggers. Why do they have to come in and tell us in Tennessee how to elect our judiciary?"[28] Apparently others agreed with this sentiment; all three justices won their retention elections. But the vote was relatively close and together they spent over $1 million in their own campaigns to defend their judicial records.[29]

A similar story unfolded in 2016 in Kansas, where the Republican-dominated legislature and the state supreme court continued their longstanding clash over public education funding. Up for retention were five of the nine justices and the campaigns for and against them were expected to cost several million dollars. As a veteran observer of Kansas politics noted, "Without a doubt, we are going to see a tremendous amount of money spent on judicial elections—retention elections—in Kansas."[30]

The issue here is not just that judicial elections are expensive, but that some of the donors to the candidates, and virtually all of the groups engaging in independent spending, appear before the courts in one or more cases. An episode in West Virginia in 2004 illustrates the problem. In a heated race between incumbent West Virginia Supreme Court of Appeals justice Warren McGraw and challenger Brent Benjamin, a private individual spent over $3 million to run an independent ad campaign supporting Benjamin's candidacy.[31] This individual was Don Blankenship.[32] At the time, he was the chief executive officer of Massey Energy, one of the country's largest coal companies, and it had a $50 million judgment pending against it in the state supreme court. Aided by Blankenship's independent spending on his behalf, Brent Benjamin defeated Warren McGraw. When the Massey Coal case was reheard by the state supreme court, Justice Benjamin opted not to recuse himself, contending that the $3 million in independent spending in support of his candidacy did not impact his ability to remain unbiased on the legal questions raised. The court then struck down the $50 million award on a 3 to 2 decision, with Justice Benjamin voting with the majority.

The questions raised by this case highlight the inherent tension between judicial independence and judicial accountability that exists where judges are elected.[33] Ultimately, the U.S. Supreme Court determined that the amount of independent spending in the West Virginia case was so excessive that Justice Benjamin should have recused himself.[34] But this does not resolve the issue in numerous other state judicial elections. At what point does the amount of campaign contributions and spending become excessive?

4. Primary election rules

One of the most obvious ways in which state electoral laws affect national politics is through the rules for nominating candidates—that is, deciding which candidate will represent each political party in the general election. The rules are complex, involving 1) who can vote in the primary, 2) when the primary is held, and 3) what determines a winner in the primary. Moreover, the rules may not be the same for each party in the same state, particularly in regard to who can vote. Finally, the rules may differ within a state between presidential nominations and other nominations. Indeed, the presidential and nonpresidential nomination systems within a state are different enough that we will discuss the presidential system by itself in a later section. For now, we concentrate on the nomination system for offices other than president.

Each state decides when to hold its primary election. The primary calendar for 2016 is shown in table 6.2. States decide for themselves when to hold their

TABLE 6.2
Calendar of Primary Elections for State Offices, 2016

Early Months	May	June	July	August	September
March 1: AL, AR, TX	3: IN	7: CA, IA,MT, NJ, NM, SD		2: KS, MI, MO, WA 4: TN	13: DE, NH, RI
March 8: MS	10: NE, WV	14: ME,NV, ND, SC, VA		9: CT, MN, VT, WI	20: MI
March 15: IL, NC, OH	17: ID,KY,OR	28: CO, NY, OK, UT		13: HI 16: AK, WY	
April 26: MD, PA	24: GA,			30: AZ, FL	
					Nov. 8: LA*

Note: A few states hold nominating conventions instead of primary elections.

*Louisiana conducts a "blanket primary" in the sense that all candidates, regardless of party affiliation, run in the same contest. If no one receives a majority of the votes, the top two candidates then face one another in a runoff on December 10.

nominating events (primary elections, conventions, etc.). Note that this is the primary calendar for the nomination of candidates for state office, not the presidential primary in each state. Some states hold their presidential primary at the same time, others do not. For example, the Arizona state primary was August 30, 2016, but the state held its presidential primary March 1—almost six months earlier.

In 2016, state primary elections were spread over a seven-month span, from March 1 (Alabama, Arkansas, and Texas) to September 20 (Massachusetts). The most popular months for primary elections were June (fifteen states) and August (fourteen states). Seven states held primaries in March and another seven held theirs in May.

Each state (or state party) decides who can vote in the primary election. Primary elections (or conventions in a few states) determine the party nominees for the general election. One of the issues each state must address, therefore, is who should be allowed to vote in the primary election: anyone who is registered to vote in the general election or only those who are registered as members of the political party. The parties themselves usually argue that only those who are registered members of the party should be able to determine who the party nominees will be. For state parties, it is a matter of the "right of association." Others, however, argue that the choices available in the general election are determined by the results of the primary election, therefore everyone who is interested should have the right to help make those choices. These two arguments represent the philosophies behind the closed primary and the open primary. In truth, there are several shades of open and closed; in some states the primary is closed only to registered members of the other party but not to independent or unaffiliated voters. One authoritative source claims that only eleven states are truly open and another eleven states are truly closed (see table 6.3).

The large "hybrid" systems category masks considerable variation among the included states. There are two significant differences. First, how are unaffiliated voters treated? Most hybrid systems are closed to members of the opposition party but allow independents (usually called "unaffiliated" or "decline to state" voters) to participate in the primary. Second, do both parties use the same rules? For states in this "hybrid" category, the answer is often "no." In Alaska, for example, only those who are registered Republicans, nonpartisans, or undeclared can vote in the GOP primary, while all registered voters can vote in the Democratic primary.[35]

Finally, there are a few states that use a system called a "top-two" primary (also known as a "Cajun Primary" because Louisiana was the first state to adopt it). In a "top-two" system, all the candidates for a particular office are listed together on the ballot, regardless of party affiliation. The two top vote-

TABLE 6.3
Primary Election (Nominating) Systems

Truly Open (11 states)	*Truly Closed* (11 states)	*Hybrid* (24 states)	*Top-Two* (4 states)
Alabama	Delaware	Alaska	California
Arkansas	Florida	Arizona	Louisiana
Georgia	Kansas	Colorado	Nebraska
Hawaii	Kentucky	Connecticut	Washington
Michigan	Maine	Idaho	
Minnesota	Nevada	Illinois	
Missouri	New Jersey	Indiana	
Montana	New Mexico	Iowa	
North Dakota	New York	Maryland	
Vermont	Pennsylvania	Massachusetts	
Wisconsin	Wyoming	Mississippi	
		New Hampshire	
		North Carolina	
		Ohio	
		Oklahoma	
		Oregon	
		Rhode Island	
		South Carolina	
		South Dakota	
		Tennessee	
		Texas	
		Utah	
		Virginia	
		West Virginia	

Source: National Conference of State Legislatures, "State Primary Election Types" (updated June 2014), http://www.ncsl.org/legislatures-elections/elections/primary-types.aspx, accessed May 30, 2012.

getters, even if they are from the same party, face each other in the general election. Thus as noted at the beginning of this chapter, it is possible to have two Republicans (or two Democrats) run against one another in the general election. All registered voters, regardless of party affiliation, are permitted to vote in a "top-two" primary.

There are practical effects to the distinction between open and closed primaries. Among those states that conduct truly open primaries for both parties, there is no reason to require voters to register by party. In these states, parties, interest groups, and candidates find it more difficult to target specific voters.[36] While they may have a list of who voted in previous primaries, they do not have a list of who voted in *which* primary (the Republican or the Democratic one). Consequently, communicating with voters is less efficient (and therefore costlier). In a strictly closed system in which voters register by party, a readymade list of contacts exists.

The open versus closed nature of the primary may also affect the nature of the message a candidate seeks to deliver. In a strictly closed primary, Republican candidates may be more likely to take more conservative issue positions, while Democratic candidates may espouse a decidedly liberal point of view. After all, the eligible voters in a strictly closed primary are likely to be among the more conservative elements in the Republican primary and the more liberal elements in the Democratic primary. Because independents and others cannot participate, the candidates, in essence, preach to the choir—the party faithful. But in open or top-two primary systems, the electorate represents a broader spectrum of policy positions. It was this assumption that led California voters to adopt the top-two primary in 2010. The first election under the new system was held in 2012, and while it is too early to make definitive declarations, some analysts think it has led to a change in the way candidates present themselves to the electorate. A recent report from an independent California think tank suggests there has been a modest increase in the election of moderate candidates.[37]

5. Voter eligibility and access rules

In some regards, federal policies have diminished the amount of latitude that states have in determining eligibility. In particular, several amendments to the U.S. Constitution were adopted to specifically prohibit discriminatory practices of some states (for example, the Fifteenth and Nineteenth Amendments, which prohibited the states from denying the right to vote based on race or sex, respectively) or to establish a national standard (for example, the Twenty-Sixth Amendment, which standardized the legal voting age at eighteen years). Federal influence over voter eligibility and access certainly is not limited to the several constitutional amendments. Congressional actions such as the 1965 Voting Rights Act (and its subsequent renewals) and the 1993 National Voter Registration Act (commonly known as the Motor-Voter Bill) are well-known examples of significant federal mandates. The 2002 Help Americans Vote Act (HAVA), while not specifically targeted at voter eligibility and access, is another example of federal action in the electoral process, in this case seeking to upgrade and partially standardize the mechanics and administration of voting in the states.

In 2013, the U.S. Supreme Court reconsidered certain aspects of the 1965 Voting Rights Act (VRA).[38] A key provision of the 1965 VRA was Section 5, which provided for federal oversight of the administration of electoral laws in states where discriminatory practices had previously existed. For the most part, Section 5 applied to southern states. In striking down the essence of Section

5, the Court reduced federal control over the electoral law decisions of those states. This in turn has led a number of these states to change electoral laws in ways that will likely impact voter participation in some instances. In particular, some states have reduced early voting periods and increased the requirements for registration and voting. There are partisan implications for these changes; almost all were passed by states with Republican legislative majorities. In the states the Democrats control, laws have been passed to make it easier for people to register and vote. The most notable recent reforms were passed in California, Oregon, and Vermont, each of which adopted legislation creating automatic voter registration systems. Such laws are anticipated to increase voter participation and the share of the vote received by Democratic Party candidates. In this, as in so many other instances, not only do states matter, but which party is in control of the state also matters. But it is also worth noting that in 2016, GOP-leaning Alaska voters adopted such a measure, and West Virginia lawmakers managed to pass a bipartisan voter reform bill combining an automatic registration process of the sort supported by Democrats with voter identification requirements along the lines that Republicans back.[39]

Whether or not a state encourages early voting (especially by mail, as several states do) has important consequences beyond just the partisan consideration. The consequence for the potential voter is obvious—it makes voting much more convenient. A voter can read campaign material and fill out the ballot at his or her convenience, then slip the ballot in the privacy-protected envelope and drop it in the mailbox.

For the political parties and the candidates themselves, early voting adds to their planning and strategic burdens. In states where a lot of people vote early, candidates must time their campaigns to coincide with when the ballots are made available to the voters—usually about three weeks prior to the actual Election Day. This means media buys and targeted mailings must be undertaken earlier and presumably sustained for a longer period of time.

All of these differences we have discussed do not exhaust the ways electoral rules vary across the states. Nevadans, for example, find a line on their ballots for "None of These Candidates" in U.S. presidential, U.S. Senate, and statewide contests (governor, lieutenant governor, secretary of state, state treasurer, state controller, attorney general, and justice of the supreme court). Relatively few voters vote that line in presidential races, but almost 20 percent do in judicial contests.[40] Vermont law requires that any statewide election for a state office where no candidate secures a majority of the vote is to be determined by the state legislature. Thus when the incumbent governor, Democrat Peter Shumlin, finished first in the 2014 election with 46.4 percent of the vote, he did not automatically win. Instead because he failed to attain a majority the contest was turned over to the state legislature to decide. It was the twenty-fourth time the Vermont legislature was forced to pick the winner. In early 2015, the 180 legislators chose Shumlin. (No second-place finisher has been selected by the state legislature since 1853.)[41] The point to keep in mind is that the electoral process differs from state to state in both large and small ways.

Redistricting

The American preference for single-member legislative districts and the "one person, one vote" conception of political equality means that redistricting is an important feature of state politics. Redistricting involves the redrawing of legislative district lines after each new federal census is released. It may seem obvious that the state is required to redraw those state legislative districts once new census data are available; after all, since the reapportionment revolution of the 1960s, we expect each legislative district to have roughly the same population as every other district within the state. But what may not be so obvious is this: states are also charged with drawing the *congressional* lines within the state as well. In other words, every ten years all congressional districts are redrawn by the states.[42]

In most states, the ultimate redistricting authority is the state legislature.[43] In other words, redistricting is achieved through statute—the legislature passes a bill laying out the boundaries of each legislative district and the governor signs it into law. Given the highly political nature of the issue, partisan control of the legislature and the governor's office are important advantages. If one party controls all three points of action—the lower state house, state senate, and governor's office—that party is in a strong position to implement a redistricting plan that benefits its interests and harms the opposition party. This is commonly referred to as a gerrymander, after the way Massachusetts governor Elbridge Gerry's party drew state legislative district lines to its advantage in 1812. These lines are critical because they (usually) stay in effect for a decade—until the next census.[44] And remember also that the state is drawing the lines for both the state legislature and the congressional districts within that state. For these reasons, state elections held in the "zero year" of a decade (2010, 2020, etc.) can have important consequences for partisan fortunes in both the state legislature *and* the U.S. House of Representatives. Because the census data are made available in the "one year" (for example, 2011) and in most cases have to be used in redrawing district lines in the "two year" (for example, 2012), the election in the "zero year" determines who will be in control of the redistricting process.

There is a growing minority of states in which the redistricting process has been put outside the immediate control of the legislature.[45] In these places, the process is usually controlled by an outside (independent) commission that has been granted authority to draw the lines. While these independent commissions are still subject to political and partisan pressures (that is, they are usually not entirely "independent"), it is usually true that they are not as overtly partisan. In other words, in terms of the partisan implications for redistricting, the state election results in the "zero year" are not quite as important in those states with independent redistricting commissions.

It is clear that the Republican Party understood the importance of the 2010 state elections for the upcoming redistricting process for both state legislative districts and congressional districts.[46] Employing a strategy they called REDMAP (Redistricting Majority Project), the party identified the legislative chambers most likely to flip party control. They spent more than $30 million on state legislative races in 2010, hoping to turn some Democratic-controlled state legislative chambers into Republican-controlled chambers. They were immensely successful, winning over seven hundred additional legislative seats, gaining control of numerous chambers, and greatly enhancing the party's role in the redistricting process.

One can see the effect of REDMAP on the political dynamics of redistricting from table 6.4. Presumably, states listed in the first column are less sensitive to changes in partisan control of the executive and legislative branches because primary responsibility for redistricting is initially controlled by outside commissions. A notable exception is Ohio because there the seven-person commission is composed of three statewide elected officials (governor, secretary of state, and state auditor) and four people chosen by legislative leaders.

The second column shows there are five states in which, prior to the 2010 election, Democrats had unified control (that is, a Democratic governor and a Democratic majority in both houses of the legislature) but in which the Republicans won a majority in at least one legislative chamber and/or the governor's office. In other words, the state went from unified party control to divided party control. The political implication is that in that circumstance the two parties must negotiate and compromise in a bipartisan manner to reach consensus on a redistricting plan. Had Democrats retained unified control, they would have controlled the redistricting process. Among the states that moved from unified Democratic control to divided control were New York and North Carolina.

The third column represents states that moved from divided control prior to the election to unified Republican control after the election. These are states in which Republicans gained power over the process whereas previously—under divided control—they would have had to compromise. There are seven states in this category, including Michigan. Effectively, however, there are eight states in this category because of the way the Ohio commission was selected.

TABLE 6.4

The Effect of the 2010 State Elections on Who Controls the Redistricting Process

States with Redistricting Commissions	BLUE TO PURPLE: Moved from Unified Democratic to Divided control	PURPLE TO RED: Moved from Divided to Unified Republican	BLUE TO RED: Moved from Unified Democratic to Unified Republican	PURPLE TO BLUE: Moved from Divided to Unified Democratic
AK	NH	AL	WI	CT
AZ	NM	IND		
AR	NY	KS		
CA	NC	MI		
CO	OR	OK		
HI		TN		
IA***		WY		
ID				
ME*				
MO				
MT				
NJ				
OH**				
PA				
VT*				
WA				

States not listed are states in which there is no change in the partisan influence over redistricting (n=20, including Nebraska).

*Advisory Committee—legislature may accept alternative plan.

**Ohio board includes governor, secretary of state, auditor, and one each chosen by political party leaders. All three statewide offices are now controlled by Republicans, giving them a 4 to 1 partisan advantage on the commission.

*** Iowa's is not actually an independent commission, but plans are drawn by nonpartisan legislative staff and legislature votes on the plan. It is included here under "commission" because legislature does not have direct control of drawing plans.

One state, Wisconsin, went from unified Democratic control to unified Republican control following the 2010 election (column 4). This represents a complete reversal of who controls the process. Finally, in one state (see column 5) we see an electoral gain for the Democrats, as Connecticut moved from divided control to unified Democratic control.

From table 6.4 we can conclude that after the 2010 election Democrats were in a worse position in fourteen states (if we include Ohio) and in a better position only in Connecticut. It is important to remember that the state legislature is responsible for redistricting the congressional districts within the state as well as the state legislative districts. That the Democrats were in a worse position to influence the drawing of congressional lines in

New York, North Carolina, Michigan, Ohio, and Wisconsin is not a trivial outcome of the 2010 state elections. Some have argued that the Republicans were able to maintain their majority in the U.S. House of Representatives in 2012 precisely because the GOP had gained majorities in so many state legislatures in 2010, and therefore were able to draw favorable congressional district lines in a number of states.[47] Other variables were certainly involved, but there is little doubt that the 2012 congressional elections were influenced by the 2010 shift in state legislative chambers.[48] Moreover, it appears the Democrats learned a costly lesson from the 2010 REDMAP experience. According to one report, they are preparing for the next redistricting cycle by creating "Advantage 2020," a plan to raise $70 million to contest the 2020 state legislative elections.[49]

The States and Direct Democracy

In regard to political participation, the federal government has often taken a stronger position than many states in extending and protecting individual citizens' right to vote. Previously we mentioned four amendments to the U.S. Constitution that were designed to expand the right to vote to citizens who were being denied that right by some states. The discriminatory actions taken by some American states to discourage racial and ethnic minorities from voting are well documented. We should remember, however, that African Americans were voting in some northern states long before passage of the Fifteenth Amendment, that women were voting in many western states long before passage of the Nineteenth Amendment, and that eighteen- or nineteen-year-olds could vote in Georgia and several other states long before passage of the Twenty-Sixth Amendment. Nonetheless, it is generally acknowledged that the federal government has done more than many states to extend and protect voting rights.

But in regard to other forms of political participation, states are often far ahead of the national government. This is especially true of those instruments of direct democracy known as the initiative, the referendum, and the recall. Virtually all states permit at least one of these instruments and almost one-third of the states allow all three forms. The national government allows none of them. One might argue that some of the states are more democratic than the federal government in the sense that at the state level the public has a greater ability to inform, direct, or constrain the policy actions of elected officials.

The Recall. Between March 2011 and June 2012, the biggest election story in the United States, other than the presidential campaign, played out in Wisconsin. It was quite a story—perhaps unprecedented in American history.

As part of the Republican electoral sweep in 2010, the Wisconsin Assembly, the Wisconsin Senate, and the Wisconsin governorship were suddenly all firmly in the hands of Republicans. Under the leadership of the new governor, Scott Walker, the legislature made sweeping changes in the collective bargaining rights and the benefits packages of the state's public employee unions. The legislation did not pass without a fight; daily public demonstrations at the state capitol became national news. As the legislation was scheduled for a vote in the state senate, fourteen Democratic state senators actually fled the state to break a quorum and prevent action on the bill in the Senate.[50] Meanwhile, as a Reuters news report stated, "Capitol police estimated 25,000 people, many carrying signs protesting the Republican plan, converged on the state Capitol building on Thursday, including 5,000 packed inside. The protests, which began on Monday, have grown in numbers every day this week, police said."[51]

Ultimately, the Democratic senators returned and, amid emotional outcries from the crowds in and around the capitol, the anti-union legislation narrowly passed on strict party line votes in both chambers and was then signed by the governor. Within days, petitions to recall some state senators were being circulated—under state law only those elected officials who had been in office for at least one year could be subject to a recall. By the summer of 2012, recall elections were held against thirteen state senators (ten Republicans and three Democrats), the lieutenant governor, and—most famously—Governor Scott Walker. Never had there been so many recall elections held in the span of a year than occurred in Wisconsin. Ultimately, only three of the fifteen officials were defeated in the recall elections—all Republican state senators. A fourth Republican state senator resigned rather than face a recall vote. After a brutal and expensive campaign, Scott Walker retained his office with 53 percent of the vote. Over $125 million was spent on the Wisconsin recalls, including at least $75 million on the governor's recall alone.

One of the reasons that so much attention and so much money were lavished on the Wisconsin recalls is that the issues in play had national implications. Collective bargaining, public employee retirement obligations, and state budget constraints were issues playing out not just in Wisconsin, but in Indiana, Michigan, and Ohio as well. In effect, the recall elections in Wisconsin served as a plebiscite on public policy in a way that only happens at the state (or local) level in the United States.

While thirty-six states allow for the recall of local officials, only eighteen states permit the recall of state officials. The procedures vary among these states, but generally the requirement is that a petition calling for a recall election is circulated and a specific number of valid signatures must be gathered. If the petitioners meet this standard, a special election is called to remove the official from office. The process may be simple to comprehend, but it is rarely successful. Only twice have governors been recalled from office (the most famous example being the recall of Gray Davis in California in October 2003, resulting in the choice of Arnold Schwarzenegger as the new governor). Since 1990, only eleven state legislators have been recalled (Arizona, California, Colorado, and Wisconsin offering the most recent examples) and at least one other governor (Evan Mecham, R-AZ) was facing a recall election when he was impeached by the state legislature.[52] The most recent gubernatorial recall effort was in 2016, targeting Governor Rick Snyder of Michigan in the wake of the Flint water crisis. That same year recall petitions circulated aimed at recalling four Michigan legislators who had voted for an increase in vehicle registration fees and the gasoline tax.

While it may be true the recall is only occasionally successfully executed, the mere threat of its use can influence public policy. As one knowledgeable observer of politics in Michigan recently commented, "Make no doubt about it, threat of a recall has a tremendous impact on the State Legislature, in both parties."[53]

The Referendum. While there are several versions of the referendum, the common element is that a policy proposal (a potential law or constitutional amendment) is submitted (referred) to the voting public for approval. It is also a common practice (indeed, it is constitutionally required in some states) to submit any proposal for bonded indebtedness to the public for a vote. None of this, of course, is allowed at the federal level.

The referendum process exists in all states—save, arguably, for Delaware—most commonly for adoption or rejection of amendments to the state constitution.[54] Note that at the federal level, constitutional amendments are not submitted directly to the public for a vote. In about half the states, members of the public can directly challenge a law passed by the state legislature by requiring a *popular referendum* on the law. This requires the gathering of signatures on a petition and, if the threshold for the required number of signatures is surpassed, the issue is put to public vote in the next election. As one authority on state politics notes, "The popular referendum is effectively a public veto of a law."[55]

Granting the right of approval or rejection through a referendum vote is an important form of direct democracy that does not exist at the federal level. In this sense, state governments afford their citizens the opportunity to have a direct impact on public policy in a way that the national government does not. Indeed, about 30 percent of the items brought forth by referendum are rejected by the citizens. For example, in 2011 Maine voters used the popular referendum—called the "People's Veto" in that state—to repeal a law passed by the state legislature abolishing election day voter registration. In 2012, a total of twelve public referenda made state ballots, the highest number in many years. Of these proposed laws, five were rejected, including three in Idaho and one in South Dakota in which voters rejected laws passed by their legislatures that would have put strict limits on teachers' unions.

Again, state referenda can carry considerable weight nationally. In 2011, Ohio voters rejected a bill (Senate Bill 5) that the Ohio state legislature had passed earlier in the year. The measure was similar to the one that had passed in Wisconsin that led to the recall frenzy discussed earlier. In the Ohio case, the bill limited collective bargaining options for public employee unions, eliminated the mandatory payment of union dues, and required public workers to contribute more to their pension funds—provisions similar to those that had passed in Wisconsin.[56] But instead of pursuing recall elections of the officials involved—which is not an option under Ohio law—Ohioans sought to repeal the law through the popular referendum process. They were successful, striking down the law by 62 percent to 38 percent. As in Wisconsin, huge sums were spent on the referendum election—about $54 million.[57]

Ohio voters had the ability to pursue a straightforward path of holding a referendum election on the anti-union bill. Why did their counterparts in Wisconsin take the recall route on their anti-union bill, a process that required a series of elections strung out over more than a year? The answer is simple: the popular referendum does not exist in Wisconsin. Thus the only immediate avenue open to challenging the law in Wisconsin was an attempt to recall the public officials involved in passing it. Rules matter and different states have different rules.

The Initiative. There are also several versions of the initiative, but the most important point is that in some states the initiative can be a powerful instrument of direct democracy. As one expert source on the subject proclaims, initiatives "are the most potent form of direct democracy."[58] Indeed, some of the most important and controversial public policies today—minimum wage laws, immigration, abortion, marijuana use, and gun control—have been the subject of the initiative process in one state or another. Tax limitations and expenditure mandates are also common topics addressed through the initiative process.

Only about half the states (twenty-four, to be exact) provide for the direct initiative. About half the population of the United States lives in states with the direct initiative; California and Florida being the two largest states with the process. Sponsors of a proposal must gather the requisite number of signatures on petitions in order to get their proposal on the ballot in next regularly scheduled election. The direct initiative, therefore, is an instrument of political participation that allows the public to bypass the state legislature and the legislative process altogether. It can become a tactical weapon for ideological groups that feel unrepresented. In recent decades, conservatives

often turned to the initiative process.[59] But with the majority of state legislatures now under Republican control, some liberal groups "are using state
ballot initiatives as their weapon of choice for 2016."[60]

Elizabeth Garrett uses the term "hybrid democracy" to describe the initiative states.[61] We think this an apt term; it captures the idea that these states
have a policymaking process that combines the traditional American pen-
chant for representative government by elected officials with the element of
direct democracy through the initiative. Clearly, the policy process has the
potential to be different in these states.

The ease or difficulty by which initiatives can be employed varies; in states
like California, Oregon, and North Dakota it is much easier to use than in
Illinois or Wyoming.[62] The most important difference is the proportion of
valid signatures that must be gathered. In some states the requirement is 5
percent of the number of votes in the last statewide election (for governor,
typically). In other states the requirement is 10 percent or even 15 percent. In
a few states there are requirements that the signatories must be geographically
dispersed (a certain number of signatures must come from a certain number
of counties or congressional districts, for example), which increases the difficulty of meeting the standards for acceptance onto the ballot. Because of
these variables, the use of the initiative as a method of policymaking is more
likely in some states than others. For example, between 1996 and 2013 in California, an average of thirteen measures qualified for the ballot every two-year
election cycle; Oregon averaged nine, while Colorado and Washington each
averaged about seven.[63]

In about sixteen initiative states the instrument can be used to amend the
state constitution, while in the remaining eight initiative states it can only be
used to create statutory law. This is an important distinction. Any changes
made to the state constitution through the direct initiative can only be altered
or overturned by the courts. But initiatives that simply create statutory law
can be changed by legislative action.

Donovan and his colleagues provide a useful summation of the role that
instruments of direct democracy play in the political environments of some
states. They note, "Direct democracy—specifically, the initiative process—has
important effects where it is used. It . . . may alter participation levels and the
issues voters use when evaluating candidates. There is some evidence that
direct democracy may lead state policies to be more representative of what
voters in a state prefer."[64]

There are both positive and negative aspects of direct democracy in the
states and they are frequently debated and discussed among political practi-
tioners, political scientists, and journalists. While the initiative and referendum provide opportunities for voters to influence a variety of public policies,

sometimes the task can be daunting. California voters found seventeen propositions on their ballot in November 2016. The propositions covered a wide range of issues, including several that conflicted. For example, one proposal would ban capital punishment in California, while another would speed up the execution process for death row inmates. Other measures asked voters to approve a $2 increase in the tobacco tax, to require background checks for the purchase of ammunition, to legalize recreational marijuana, and to overturn a ban on bilingual education in public schools that had passed in 1998. As one observer of California politics commented, "It's incredible the amount of substance and complexity in the November ballot. It's going to be overwhelming for voters to deal with."[65] But there are shortcuts such as support or opposition from particular politicians or interest groups voters can employ to reach what is, from their political perspective, the correct voting decision on such measures.[66]

Again, our larger point is that any discussion about direct democracy takes place in the context of state politics, not national politics. There are no instruments of direct democracy at the national level in the United States. At the state level, as states appear to be realigning or sorting on the basis of political ideology and culture, the initiative, referendum, and recall may be especially useful in fostering innovative policies. They are, in effect, important instruments in the laboratories of democracy. Strikingly different policies in regard to the use of marijuana, end-of-life decisions, abortion, environmental regulation, and the definition of animal cruelty exist among states in part because of the initiative and referendum procedures in some of them.

Term Limits and the States

At the end of the 1980s a movement began to limit the number of terms lawmakers could serve in office. It first met with success with the passage of term limit initiatives in California, Colorado, and Oklahoma in 1990. Two years later, again through the initiative process, limits were placed on legislative terms in Arizona, Arkansas, Florida, Michigan, Missouri, Montana, Ohio, and South Dakota. By the end of 1994, term limits were in place in nineteen states. Almost all of these laws were the product of the initiative process. Several states eventually repealed their term limit or the state supreme court determined they violated the state constitution, so that today there are fifteen states with term limits on their state legislators.

In important respects, the term limitation laws that were adopted differed from state to state, with some states imposing stricter limits on state legislative service than other states. But one thing that all the term limit initiatives contained was a term limit on members of Congress as well as on state legislators. Here, then, is a case in which almost 40 percent of the states (and about 80 percent of the states with the initiative from of direct democracy) used a state-based process to define a federal office. While the precise nature of the term limits on state legislatures differed from state to state, almost all of them placed the exact same limit on the their members of Congress: six years (three terms) in the House of Representatives and twelve years (two terms) in the Senate. Few people recall that the original term limit laws passed in the states included provisions limiting congressional terms as well. This has been forgotten because in 1995 the U.S. Supreme Court struck down the part of each of state initiative that imposed limits on members of Congress, finding that states (and Congress itself) cannot impose an additional qualification for federal office beyond those in the Constitution, only a constitutional amendment could do so.[67] Thus what many viewed as an effort to limit congressional terms through the use of a state-based instrument of direct democracy ultimately had no direct effect on the federal office but a substantial effect on state legislative office in some states.

Nonetheless, it would be a mistake to assume that state legislative term limits have no impact on Congress; one report finds that members of Congress from term-limited states are more likely to be former state legislators than members from non-term-limited states: 61 percent of members who represented states with legislative term limits were former state legislators compared to only 46 percent of members from non-term-limited states.[68] The presumption is that term-limited legislators who do want to end their political careers are forced to seek other offices for which to run, and a congressional seat would be an obvious next step.

Because term limit laws differ, the effect of the law is not the same for all the states that impose them.[69] In those states in which the limit is generous (twelve years in each chamber in Louisiana, Nevada, and Oklahoma), the effects are different than in states where the limit is especially stringent (six years in the lower chamber in Michigan). A strict term limit can actually accelerate the already substantial effect of a "wave election," such as that experienced in 2010. A good example is Michigan: when the state legislature convened in January 2011, 54 percent of the state representatives and 76 percent of the senators were newly elected—an extraordinary level of turnover by any standard.

The Presidential Election and the States

The method by which Americans choose their chief executive is unique. Some might even characterize it as bizarre. It consists of two distinct and decidedly different phases—the nomination phase and the general election phase. The two phases evolved separately. But each, in its own way, emphasizes the role of the states in choosing the national executive.

The Presidential Primaries. The first step—the nomination phase—is actually a series of steps defined by a combination of national party rules, state party rules, and state election laws. There is no mention of any nomination phase in the U.S. Constitution. The system has evolved over time and the current process bears almost no resemblance to the system of 1800, and only faint resemblance to the system of 1900 or even 1950. Indeed, the nomination system continually morphs (see table 6.5). For our purposes, the key things to understand about the current nomination system are the following.

First, each state party is allocated a certain number of delegates by the national party. Most of these delegates are pledged to support a particular candidate, and they are authorized to attend the national nominating convention and vote for that candidate. There are several ways delegates may be selected, the most common of which are caucuses or primary elections. In 2016, about a quarter of the state parties used a caucus nominating system, along the lines of Iowa's. But in most states primary elections are held.

Second, the decision about how many delegates can participate at the nominating convention is a matter for each national political party to decide. Republicans tend to have smaller nominating conventions than Democrats; in 2016 there were 2,472 delegates to the Republican convention while the Democrats had 4,763 delegates.

Third, the manner in which the delegates are allocated to each state is different for each party and it is not based solely on state population. The Democratic Party in particular tends to allocate additional delegate seats to

TABLE 6.5
**Growth in States' Use of Primary Elections to
Select Delegates to the Presidential Nominating Conventions**

Year	Number of States Holding Primary*	Percent of Delegates Chosen through Primaries**
1948	14	36
1968	15	39
1988	36	72
2008	42	75

*This represents the larger number between the number of states holding Republican primaries and the number of states holding Democratic primaries. In 1948, fourteen state Democratic parties held primaries, while twelve state Republican parties did so.
**Calculated as the average of the Republican and Democratic Party delegates chosen through primary elections.
Source: Calculated by authors using data in Harold W. Stanley and Richard Niemi, eds., *Vital Statistics on American Politics, 2009–2010* (Washington, DC: CQ Press, 2009), 55.

those states that tend to vote for its candidates—basically, a reward for voting for the party in the past. To a lesser extent, the Republicans do this also.

Fourth, the manner by which delegates within a state are allocated to various candidates also differs. Depending on state law, each party in a state can choose to have nominating caucuses, nominating conventions, or nominating primaries. Over time the system has evolved that most of the nominating events are now primary elections. In 2016, twelve states held caucuses for the Republicans and twelve states held caucuses for the Democrats (although not exactly the same twelve states for each party); all the rest held primary elections.[70] Each party within a state must also decide if they will allocate delegates proportionally or in a winner-take-all fashion.

For the most part, the national Democratic Party requires that the delegates within a state be divided proportionally by the primary vote: if candidate A received 30 percent of the vote in the primary, she would receive roughly 30 percent of the delegates from that state. In contrast, while the Republican Party required all early voting states to allocate delegates proportionally, in later voting states each state Republican Party was allowed to determine for itself how its delegates would be allocated.[71] In 2016, seventeen state Republican parties decided on a winner-take-all allocation.[72] Moreover, sometimes state parties allocated delegates based on the statewide vote, sometimes they allocated on the bases of congressional district or state legislative district vote, and sometimes they used a combination or hybrid approach.

Fifth, there are also differences by state and party as to who can participate in the nominating event. Some state parties restrict participation to registered members of the party (a closed system), while some state parties allow independents to participate as well (open primary). Closed primaries are slightly more common than open ones. In 2016, Republicans held closed primaries in twenty-seven states; Democrats held closed primaries in thirty-one states.

Sixth, since 1972, the first two nominating events are the Iowa caucuses, followed within eight days by the New Hampshire primary elections. Because they host the first events in which delegates are allocated, these two states attract a substantial amount of money and attention from the candidates and the media. Usually any candidate who does better than projected in Iowa and New Hampshire is bestowed instant credibility and the appearance of momentum. Any candidate who does worse than expected may find it difficult to recover. In effect, these two small states exert disproportionate influence on the presidential nomination system. In this regard, a noteworthy observation is that in important ways Iowa and New Hampshire are not reflective of the national electorate because they have much smaller racial and ethnic minority populations.[73]

Each state, usually through legislative statute, determines when it will hold its presidential nominating event, sometimes ignoring national party rules. And within a state, the two parties might not share the same primary date or even method of selection. For example, in 2016, Idaho Republicans held a closed primary election on March 8, while Idaho Democrats held an open caucus on March 22.

Starting in the 1980s, many states have moved their primaries or caucuses to an earlier date, hoping to increase their influence on the nomination process. And as one state moved forward, other states would subsequently move their events even earlier on the calendar. A sort of "calendar creep" occurred, a process known as "frontloading." Increasingly, we see states moving their primaries to the early months of the presidential election year (from say April to February). Calendar creep has changed the dynamics of the presidential nominating process. In 1976, only 10 percent of the delegates were selected by early March; by 2008, over 70 percent had been chosen by then.[74]

Overall, one can see that the nomination phase is really a series of state-based political events. And each state (or state party organization, in some cases) makes important decisions about the manner, timing, and mechanics of its particular nominating events. Some states, notably Iowa and New Hampshire, exert disproportionate influence in the process because they get to hold the earliest contests. Clearly, states matter when it comes to establishing rules for choosing presidential nominees.

The General Election and the Electoral College. In the presidential selection process, the nomination phase and the election phase are distinct. The field of candidates is different, the rules are different, the strategies employed are different, and the length of the campaign is different.[75] But what does not differ is the strategic role of the states. As Darrell West notes, "Candidate behavior is conditioned by the rules of the game. Presidential elections in the United States are determined by the state-based Electoral College. . . . This electoral structure has enormous implications for advertising strategies. Most candidates . . . focus on the fifteen to twenty states that swing back and forth between the two major parties."[76]

At the beginning of this chapter, we noted that the president is not elected by a nationwide popular vote but in a series of fifty-one concurrent elections (each of the fifty states plus the District of Columbia). The purpose of these concurrent elections is to choose each state's electors for the Electoral College. The number of electors from each state is equal to that state's congressional delegation (seats in the House of Representatives plus two senators). Thus more populous states like California (fifty-five electors) and Texas (thirty-eight) have many more electors than Montana (three) or South Dakota (three).

One might expect presidential candidates to spend far more time, money, and effort in the large states like California and Texas because there are many more electoral votes to be won in those states. So why is it that in the past few presidential elections the candidates have spent about as much time in New Mexico and Nevada as they have in California and Texas? It is because of a combination of three things: 1) a competitive presidential election, 2) a series of noncompetitive state elections, and 3) something called the "unit rule." The unit rule is the same thing as "winner-take-all." It is up to each state to decide how to allocate its Electoral College votes, and all but two states (Maine and Nebraska) choose to assign all their electors to the winner of the popular vote in the state. Thus the plurality winner in a state gets all of the electoral votes. Note that the allocation of presidential electors is a state decision.

One of the closest state races for president in 2016 was in Michigan, where Donald Trump received 2.28 million votes to Hillary Clinton's 2.27 million. With more than 4.45 million votes cast, Trump won by about 13,000 votes. That is less than one-half of one percent of all the votes cast, but because Michigan allocates its electors using the unit rule, Trump received 100 percent of its Electoral College votes—all sixteen electors.

States use the winner-take-all rule because they think it increases their Electoral College clout. But this is only true in those states where the popular vote is expected to be close. If the popular vote in a state—even a large state like California—is expected to be one-sided, then the candidates will not spend much time or money there. For one candidate the state is a given, for the other it is a lost cause. Either way, why spend precious resources pursuing a sure thing or a lost cause when there are states still up for grabs? And in an election in which the Electoral College vote is expected to be close, every state and its unit of electoral votes (even New Hampshire's paltry four votes) can be important. Consequently, while Washington State (twelve electoral college votes) and Virginia (thirteen electoral college votes) have almost identical value in Electoral College math, presidential candidates Obama and Romney made a combined forty-seven trips to Virginia and only three trips to Washington between June and November of 2012.[77] This happened because Washington was deemed a safe Democratic state while Virginia was one of the prized battleground states. In presidential electoral politics, some states matter more than others because they are competitive.

The same phenomenon occurred in 2016, when candidates Trump and Clinton spent most of their campaign time in just a few states. These states included Florida, Michigan, Ohio, North Carolina, Pennsylvania, and Virginia—all populous states that were competitive. But they also spent considerable time in small competitive states like Nevada and New Hampshire.

Neither candidate spent much time at all in California, New York or Texas—three of the most populous states—because each of these states were "safe" for one candidate or the other.

The other oft-noted aspect of this system is that it is possible for a candidate to receive more overall popular votes nationwide and still lose in the Electoral College. Indeed, this happened at least four times, the most recent instance being the 2000 election in which the Democratic candidate, Al Gore, received slightly more popular votes nationwide but the Republican George Bush won slightly more votes in the Electoral College. And it is the Electoral College vote that matters.[78]

Many people call for an overhaul of the way we elect our president in the United States. Most of them would abolish the Electoral College and replace it with a direct national popular vote. But there are others who defend the unique contrivance of the Electoral College, arguing that it is an important reflection of a federal system of government—one in which the states play a key role in the selection of a federal office.[79] Indeed, it is likely that elected officials who consider the various proposals to reform the system will always calculate whether their state wins or loses under any changes.

State Elections in a Polarized Federal System

In this book, we have made the case that states matter in the policymaking process. And in this chapter we argue that states are important electoral units in the United States. Logically, then, we can expect that voters are attentive and active participants in state elections. Unfortunately, this is often not true. State elections, which should be about state issues and holding elected state officials accountable for their record in office, often appear not to be about that at all. There are a series of variables—some perhaps causal, others perhaps just confounding—that help explain why this happens. At a minimum, we need to discuss party polarization, electoral competition (or lack thereof), and the effect of national factors.

Polarization. In the past few years, a great deal has been written about party or ideological polarization in the United States.[80] Much of the attention is devoted to polarization at the national level, especially Congress. But there is ample evidence that political polarization exists at the state level as well. Indeed, some state legislatures appear to be even more polarized than the U.S. Congress.[81] Note that polarization in this context simply means the ideological distance between the political parties in a given legislature. It does not necessarily induce gridlock; in fact, one can have highly polarized political parties but very "productive" policymaking, especially if one party holds the governor's seat and large majorities in both chambers of the state legislature. But in terms of electoral choice, polarized parties are likely to offer candidates who are considerably more liberal or more conservative than the median voter. Assuming that the median voter prefers middle of the road or "moderate" policies, he or she may find him- or herself voting for a candidate who does not match his or her policy preferences, but simply meets a "lesser of two evils" criterion. In other words, the median voter may feel dissatisfied and not adequately represented.

Electoral Competition. For statewide office, such as governor, elections remain competitive in many states. But in some states, one party dominates. As of June 2016, there were seven statewide partisan executive offices elected in California, and all were held by Democrats.[82] Even more impressive is the fact that all twenty-seven statewide elected officials in Texas were Republicans.[83]

Below the statewide level, many state legislative districts are so dominated by one party that the other major party does not even field a candidate. Depending on the year and circumstance, between 35 percent and 40 percent of state legislative races are uncontested. In some places, the situation is even direr. The state with the least competitive districts may be Georgia: 80 percent of the seats for its state house of representatives were uncontested by one of the major parties in 2014 and again in 2016. In other words, 80 percent of the candidates were effectively elected *before* the general election was even held, leaving voters in those districts with no meaningful choice to make in the election for their state representative.

Even if a legislative race is contested, there is no guarantee that it is competitive. One commonly used measure of a "competitive election" is that the winning candidate's margin of victory was no greater than 10 percent of the votes cast. Recent research shows that only about 12 percent of state legislative races across the country are competitive by this standard—that is, only one out of every eight legislative contests.[84] The specific trends differ across the states, but overall the number of competitive districts has declined over the last generation.[85] While elections for governor are usually more competitive than state legislative races, they too have experienced a decline in competitiveness in recent years.[86]

The Intertwining of National Politics and State Elections. We have long known that state elections are influenced by national issues and trends.[87] Presidents have "electoral coattails" that help members of the president's party in down-ticket elections, and those coattails are "withdrawn" in midterm elections, when the president's party usually loses seats in the U.S. House and in state legislatures. The extent of presidential coattails and the subsequent mid-term reaction against the president's party vary by year, state, and circumstance. But such national forces appear to be growing in state elections, and especially in state legislative elections. Katharine Javian studied the effect of national factors on state legislative elections for the period from 1970 to 2010 and concluded "national contextual factors related to the president's party, evaluations of the president, and the presidential election cycle are important predictors of state legislative election outcomes."[88] Others have come to the same verdict.[89] After examining a variety of factors, including the number of uncontested races, the ideological position of the incumbent legislator, the popularity of the governor and the president, and the condition of the economy, Steven Rogers concludes that for the most part the public does not hold state legislators accountable. He contends, "Elections do not appear to hold state legislators accountable for state-level policy outcomes, their legislative records, or their general performance . . . instead of serving as a referendum on state legislators' own action, state legislative elections are dominated by national politics."[90]

Why is it the case? There are a series of variables that converge to create this situation. First, many people are not knowledgeable about state politics or about how important states are in the policymaking scheme. Only one of four voters knows who their state legislator is; even more discouraging is the fact that less than half can correctly identify which party controls their state senate or state house.[91] They are better at identifying the governor's party affiliation. Second, some voters appear to have a weak grasp on what the states do, what the national government does, and which officials are elected at which level. Because state elections and national elections are often held at the same time, it appears that issues associated with candidates for the national level seep into the voter's calculus for choosing among candidates in state elections. This has been called "the distraction hypothesis": elections for national offices (especially the presidential election) distract potential voters from state issues and conditions, even when voting for candidates for state office.[92] In other words, the existence of a federal system makes the potential voter's job more difficult. As some have argued, the states are less visible to the average citizen than either the national government or their local governments. This reality is made worse by the diminished media coverage of state politics.[93]

All of this is ironic. In chapters 1 and 2 we showed that states matter, especially in a period in which the national government appears polarized and gridlocked. In chapters 3 and 4 we showed that state institutions and officials are more capable and better equipped to be effective policymakers than they were in the past. In chapter 5 we demonstrated that states set many important public policies and that these policies vary by state. Earlier in this chapter we made the case that American elections are organized around the states. We also noted that many states have the initiative, referendum, and recall, mechanisms the national government does not have to translate public opinion into public policy. But—and here is the irony—voters often have limited or no real choice among candidates for state office and they often appear to be uninterested in or inattentive to state elections. Thus while states matter, indeed increasingly so, the choices provided for the voters in state elections are either nonexistent (uncontested or uncompetitive elections), distasteful (too ideologically extreme), misunderstood (confused by federalism), or simply unnoticed (lack of knowledge about or lack of interest in state politics).

Conclusion

It is a curiosity of the American federal system that each level—national and state—has been at the forefront of "democratizing" the political system, but in different ways. Generally speaking, the national government has led the way in opening the franchise—the right to vote—to more classes of people. One need only think of the effects of the Fourteenth, Fifteenth, Nineteenth, Twenty-Fourth, and Twenty-Sixth Amendments to the U.S. Constitution and the effects of the 1965 Voting Rights Act to understand how the national government expanded the definition of citizenry, in terms of who could vote, beyond what the states (or at least some states) were willing to do.

Many states have allowed their citizens greater opportunities to directly influence public policy than what is permitted at the national level. One need think only of the instruments of direct democracy available at the state levels that are not available at the national level to appreciate the difference. The multitude of judicial elections at the state and local level, in contrast to the manner in which federal judges are chosen, is another example of significant differences.

The main theme of this chapter is the variety of ways in which electoral rules and procedures that are defined at the state level impact the way politics plays out at the national level. All federally elected officeholders are chosen under rules influenced by the states. Rules matter, particularly electoral rules. And electoral rules among the states are something of a hodge-podge. They differ from one state to another in one or more of the following ways:

- Who can vote (voter eligibility)
- The process by which they get registered to vote (and they do not register at all in North Dakota)
- How they vote (ballot structure, absentee/mail voting)
- For whom they can vote (open versus closed primaries, which offices are elected)
- When they vote (presidential year, off-year, odd-year)

- How often they vote (terms of office)
- For what they can vote (just candidates or candidates and issues)

States also differ rather dramatically in terms of the relative strength of each the two major political parties. While nationally the two parties are currently roughly equal in strength, that is not the case in many states today. Some states are heavily Republican, some are heavily Democratic, and a smaller number are competitive and hotly contested between the two parties. At the intersection of these two issues—state party strength and state electoral rules—we find the Electoral College and the campaign for the presidency. In numerous ways, some obvious, others less so, state electoral and party systems matter.

Notes

1. http://www.reuters.com/article/us-usa-election-california-senate-idUSKC N0YT16J.

2. While Cruz had never run for office before, it would be inaccurate to describe him as a political novice. A Harvard-educated lawyer, he had clerked for former U.S. Supreme Court Chief Justice Rehnquist and had been appointed Solicitor General of Texas.

3. http://www.politifact.com/texas/statements/2015/apr/27/ted-cruz/ted-cruz -says-half-presidents-were-previously-gove/. Five former presidents served in both the governor's office and the U.S. Senate.

4. Doreen Barrie and Roger Gibbins, "Parliamentary Careers in the Canadian Federal State," *Canadian Journal of Political Science* 22 (1989): 137–45.

5. Klaus Stolz, "Moving Up, Moving Down: Political Careers Across Territorial Levels," *European Journal of Political Research* 42 (2003): 223–48.

6. Peverill Squire, "Electoral Career Movements and the Flow of Political Power in the American Federal System," *State Politics and Policy Quarterly* 14 (2014): 72–89.

7. "Voting Wrongs," *The Economist*, May 28, 2016, 13.

8. In 1992 there were 510,497 elected officials, a figure that almost certainly has increased over the years. The figure is reported in Frank Shelly, J. C. Archer, F. M. Davidson, and S. D. Brunn, *Political Geography of the United States* (New York: Guilford Press, 1996), 123.

9. There are some excellent discussions of these matters, however. See Douglas Rae, *The Political Consequences of Electoral Laws* (New Haven, CT: Yale University Press, 1967). Also see David M. Farrell, *Electoral Systems: A Comparative Introduction*, 2nd ed. (New York: Palgrave, 2011); Pippa Norris, *Electoral Engineering: Voting Rules and Political Behavior* (New York: Cambridge University Press, 2004); and Michael Gallagher and Paul Mitchell, eds., *The Politics of Electoral Systems* (New York: Oxford University Press, 2005).

10. See Peverill Squire and Gary Moncrief, *State Legislatures Today*, 2nd ed. (Lanham, MD: Rowman & Littlefield, 2015), 21–22.

11. Richard G. Niemi, Jeffrey S. Hill, and Bernard Grofman, "The Impact of Multimember Districts on Party Representation in U.S. State Legislatures," *Legislative Studies Quarterly* 10 (1985): 441–55.

12. http://ncsl.typepad.com/the_thicket/2012/09/a-slight-decline-in-legislatures -using-multimember-districts-after-redistricting.html.

13. Stephen Calabrese, "Multimember District Congressional Elections," *Legislative Studies Quarterly* 25 (2000): 611–43.

14. Elizabeth Kolbert, "Drawing the Line," *The New Yorker*, June 27, 2016, 70; Jamie Carson, M. Crespin, C. Finocchiaro, and D. Rohde, "Redistricting and Party Polarization in the U.S. House of Representatives," *American Politics Research* 35 (2007): 878–904.

15. In fact, history reveals that MMDs were eliminated by some states because they led to one party dominating elections. See Thomas Schaller, "Multi-Member Districts: Just A Thing of the Past?" http://www.centerforpolitics.org/crystalball/articles/multi -member-legislative-districts-just-a-thing-of-the-past/.

16. See Didi Kuo, "Electoral System Reform in the United States," Conference Report, Program on American Democracy in Comparative Perspective, Stanford University, Center on Democracy, Development, and the Rule of Law, June 3, 2014, https://fsi.stanford.edu/sites/default/files/electoral_system_report.pdf.

17. James Langan, "A Cure that Is Likely Worse than the Disease." *William and Mary Law Review* 46 (2005): 1569–95, http://www.uvm.edu/~dguber/POLS125/ articles/langan.htm.

18. L. Sandy Maisel and Mark D. Brewer, *Parties and Elections in America*, 5th ed. (Lanham, MD: Rowman & Littlefield, 2010), 199.

19. That is, nine states have four-year electoral cycles that are held at the same time as the presidential election. But because New Hampshire and Vermont have elections every two years, there are actually eleven states holding gubernatorial elections during the presidential election year.

20. One expert finds that 87 percent of judges in state court systems face the electorate in one way or another. See Roy A. Schotland, "Judicial Elections," in *Guide to Political Campaigns in America*, ed. Paul Herrnson (Washington, DC: CQ Press, 2005), 391.

21. http://www.opensecrets.org/news/2011/04/wisconsin-supreme-court -elections-b.html.

22. Jon Frandsen, "Cash Flows into Judicial Races: What's Being Bought?" *Stateline*, June 14, 2016, http://www.pewtrusts.org/en/research-and-analysis/blogs/ stateline/2016/06/14/cash-flows-into-state-judicial-races-whats-being-bought.

23. Schotland, "Judicial Elections," 393.

24. Schotland, "Judicial Elections," 394.

25. David Rottman, "Judicial Elections in 2008," Council of State Governments, *Book of the States 2009*, 291.

26. Rottman, "Judicial Elections in 2008," 391.

27. November 9, 2010 post, "2010 Judicial Elections Increase Pressure on Courts," *Legal News*, November 9, 2010.

28. Alan Blinder, "Conservatives See Potential in Tennessee Judicial Race," *New York Times*, August 5, 2014, http://www.nytimes.com/2014/08/06/us/conservatives -target-tennessee-justices-in-expensive-race.html?_r=0.

29. Blinder, "Conservatives See Potential."

30. Sam Zeff, "Get Ready for a Raucus Kansas Supreme Court Retention Race," *KCUR Radio*, May 24, 2016, http://kcur.org/post/get-ready-raucous-kansas-supreme -court-retention-race#stream/0. The quote is from KU political science professor Burdette Loomis.

31. See Todd Donovan, Christopher Z. Mooney, and Daniel A. Smith, *State and Local Politics: Institutions and Reform*, 2nd ed. (Belmont: Wadsworth, 2011), 335–37.

32. This is the same Don Blankenship who was convicted and sentenced to prison in 2016 on a federal misdemeanor charge of conspiring to violate safety standards be- fore the explosion at the Upper Big Branch mine that killed twenty-nine workers. The charge was not related to the campaign finance issue discussed in the text. See Allen Cone, "Coal King Reports to Prison After Appeal Denied," *United Press International*, May 13, 2016, http://www.upi.com/Top_News/US/2016/05/12/Coal-king-reports-to -prison-after-appeal-denied/9401463073932/.

33. Melinda Gann Hall, "State Courts: Politics and the Judicial Process," in *Politics in the American States*, ed. Virginia Gray and Russell Hanson, 9th ed. (Washington, DC: CQ Press, 2008), 245.

34. Caperton v. A.T. Massey Co, Inc. 129 S.Ct 2252 (2009).

35. https://www.elections.alaska.gov/ei_primary.php.

36. Maisel and Brewer, *Parties and Elections in America*, 211–12.

37. Eric McGhee, "Assessing the Top Two Primary," Public Policy Institute of California, June 9, 2016, http://www.ppic.org/main/blog_detail.asp?i=2070.

38. Shelby County v. Holder 570 U.S.__ (2013)

39. http://www.governing.com/topics/politics/gov-week-politics-voter-registration -wisconsin-primary.html.

40. Adam Brown, "Losing to Nobody? Nevada's 'None of these Candidates' Ballot Reform," *Social Science Journal* 48 (2011): 364–70.

41. http://www.governing.com/topics/politics/gov-vermont-peter-shumlin -election.html; "Shumlin Defeats Milne in Legislature Governor Vote," *Burlington Free Press*, January 9, 2015.

42. To be completely accurate, only 428 districts are currently redrawn by the states because seven states have only one congressional district each. In those in- stances the congressional district is the entire state and does not have to be redrawn.

43. The current number is thirty-seven states. This includes states in which there is a "backup commission" that takes over the process if the legislature does not com- plete the redistricting task by a specific date. Moreover, there are some states in which a commission is used to draw state legislative lines but in which the legislature has responsibility for drawing congressional districts within the state.

44. While this is generally true, it is possible for redistricting to be done more than once every decade. Perhaps the best known instance of this was when the Republican

Party won majority control of the Texas Legislature in 2003 and moved to redistrict despite the fact that the legislature had just effected a new redistricting plan (under the then-majority Democrats) in 2002.

45. By our count eighteen states fit under this definition. But there is some latitude for interpretation of the phrase "outside the control over the legislature." For example, in Maine, New York, Rhode Island, Vermont, and Virginia the redistricting commissions are advisory; they recommend plans but the legislature has the authority to reject the recommendation and adopt a different plan.

46. This discussion relies in part on Herman Schwartz, "Democrats: It's the States, Stupid!" *Reuters*, July 14, 2013, http://blogs.reuters.com/great-debate/2013/07/14/democrats-its-the-states-stupid/ and Elizabeth Kolbert, "Drawing the Line," *New Yorker*, June 27, 2016, 68–70.

47. See, for example, Sam Wang, "The Great Gerrymander of 2012," *New York Times*, February 2, 2013, http://www.nytimes.com/2013/02/03/opinion/sunday/the-great-gerrymander-of-2012.html?pagewanted=all.

48. See "Not Gerrymandering, but Districting: More Evidence on How Democrats Won the Popular Vote but Lost the Congress," *The Monkey Cage*, accessed March 27, 2013, http://themonkeycage.org/2012/11/15/not-gerrymandering-but-districting-more-evidence-on-how-democrats-won-the-popular-vote-but-lost-the-congress/.

49. Kolbert, "Drawing the Line," 71.

50. On breaking quorum in this case and others, see Peverill Squire, "Quorum Exploitation in the American Legislative Experience," *Studies in American Political Development* 27 (2013): 142–64.

51. Jeff Mayers, "Democrats Flee Wisconsin to Protest Union Curbs," *Reuters*, February 17, 2011.

52. For a list of recalled state legislators, see http://www.ncsl.org/legislatures-elections/elections/recall-of-state-officials.aspx.

53. Pete Nichols, "Tax Hike Opponents Lecture on Recall Rights," *The State News*, July 2007.

54. According to Jennie Drage Bowser, formerly of the National Conference of State Legislatures, Delaware's referendum authority is extremely limited, applying only to the question of whether or not "Bingo" should be licensed or prohibited. See NCSL, "Legislative Referendum: Constitutional Provisions," information sheet dated January 2012.

55. Donovan, Mooney, and Smith, *State and Local Politics*, 114–15.

56. Initiative & Referendum Institute, *Ballotwatch*, December 2011, No. 2, 1.

57. Unlike Wisconsin, where the pro-union forces were outspent in the effort to recall Governor Walker, in Ohio they held a commanding advantage in campaign expenditures. The pro-union groups outspent the anti-union coalition by more than 3:1.

58. Initiative and Referendum Institute, accessed August 27, 2010, http://www.iandrinstitute.org/BW%202008-3%20Results%20v4.pdf.

59. Arthur Lupia and John Matsusaka, "Direct Democracy: New Approaches to Old Questions," *Annual Review of Political Science* 7 (2004): 474–74.

60. Liz Essley Whyte, "How Democratic are Ballot Initiatives," *The Atlantic*, http://www.theatlantic.com/politics/archive/2016/01/ballot-initiatives-2016/422385/.

61. Elizabeth Garrett, "Hybrid Democracy," *George Washington University Law Review* 73 (2005): 1096–130.

62. Shaun Bowler and Todd Donovan, "Measuring the Effect of Direct Democracy on State Policy: Not All Initiatives Are Created Equal," *State Politics and Policy Quarterly* 4 (2004): 345–63.

63. Squire and Moncrief, *State Legislatures Today: Politics under the Domes*, 185.

64. Donovan, Mooney, and Smith, *State and Local Politics*, 148.

65. Mark Baldassare, president of the Public Policy Institute of California, quoted in www.sfgate.com/bayarea/article/November-ballot-crowded-with-weighty -measures-8335746.php.

66. Arthur Lupia, "Shortcuts versus Encyclopedias: Information and Voting Behavior in California Insurance Reform Elections," *American Political Science Review* 88 (1994): 63–76.

67. U.S. Term Limits, Inv. V. Thornton, 514 U.S. 779 (1995).

68. Karl T. Kurtz, "An Unexpected Benefit of Term Limits," *The Thicket* (National Conference of State Legislature's blog), April 23, 2009, http://ncsl.typepad.com/ the_thicket/2009/04/an-unexpected-benefit-of-term-limits.html.

69. Marjorie Sarbaugh-Thompson, "Measuring 'Term-Limitedness' in U.S. Multi-State Research," *State Politics and Policy Quarterly* 10 (2010): 199–217.

70. It should be noted that both parties also allocate delegates to the District of Columbia, Guam, the Northern Mariana Islands, Puerto Rico, the Virgin Islands, and American Samoa, although their residents cannot vote in the presidential election.

71. https://www.gop.com/the-official-guide-to-the-2016-republican-nominating -process/.

72. Some of these are statewide winner-take-all (whoever receives the most votes statewide receives all the delegates), some of these are district winner-take-all (whomever gets the most votes in each congressional district gets all three district votes). About half of the GOP delegates at the 2008 convention were selected through some form of winner-take-all rule. See Justin Sizemore, "Political Conventions in 2008," in *The Year of Obama*, ed. Larry Sabato (Boston: Longman/Pearson, 2010), 13.

73. Stephen Wayne, *Is This Any Way to Run a Democratic Election?* 4th ed. (Washington, DC: CQ Press, 2011), 179.

74. Barry Burden, "The Nominations: Rules, Strategies, and Uncertainty," in *The Elections of 2008*, ed. Michael Nelson (Washington, DC: CQ Press, 2010), 25.

75. Maisel and Brewer, *Parties and Elections in America*, 319.

76. Darrell West, *Air Wars*, 5th ed. (Washington, DC: CQ Press, 2010), 19.

77. "Presidential Campaign Stops: Who's Going Where," *Washington Post*, http:// www.washingtonpost.com/wp-srv/special/politics/2012-presidential-campaign -visits/.

78. The elections of 1824, 1876, and 1888 all resulted in the selection of a president who had not won the popular vote. While the evidence is not definitive, the 1960 election might also fall into this category. See, for example, Stephen Medvic, *Campaigns and Elections* (Boston: Wadsworth/Cengage, 2010), 48.

79. Martin Diamond, *The Electoral College and the American Idea of Democracy* (Washington, DC: American Enterprise Institute, 1977).

80. A good summary is provided in Steven Schier and Todd Eberly, *Polarized: The Rise of Ideology in American Politics* (Lanham, MD: Rowman & Littlefield, 2016).

81. See, for example, Boris Shor, "Party Polarization in America's State Legislatures: An Update," in *The State of the Parties*, ed. John Green, Daniel Coffey, and David Cohen, 7th ed. (Lanham, MD: Rowman & Littlefield, 2014), 121–36.

82. https://ballotpedia.org/California_state_executive_offices.

83. http://www.sos.state.tx.us/elections/voter/elected.shtml.

84. Carl Klarner and Heather Evans, "The Polarization and Nationalization of State Elections, 1971–2014," http://klarnerpolitics.com/.

85. Klarner and Evans, "The Polarization and Nationalization of State Elections, 1971–2014." Also see Keith Hamm and Gary Moncrief, "Legislative Politics in the States," *Politics in the American States*, ed. Virginia Gray, Russell Hanson, and Thad Kousser, 10th ed. (Washington, DC: CQ Press, 2013), 172–75 for a similar interpretation using a different measure of "competitive."

86. Klarner and Evans report that since 2003, only about 40 percent of all gubernatorial elections qualify as competitive. See Klarner and Evans, "The Polarization and Nationalization of State Elections, 1971–2014."

87. See, for example, James E. Campbell, "Presidential Coattails and Midterm Losses in State Legislative Elections," *American Political Science Review* 80 (1988): 45–63; John Chubb, "Institutions, The Economy, and the Dynamics of State Elections," *American Political Science Review* 82 (1984): 133–54. Also see William Berry, Michael Berkman, and Stuart Schneiderman, "Legislative Professionalism and Incumbent Reelection," *American Political Science Review* 94 (2000): 859–74. For the role of gubernatorial coattails, see Robert Hogan, "Gubernatorial Coattail Effects in State Legislative Elections," *Political Research Quarterly* 58 (2005): 587–97.

88. Katharine Javian, "The Influence of National Contextual Factors on State Legislative Election Outcomes," paper prepared for the 2012 American Political Science Association annual meeting scheduled for New Orleans in September 2012. Also see Katharine Javian, "Party Voting in the American States: How National Factors and Institutional Variation Affect State Elections" (PhD dissertation, Temple University, August 2012).

89. See Klarner and Evans, "The Polarization and Nationalization of State Elections, 1971–2014." Also see Carl Klarner and C. Lockwood Reynolds, "Driven to Distraction: State and National Forces in State Legislative Elections," paper prepared for the 2014 annual meeting of the State Politics and Policy Conference, Iowa City, May 2014.

90. Steven M. Rogers, "Accountability in a Federal System" (PhD dissertation, Princeton University, 2013), 4.

91. Steven Rogers, "Accountability in a Federal System," 34–35.

92. Klarner and Reynolds, "Driven to Distraction," 22.

93. Jeffrey Lyons, William Jaeger, and Jennifer Wolak, "The Roots of Citizens' Knowledge of State Politics," *State Politics and Policy Quarterly* 13 (2012): 185–86.

7

State Fiscal Systems

States matter because

- About 10 percent of the average citizen's income goes to pay state and local taxes
- The way a state puts together its tax system determines which citizens carry more of the tax burden
- The ability of local governments to tax and spend is controlled by state policymakers
- Public education in the United States is largely funded by the states and their local governments
- The sales tax is almost exclusively a state tax
- Unlike the federal government, states have balanced budget requirements
- State fiscal systems are pro-cyclical, which magnifies the effects of economic cycles
- Underfunded public employee pension funds pose a significant future problem in some states
- State fiscal systems are likely to become more reliant on their own revenue sources in the coming years

S TATE LEGISLATURES PASS A LOT OF BILLS. The only bills they are actually required to pass are those setting the state budget. But in 2015 at least eight states were unable to pass a budget on time. The following year showed no improvement. Across the country, 2016 was a year of state budget problems. It seemed every headline about budgets brought bad news. Here is a just a sample, all of which appeared within the first few months of 2016:

- "Oklahoma Legislators Lay Budget Problems on the Line: 'It's not Pretty'"[1]
- "Illinois Budget Standoff Nears One-Year Mark"[2]
- "Kansas Confronts Yet Another Budget Crisis"[3]
- "Louisiana's Budget Is a Hot Mess"[4]
- "Gov. Bentley: Alabama in a Budget Crisis"[5]
- "It's a Ticking Time Bomb: Wolf Unveils Pennsylvania Budget Amid Historic Gridlock"[6]
- "Alaska Faces a Clear Budget Deficit Without an Evident Solution"[7]

Troublingly, these are headlines that appeared five or six years *after* the Great Recession ended. For the most part, the states had actually emerged from the recessionary doldrums and experienced at least a modest economic recovery. So why the headlines about crises and missed budget deadlines? For some states, the new budget problems are the product of external factors; for example, the precipitous drop in oil prices had a major effect on the revenues and budgets in states like Oklahoma, Louisiana, and, especially, Alaska.

For other states, the "crisis" was more about a clash of political philosophies concerning the role of the state in taxation and government programs. Epic battles occurred in several states, most notably in Illinois (with a Democratic legislature and a Republican governor) and Pennsylvania (with a Republican legislature and a Democratic governor). An ideological standoff prevented Illinois from producing a full budget for over a year, while Pennsylvania only settled its budget after a nine-month stalemate.[8] During the impasse school districts in Pennsylvania were forced to borrow money from banks to stay open.[9] In Illinois, some social service programs were shut down and a child advocacy group led by the governor's wife was among the organizations that sued to get the state to release promised funds.[10]

In still other states, the budget "crisis" was self-inflicted, largely due to the accumulating effect of personal income tax reductions that did not produce the anticipated increase in state economic growth. Louisiana and Kansas were the prime examples of unfulfilled economic promises.

Public budgeting is inherently political.[11] This includes state and local budgeting. To a large extent, budgets represent policy preferences with dollar signs attached. Often they represent compromises between different policy preferences. They represent negotiations and decisions involving the level of taxation, the level of regulation, what services to provide, and the level of those services to be provided. State budgets involve intergovernmental relations in two ways. First, state budgets are affected by the availability and requirements of federal grants. Second, state budgets include state aid to local governments. To appreciate all this, we must examine state and local fiscal systems. There are three broad topics to cover: public budgeting cycles, revenue sources, and expenditures. And as always, there are differences in the way states handle each of these.

A key issue in the future for the states will be their degree of financial independence. This is the central truth about fiscal federalism: when the level of federal aid is high, the independent policymaking authority of the states is lower. In contrast, when the level of federal aid is lower, the independent policymaking authority of the states is higher, but the fiscal capacity of the states to pay for those policies is diminished. In other words, financial dependence is associated with less policymaking independence. The main reason for this relationship is that most federal aid comes "with strings attached"; the state (or local governments) must comply with specific rules and procedures in order to receive the funds.

As we have noted throughout this book, the fiscal problems of the national government have a trickle-down effect on the states. What federal fiscal aid exists in the future will be largely consumed by the entitlement category—especially Medicaid at the state level. This means states will likely have to go it on their own in even more policy areas than they have in recent decades. It is essential that citizens of each state understand the ways that state and local finances are tied to policy decisions and how the decisions policymakers make affect what state and local governments take (in the form of taxes and fees) and what they provide (in the form of services and protections). These are difficult decisions for which there are no simple solutions. As a Republican West Virginia senator and chair of the State Senate Finance Committee recently noted, "The anti-tax people are convinced there are millions and millions and millions of dollars of government waste that could be squeezed out if there's political will to do it." But as the senator noted, the "difficulty arises when the discussion moves from cutting spending in general to determining which specific programs are to be cut."[12]

Types of Budgets and Budget Cycles

There are several ways to distinguish budgets. One of the most common is a division between operating budgets and capital budgets. For states, most of their expenditures are payments to personnel or to purchase goods or services. These are part of the operating budgets—think of them as the price of ongoing government operations. But some types of expenditures are for long-term projects involving the acquisition of property and the building of something on that property. Thus capital budgets are about physical items—highways, bridges, university campus buildings, etc. For the most part, capital budgets involve one-time items—once a building is built, it is no longer in the capital budget. But operating budgets are ongoing. Once a program is started, the personnel have to be paid every year. For states, one of the most important distinctions between operating and capital budgets is that states can only go into debt (that is, borrow money through government bonding) for capital budgets, not operating budgets.

General Fund and Total Funds Budgets. But when talking about state budgets, there is another important way to distinguish between types of budgets, and it has to do with the control the state has over the way the funds are allocated. There are two of these too, and in most states they are called the general fund budget and the total budget. The general fund budget typically makes up 40 percent to 50 percent of the total budget. Although it is only half (or less) of the total budget, the general fund is the one that gets most of the media attention. The reason is simple enough; the general fund is *discretionary* money—meaning it can be spent in a variety of ways, and the state legislature and governor negotiate over its distribution. *Nondiscretionary* funds are monies that are "locked in"—they must be spent on specific programs or items. The state legislature and governor have no choice in how the money is allocated. It is mandated by the state constitution, state law, and court order or, in the case of federal grants-in-aid, by the federal government. For example, in most states, revenue from the state gasoline tax (more formally known as the "motor fuels tax") must go to the state transportation department or state highway department. This money cannot be diverted or reallocated by the legislature or the governor to schools or prisons or something else. Given that there is no discretion, there is no argument over who (what department) gets the money. Figures 7.1 and 7.2 show a typical state general fund budget and total fund budget.

Discretionary funds can be moved from one account to another. Consequently, there is almost always an argument in the legislature over who gets what share of general fund money. Thus the media focuses almost entirely on the fight over the general fund appropriation; it is often characterized as "slices of the (budget) pie" and the story is who is getting a larger or smaller piece. Some types of programs and interests tend to be funded through nondiscretionary funds (for example, highways), while others (for example, public education) are mostly financed through discretionary, general funds. From the point of view of program beneficiaries, nondiscretionary funds are more desirable than discretionary funds.

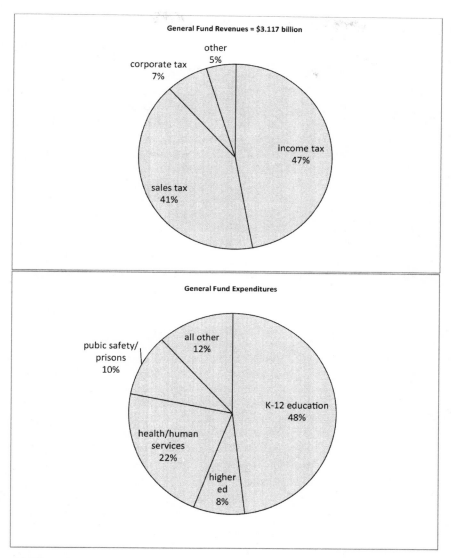

FIGURE 7.1
Idaho General Fund Revenues and Expenditures, FY2016

Federal aid—also known as fiscal federalism or federal intergovernmental transfers—is an important component of the nondiscretionary part of the total state budget. Almost all of these funds are accompanied by mandates—rules and regulations on how the money is to be spent. We will say more about fiscal federalism later in the chapter.

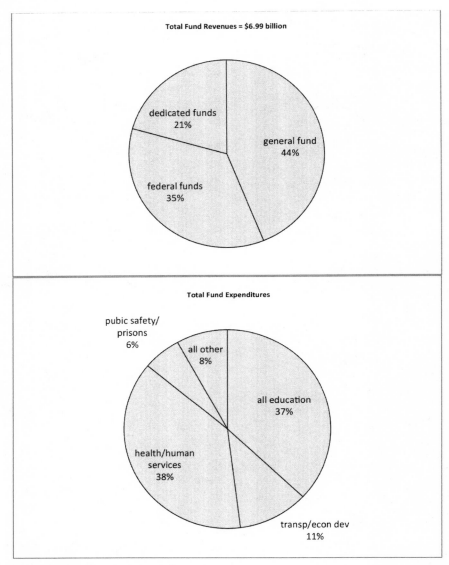

FIGURE 7.2
Idaho Total Fund Revenues and Expenditures, FY2016

Fiscal Years and Budget Cycles. For most of us, the major annual time refer-
ent is the calendar year: it begins January 1 and ends December 31. So when
someone makes reference to the year "2018," we take that to mean January
1, 2018, through December 31, 2018. But there are other "years." There is
the "academic year," which begins in August or September of one year and

ends in May or June of the following year. And then there is the "fiscal year." The fiscal year is when the budget expenditures start anew. Anyone who has served in the military or otherwise been employed by the federal government knows that the federal fiscal year begins October 1. Thus for the federal government, fiscal year (FY) 2018 begins on October 1, 2017, and ends on September 30, 2018.

Almost all states operate on fiscal years that run from July 1 to June 30. For these states, FY 2018 begins July 1, 2017, and ends on June 30, 2018. Only four states do not operate on this calendar. Alabama and Michigan use the same fiscal year as the federal government (beginning October 1), while New York begins the fiscal year on April 1 and Texas begins on September 1.[13] The overlap of fiscal years with the legislative session and the calendar year in a "typical" state is depicted in figure 7.3. Most states have legislative sessions that begin in January and run three or four months. There are, however, numerous exceptions. A few states have legislatures that operate full time—essentially for the entire year. And a few states meet only every other year or begin their session in March rather than January. But the majority of states operate in the time cycle depicted in figure 7.3.

In terms of the budget process, what this means is that the governor and the legislature are setting the fiscal year 2018 budget in the early part of calendar year 2017. Thus in January through about March of 2017, policymakers are projecting revenues for a period about sixteen to eighteen months in the future—until June 30, 2018. Because budgets are always forecasts, they are prone to error and are almost never correct. How could they be? State revenues are sensitive to economic trends and the best that policymakers can do is make an educated guess as to what the condition of the economy will be a year or a year and a half in the future. The truth is that the forecasts of future revenues are usually reasonably accurate, although the forecasts are often colored by political considerations (conservatives may use more pessimistic economic growth forecasts than liberals, for example, while opting for more optimistic forecasts about the economic impacts of tax cuts). For

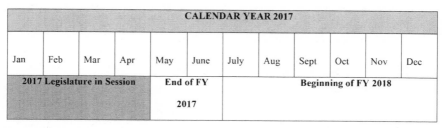

FIGURE 7.3
Calendar Year, Fiscal Year, and Legislative Session

states, the revenue forecasts are especially important because of balanced budget requirements. The important point is that spending is conditioned by revenue forecasts.

When economic conditions change rapidly, the state budget process can become chaotic. A particularly dramatic example of this is the "Great Recession" of 2007 to 2009.[14] The recession began just as most state legislatures were, in early 2008, beginning work on their FY 2009 budgets. And the data they used to make the FY 2009 forecasts were from 2006 and 2007—years of economic growth. Thus their revenue projections, and the budgets based on those projections, for FY 2009 turned out to be far too optimistic. Of course, this was not known for some months. As the National Conference of State Legislatures (NCSL) later reported, "Lawmakers were aware of the slowing economy when drafting their FY 2009 budgets, but none could have foreseen a collapse of the magnitude that has stricken state finances."[15] By the time state legislatures reconvened in early 2009 (halfway through the 2009 fiscal year), they were facing, collectively, a budget shortfall of $110 billion.[16] Some states were hit especially hard; Alabama reported a FY 2009 shortfall amounting to 12 percent, Arizona 15 percent, and California 14 percent. Other states reporting shortfalls amounting to 10 percent or more were Georgia, Nevada, New Hampshire, South Carolina, and Tennessee.[17] The FY 2010 shortfalls turned out to be even worse, approaching $200 billion. The decline in revenues in 2009 and 2010 was unusually large and largely unforeseen. Thus shortfalls were created.

The situation surrounding the Great Recession required drastic action in some instances. For several fiscal years, California had to cope with budget deficits totaling $100 billion. As one observer noted, some of the spending cuts they had to adopt were "downright breathtaking in size and scope," including eliminating some child care programs, cutting assistance for the elderly, and eliminating $1 billion in appropriations to state universities.[18]

In 2009, *USA Today* ran a story titled "Federal Aid Is Top Revenue for States."[19] In the midst of the "Great Recession," states came to rely more on money transferred from the national government than on any single revenue source of their own. It was the first time this had ever happened. It occurred again in 2010, when federal aid accounted for more than 35 percent of all state revenue.[20] In other words, while state governments rely on numerous sources of revenue for their budgets, in 2009 and 2010 they relied more on federal aid than on their own sales tax, the personal income tax, or any other single revenue source. This is unlikely to happen again anytime soon. Indeed, by 2013 federal aid had declined to 30 percent of state revenue and was no longer the largest single revenue source for most states.

The states' budget situation likely would have been even more dire if the federal government had not provided close to $800 billion in additional federal assistance as part of the American Recovery and Reinvestment Act (ARRA). These ARRA funds were intended to stimulate state economies and help shore up state education, health care, and unemployment insurance funds. These federal funds were no longer available by 2012, but were relied upon heavily by some states to help get through the difficult days of the worst economic recession in eighty years. It was also the case that many states were able to soften the budget blow in FY 2009–2011 by transferring money from their "rainy day funds"—basically state government savings accounts. But like the ARRA funds, these state savings accounts were largely depleted by the end of FY 2011. The dramatic economic downturn meant that state policymakers were faced with severely cutting back on program expenditures, raising taxes to make up the shortfall, or some combination of the two approaches.

Annual and Biennial Budgets. There is one other budget variation across the states that merits discussion. There are thirty-one states that adopt annual budgets, as the federal government does. The other nineteen states adopt biennial, or two-year, budgets. Of those states, four have state legislative sessions only every other year, but fifteen have annual legislative sessions yet they adopt two-year budgets. The arguments in favor of two-year budgets are that they give state agencies greater budget certainty and an opportunity to engage in long-range decision making. In addition, state legislatures can spend more time evaluating programs rather than budgeting. The problem, as noted earlier, is that budget forecasts over even one year are often inaccurate. Annual budgeting allows state legislatures to respond more quickly to changing economic conditions and to operate using more accurate financial data. In practice, however, it is not clear that one budget approach works better than the other.[21]

Balanced Budget Requirements. One of the key ways in which the national government and states differ is their approach to matching spending and revenue. The federal government regularly engages in "deficit spending," but the ability of states to do so is limited.[22] It was not always this way. In the early nineteenth century, states engaged in deficit spending on a regular basis. The problem was severe enough that by 1840 "some states teetered on bankruptcy from excessive debt" and at that point state constitutions were amended to place limits on state spending and debt.[23] Except for Vermont (which only has an informal norm requiring it), all states now require a balanced operating budget, although it should be noted that not all balanced budget rules are the same. The enforcement mechanism to require a balanced budget is weak in some states and stringent in others.[24] In about half the states, if policymakers cannot agree on a balanced budget, a partial shutdown of government functions is required.[25] A recent example of this occurred in Minnesota in July 2011 (the beginning of the 2012 fiscal year), when many "nonessential" services, such as state parks, road construction, and child care services, were closed for three weeks, until a balanced budget was finally passed.[26] It was the second time in five years that Minnesotans had experienced a state government shutdown. But typically, the mere threat of a shutdown is enough to bring state budget makers to some agreement on balancing the budget. Because the consequences of not reaching an agreement can be serious in many states, policymakers have a strong incentive to balance the budget.

Direct Democracy and Fiscal Policy. One of the unique features of some state electoral systems, as described in chapter 6, is the existence of the direct initiative. This is a process by which the public (or some segment thereof) can propose a law or state constitutional amendment to be decided upon by the voters in a subsequent election. Among the most prevalent types of propositions are tax limits or spending mandates, known collectively as TELs (tax and expenditure limitations). The most famous TEL is California's Proposition 13, which passed in 1978 and put a strict limit on property tax increases. That measure precipitated the tax revolt of the 1980s. Some of these propositions involve a requirement that a certain percentage of the state budget be dedicated to a specific expenditure (such as K–12 public schools). While more than half the states have one or more TELs in place, they are especially prevalent in states that permit the direct initiative. In addition to California, Colorado and Washington are two such states. States with TELs are constrained in their fiscal policies in ways not found in states without them. There is evidence that TELs and other budget rules such as strict balanced budget requirements constrain the growth in state government spending and reduce the year-to-year volatility in state expenditures.[27] But they also hamper the choices and actions available to state officials during times of economic stress.

A Note about Variation. State and subnational fiscal systems are complicated because they experience variation in three important ways. First, there is variation *between* levels of government: the revenues and expenditures at the state level look different than the revenue and expenditure patterns at the local government level. Second, there is variation *within* a particular level of government: for example, no two states generate revenue or spend money in precisely the same way. And certainly this is true at the local government level—cities, counties, school and special districts, and townships are local governments but they have different fiscal fingerprints. Finally, there is variation *over time* in the way state and local fiscal systems operate. This is largely because of changes in the supply and demand structure of public fiscal systems: where they get their money (supply) and how they must spend it (demand) change over time. With these variations in mind, we turn to an explanation of the revenue structures for state and then local governments.

State Revenues

For the most part, states must balance their budgets; expenditures cannot exceed revenues. So government spending is shaped by the revenue generated. And the revenue is generated in many ways. Most of the revenue sources are different types of taxes: personal income tax, general sales tax, tobacco tax, and so on. Lotteries generate revenue. Federal aid is yet another source. Because states need to balance their budgets, their ability to spend money is constrained by the revenue they obtain. During an economic downturn, like the Great Recession, revenues decline and, as a consequence, expenditures must be cut. The Great Recession was a particularly difficult period for state and local governments; as noted earlier, many states saw revenues drop by 10 percent or more and, as a result, substantial cutbacks occurred in state spending. Over 600,000 state and local employees were lopped off government payrolls.

While most state and local revenue sources are sensitive to economic conditions, some are more so than others. The general sales tax is affected by the economy because when the economy slows, people cut back on discretionary spending; they stop buying expensive items like hot tubs, big screen televisions, and automobiles and they reduce spending on dining out and weekend getaways. This means that government collects less sales tax money.

The revenue a state can generate through the personal income tax is even more affected by the economy. During robust economic times, unemployment is low, and more people are working, making money, and paying state income taxes. And because many states tax higher incomes at a higher rate, the income tax captures a higher percentage of economic activity in good times than in bad times. These two revenue sources are especially important contributors to the general fund budgets of most states. Local governments are also affected. A major source of revenue for cities, counties, and school districts is the property tax. In the recent Great Recession, much of the economic downturn was caused by the collapse of the housing market. As home values declined precipitously in some areas, the property tax revenue fell substantially (although with a time lag) in many cities and counties.

It is these features of state fiscal systems, along with the balanced budget requirement, that make state fiscal systems pro-cyclical. During a recession, when the economy slows, states must either raise taxes or cut programs (or both). Because these actions negatively affect spending and employment, they further slow the economy. Katharine Bradbury, an economist with the Federal Reserve Bank of Boston, sums up the macroeconomic situation succinctly: "Tax revenues, which are generated by economic activity, tend to move pro-cyclically; as a result, budget-balancing by state and local governments tends to amplify national business cycle swings."[28]

States have an array of revenue sources available to them—and to their local governments. Over time, each state has made decisions about which particular revenue sources to use and how much to rely on each of them. Each state's revenue package is a product of numerous decisions by public officials over many years. Some of these decisions involved hard-fought, well-publicized struggles over the imposition of a particular tax or the raising of a specific tax rate. Other decisions were made incrementally, as short-term adjustments to economic upturns or downturns. Consequently, each state has a unique fiscal fingerprint (see table 7.1 for a summary of the tax rates on various state and local taxes). We now turn to an examination of the revenue sources that most or all state and local governments employ.

Personal Income Tax. Only seven states (Alaska, Florida, Nevada, South Dakota, Texas, Washington, and Wyoming) do not rely at all on a personal income tax. Currently, two states (New Hampshire and Tennessee) tax personal income from interest and dividends, but not from wages, so they are taxed at a much narrower income base—and Tennessee is phasing out its tax on interest and dividends.[29] For the remaining forty-one states, the personal income tax is an important source of revenue; in many states it is the single most important source. But even among these forty-one states, there are substantial differences in how the tax is applied. A few states tax all personal income at a flat rate (for example, 3.3 percent in Indiana, 5 percent in Utah); this is known as a "proportional tax" in that everyone pays the same proportion of their income to the state. Other states have a graduated income tax structure, applying a higher tax rate at higher income levels. This system, known as a "progressive tax," means that people who make the most money are paying a higher tax rate than others. For example, New Jersey has six separate tax brackets, beginning at 1.4 percent for those making $20,000 and going up to 8.97 percent for those making over $500,000. (This means people start paying an 8.97 percent tax on each dollar they make above $500,000, not that they pay 8.97 percent on every dollar they earn if they make more than $500,000.)

General Sales Tax. Historically, the general sales tax (also known as a "consumption tax") has been an important revenue source for states and, until recently, was a revenue source that was relatively immune to the natural volatility of economic cycles. Moreover, while the sales tax is not as unpopular as some other taxes, it is increasingly a difficult tax upon which to rely. Most states that impose a general sales tax do so for physical goods (products) but not services. In this sense, a good or product is a tangible item, like a computer. A service is an activity or intangible good, such as legal representation by an attorney. Increasingly the American economy is more service-oriented than product-oriented. Consequently, over time a particular sales tax rate (say, 5 percent) captures less and less of the overall economic activity as more and more of the economic activity is service-oriented and therefore not subject to the sales tax. Furthermore, states find it difficult to monitor and recoup sales taxes on products purchased on the internet. The rapid expansion of e-commerce, therefore, represents another problem for states that rely on the general sales tax.

For the last half of the twentieth century, the sales tax was the primary revenue source for most states, generating about one-third of all state revenue.[30] But as the sales tax became less efficient at capturing revenue as the nature of the economy changed, the personal income tax surpassed the sales tax as the primary revenue source in many states. As one analyst notes, "Public finance experts generally believe that personal income tax revenue will continue to grow as a percentage of state tax revenue, while sales tax revenue will continue to decline."[31] It is, however, the case that income tax rates have been reduced recently in some Republican-controlled states. Kansas was particularly aggressive on this score, but income tax reductions also occurred in Wisconsin, Maine, Ohio, and North Carolina between 2012 and 2014.[32]

Another problem with the sales tax is that it tends to be a regressive tax, meaning the tax burden falls disproportionately on people in lower income levels. This is because poorer people must spend virtually their entire income on food, clothing, and other items that are subject to the sales tax, while people at higher incomes can save or invest some of their income and those funds are not captured by the sales tax. High income earners are also more likely to spend money on services, which are usually not subject to the sales tax.

In other words, the sales tax is actually a tax on spending rather than on income, and it is an inefficient tax on spending because it usually only captures one type of spending—goods, not services. A few states (Alaska, Delaware, Montana, New Hampshire, and Oregon) do not have a general sales tax at all. For the other states, a general sales tax between 5 percent and 6.5 percent is typical, although seven states impose a sales tax of only 4 percent while five states charge 7 percent or more.[33] In order to lessen the sting of regressivity, most states exempt purchases of prescription drugs from the sales tax, and about half the states exempt food purchases as well. It is also important to note that some states that do not have a state sales tax, such as Alaska, do allow their local governments to impose one.

Excise Taxes. Also known as "product taxes" and sometimes called "sin taxes," these excise taxes are sales taxes on specific items or goods (thus "excise" taxes are distinguishable from a "general sales" tax). The most common excise taxes are the motor fuels (gasoline) tax, the tobacco tax, and various alcohol (beer, wine, distilled spirits) taxes. In many states, these taxes are "earmarked," or dedicated, for specific expenditure funds; gasoline taxes are

TABLE 7.1
Various Tax Rates in the States

1 State	2 Personal Income Tax Rates (percent)	3 Corporate Income Tax Rates (percent)	4 State Sales Tax (percent)	5 Average Local Tax Rate	6 Gasoline Tax (cents per gallon)	7 Tobacco Tax ($ per pack of cigarettes)	8 Total State and Local Tax Rate (rank in parentheses)
AL	2.0–5.0	6.5	4	4.97	18	0.675	8.7 (39)
AK	0	0–9.4	0	1.78	8.95	2.00	6.5 (50)
AZ	2.59–4.54	5.5	5.6	2.65	19	2.00	8.8 (36)
AR	0.9–6.9	1.0–6.5	6.5	2.80	21.8	1.15	10.1 (17)
CA	1.0–12.3	8.84	7.5	0.98	35	0.87	11.0 (6)
CO	4.63	4.63	2.9	4.62	22	0.84	8.9 (35)
CT	3.0–6.99	7.5	6.35	0	25	3.65	12.6 (2)
DE	0–6.6	8.7	0	0	23	1.60	10.2 (16)
FL	0	5.5	6.0	0.66	28.4	1.34	8.9 (34)
GA	1.0–6.0	6.0	4.0	3.01	26	0.37	9.1 (32)
HI	1.4–8.25	4.4–6.4	4.0	0.35	17	3.20	10.2 (14)
ID	1.6–7.4	7.4	6.0	0.03	33	0.57	9.3 (26)
IL	3.75	7.75	6.25	2.39	20.1	1.98	11.0 (5)
IN	3.3	6.5	7.0	0	18	0.995	9.5 (22)
IA	0.36–8.98	6.0–12.0	6.0	0.79	31.8	1.36	9.2 (31)
KS	2.7–4.6	4.0	6.5	2.10	25	1.29	9.5 (23)
KY	2.0–6.0	4.0–6.0	6.0	0	26	0.60	9.5 (24)
LA	2.0–6.0	4.0–8.0	4.0	5.0	20.125	0.86	7.6 (45)
ME	5.8–7.15	3.5–8.93	5.5	0	30	2.00	10.2 (13)
MD	2.0–5.75	8.25	6.0	0	32.6	2.00	10.9 (7)
MA	5.1	8.0	6.25	0	24	3.51	10.3 (12)
MI	4.25	6.0	6.0	0	19	2.00	9.4 (25)
MN	5.35–9.85	9.8	6.875	0.39	28.6	3.00	10.8 (8)
MS	3.0–5.0	3.0–5.0	7.0	0.07	18.4	0.68	8.6 (41)
MO	1.5–6.0	6.25	4.225	3.64	17.3	0.17	9.3 (29)
MT	1.0–6.9	6.75	0	0	27	1.70	8.7 (38)

	[2]	[3]	[4]	[5]	[6]	[7]	[8]
NE	2.46–6.84	5.58–7.81	5.5	1.37	27.7	0.64	9.2 (30)
NV	0	0	6.85	1.13	23.805	1.80	8.1 (43)
NH	0*	8.5	0	0	23.825	1.78	7.9 (44)
NJ	1.4–8.97	9.0	7.0	0	14.5	2.70	12.2 (3)
NM	1.7–4.9	4.8–6.6	5.125	2.38	18.875	1.66	8.7 (37)
NY	4.0–8.82	6.5	4.0	4.49	25	4.35	12.7 (1)
NC	5.75	4.0	4.75	2.15	35.25	0.45	9.8 (20)
ND	1.10–2.90	1.4–4.3	5.0	1.82	23	0.44	9.0 (33)
OH	0.495–4.99	0	5.75	1.39	28	1.60	9.8 (19)
OK	0.5–5.0	6.0	4.5	4.32	17	1.03	8.6 (40)
OR	5.0–9.9	6.6–7.6	0	0	30	1.32	10.3 (10)
PA	3.07	9.99	6.0	0.34	50.3	1.60	10.2 (15)
RI	3.75–5.99	7.0	7.0	0	34	3.75	10.8 (9)
SC	0–7.0	5.0	6.0	1.22	16.75	0.57	8.4 (42)
SD	0	0	4.0	1.84	30	1.53	7.1 (49)
TN	0*	6.5	7.0	2.46	21.4	0.62	7.3 (47)
TX	0	0	6.25	1.92	20	1.41	7.6 (46)
UT	5.0	5.0	5.95	0.74	29.4	1.70	9.6 (21)
VT	3.55–8.95	6.0–8.5	6.0	0.17	30.46	3.08	10.3 (11)
VA	2.0–5.75	6.0	5.3	0.33	16.2	0.30	9.3 (27)
WA	0	0	6.5	2.39	44.5	3.025	9.3 (28)
WV	3.0–6.5	6.5	6.0	0.20	33.2	0.55	9.8 (18)
WI	4.0–7.65	7.9	5.0	0.41	32.9	2.52	11.0 (4)
WY	0	0	4.0	1.42	24	0.60	7.1 (48)
						average	9.9%

*New Hampshire and Tennessee tax income on dividends and interest only.
Sources for data in each column:
2. "State Individual Income Taxes" as of January 1, 2016, Federation of Tax Administrators, February 2016.
3. "Range of State Corporate Income Tax Rates" as of January 2016, Federation of Tax Administrators, February 2016.
4. "State Sales Tax Rates" as of January 2016, Federation of Tax Administrators, January 2016.
5. ""State and Local Tax Rates," Tax Foundation, 2016.
6. "State Motor Fuel Tax Rates" as of January 2016, Federation of Tax Administrators, January 2016.
7. "State Excise Tax Rates on Cigarettes" as of January 2016, Federation of Tax Administrators, January 2016.
8. "State-Local Tax Burdens, All States, 2012," Tax Foundation, 2016.

usually set aside for the highway or transportation department. Therefore the contribution of these revenues to the state general fund may be limited. Moreover, the tax rate is highly variable by state. For example, in 2016 the gasoline tax was 8.95 cents per gallon in Alaska but 50.3 cents per gallon in Pennsylvania. The state-by-state disparity in the tobacco excise tax rate is even greater: 17 cents per pack of cigarettes in Missouri to $4.35 per pack in New York.[34]

A recent development is the imposition of an excise tax on the sale of recreational marijuana in those states that have legalized marijuana for personal use. Colorado is a case in point. The state imposes a 15 percent excise tax at the point of first sale (from wholesaler to retailer). Then there is a 10 percent sales tax when the product is sold by the retailer to the consumer. This sales tax surcharge is in addition to the standard 2.9 percent general sales tax. Overall, then, there is a 25 percent tax on the sale of recreational marijuana, in addition to the regular sales tax. In 2015, Colorado generated about $70 million in this manner.[35] One might be tempted to say that the tax has become a blunt instrument in addressing the Colorado budget, generating more money in 2015 than the long-established tax on liquor. Meanwhile, the State of Washington, where the sale of marijuana for personal use is also legal, expected to generate more than $150 million from a 37 percent sales tax surcharge in 2016.[36]

Corporate Income Tax. There are forty-four states that impose income taxes on corporations that do business in the state. Another four states—Nevada, Ohio, Texas, and Washington—impose a gross receipts tax on businesses. Both a gross receipts tax and a corporate income tax are applied in Delaware and Virginia. Only South Dakota and Wyoming fail to impose either a corporate income tax or a gross receipts tax.

In the case of the corporate income tax, more states use a flat rate rather than a graduated (progressive) structure. A typical flat rate is around 6 percent, but it is as low as 4 percent (North Carolina) and as high as 9.99 percent (Pennsylvania). A minority of states have graduated corporate income taxes. Kansas, for example, has a 4 percent rate up to $49,999 and then 7 percent above that figure. Iowa actually imposes the highest rate, 12 percent on income above $250,000. In recent years, many states have reduced their corporate income tax rates as a tactic to attract new enterprises or retain existing business.[37] Consequently, corporate income taxes have declined as a percent of total state revenue for most states.[38]

Severance Tax. This is a tax on the extraction or depletion of a nonrenewable natural resource, usually a resource associated with energy production. A few states—Alaska and Texas are the obvious examples—have substantial underground reserves of oil or natural gas. Coal is another such resource. States that have such resources tax the "producer"—the coal or oil company—for extracting the resource from the state. The producer, of course, will eventually pass this tax on to the consumer as part of the total cost of the good. For a few states, this is an important part of their revenue stream. But it is usually dependent on the amount of the commodity being extracted. In 2012 in West Virginia, over $400 million (representing about 11 percent of the state budget) was derived from severance taxes on coal and natural gas.[39] But by 2016, coal and gas revenues were down by 26 percent, in part because of a lower demand for coal, creating a substantial gap in West Virginia's budget and leading to "budget crisis" headlines similar to those at the beginning of this chapter.[40]

The West Virginia situation reveals a particular problem for states that rely heavily on resource-based severance taxes: state revenues are closely tied to resource markets that are outside the state's control. For example, the severance tax on oil and natural gas generates the majority of budget revenue in Alaska, so much so that Alaska does not have a general sales tax or a personal income tax. But the plunge in oil prices and the drop in oil production in the state created a $4 billion hole in the state's 2017 fiscal year budget, leaving the governor lamenting, "We've lost 80 percent of our income in about a year and a half."[41] Or take the case of North Dakota: between 2005 and 2014, almost half of the North Dakota general fund budget came from the severance tax on its newly developed "western oil patch." As noted before, this recent "oil boom" meant that North Dakota was the only state that consistently had a budget surplus during the otherwise lean recession years. But when U.S. crude oil prices dropped from a high of $104 a barrel in 2014 to a mere $27 a barrel in January 2016, budgetary havoc ensued.[42]

Only about six or seven states, however, can count on as much as 10 percent of their budget from severance taxes even when resource markets are good. For the vast majority of states, the severance tax generates very little revenue.

Charges and Miscellaneous Revenue. User fees, license fees, and fines are often lumped together under this category. These sources tend to be regressive because they are usually a flat amount ($50 for vehicle registration, for example) rather than a percentage of income. But there are exceptions: some states charge a higher license or registration fee for luxury cars, for example. Moreover, the states vary a lot in what they charge. In Nebraska, vehicle registration and title fees amount to $25 while in Montana it can cost up to $229 to register the same vehicle—almost ten times as much.[43] The same is true of fines; failure to wear a seatbelt can cost the driver $127.50 in Iowa but only $10 in neighboring Wisconsin.[44] User fees include highway or bridge tolls, camping fees at state parks, tuition at state colleges and universities, and a host of other charges. Following the 2008–2009 recession many states increased user fees to help close their budget gaps.[45]

Lotteries, Gambling, and Other Revenue Sources. State-authorized lotteries were common in the nineteenth century but became increasingly contaminated by fraud and corruption. Interstate lotteries were outlawed by Congress and most states banned lotteries within their borders. By 1900 there were no state lotteries. This remained the case until 1964, when New Hampshire authorized a state lottery. Once New Hampshire opened the door, other states followed—New York in 1966 and New Jersey in 1970. By 1975, fifteen states had reintroduced lotteries. The modern-day adoption of state lotteries basically followed a regional pattern; once one state in a region introduced a lottery the neighboring states created their own lotteries within a few years. In 2014, Wyoming became the forty-fourth state to establish a lottery.[46] Lotteries do not generate nearly as much revenue for the states as sales and income taxes, but almost all states have adopted them, in part to capture these gambling dollars for the state. If a state does not sponsor its own lottery, its citizens who are attracted to this type of gaming may simply take their dollars across the border to a neighboring state with a lottery. A vivid example of this phenomenon occurs in the intermountain region of the United States. Prior to 2014, neither Wyoming nor Utah had a lottery, but Idaho did. The stores with the highest volume of lottery sales in Idaho are in the sparsely populated southeast corner of the state—close to the Utah and Wyoming borders. One recent analysis found that Utahans bought almost 20 percent of traditional lottery tickets purchased in Idaho.[47]

Among the states that do maintain a lottery, there is a lot of variation in the way the lotteries are administered. Typically about 62 percent of the ticket sales are returned as prize money, about 5 percent goes to administering and advertising the lottery games, and 33 percent is retained as revenue for the state. Overall, the states netted a total of about $18 billion on sales of $53 billion.[48] But there are big differences in the payout margin by state. Massachusetts (76 percent) and Minnesota (73 percent) return the highest percentages of total sales as prizes, while Louisiana, North Dakota, and Oklahoma return less than 55 percent. In other words, if you are inclined to play a state lottery, it is a better deal to play in East Grand Forks, Minnesota, than across the river in Grand Forks, North Dakota. Of course, by paying out more, Massachusetts and Minnesota retain a relatively low percentage of the revenue from lottery sales for the state coffers (around 20 percent), while Oklahoma keeps over 40 percent.

The absence of a state lottery should not be taken as a signal that a state is opposed to gambling. One of the six states that do not allow a state lottery is Nevada, where a lottery is prohibited by the state constitution. Another state without a lottery is Mississippi, which, like Nevada, offers plenty of other opportunities to gamble.

A related source of state revenue that has gained in popularity in recent years is casino gambling, which generates money for states from licenses and taxes on the profits. For many years, gambling was illegal in every state except Nevada (which legalized it in 1931). In 1976, New Jersey legalized gambling in Atlantic City as part of an effort to revive the downtrodden resort community. In 1989, Iowa responded to budgetary problems by permitting gambling on riverboats plying the rivers along the state's borders. Riverboat gambling quickly became adopted by several other states along the Mississippi as they too searched for new revenue streams. By 2015, twenty-three states had legalized commercial casino gambling, generating about $8 billion in tax revenue.[49] In addition, twenty-eight states have agreements allowing American Indians to operate casinos on tribal lands, generating another $2.4 billion in tax revenue.[50] Only Hawaii and Utah do not allow any form of wagering, thereby forswearing that potential source of state revenue.

The states have miscellaneous other revenue sources, among them state-run enterprises such as state liquor stores (in thirteen states) and insurance trust funds.[51] North Dakota is the only state that owns its own state bank; it has proven lucrative.[52] For the most part, these are not major revenue generators and the funds they produce are usually earmarked for specific expenditure accounts (and therefore are not part of the discretionary general fund account).

Federal Aid. For generations now, federal grants-in-aid to states and, to a lesser extent, to local governments have been an important part of the total subnational revenue package. The first significant transfer of funds from the national to subnational governments began during the Great Depression of the 1930s.[53] As table 7.2 shows, the proportion of federal aid to state and local

TABLE 7.2
Federal Grants-in-Aid
as a Percentage of State
and Local Expenditures

Year	Percent
1960	14.3
1970	19.6
1980	27.3
1990	18.7
2000	21.8
2010	26.4
2015	25.1

governments has increased over time, but not in a monotonic manner. In 1960, 14.3 percent of the funds spent by state and local governments came from the national government as federal aid. This figure steadily increased during the 1960s and 1970s, first under Lyndon Johnson's "Great Society" and then Richard Nixon's "New Federalism." By the time Ronald Reagan became president, state and local governments relied on federal aid for over 27 percent of their expenditures. In other words, state/local dependence on federal aid basically doubled between 1960 and 1980. Under the Reagan administration, there was an effort to roll back the magnitude of the reliance on fiscal federal dollars—in part because of the president's desire to reverse the growing state dependence on the federal government and in part because of growing concerns over the size of the federal deficit. This effort was largely successful and by 1990 the state/local reliance on federal aid had declined.

But by 2000 the figure crept back up a bit, largely due to an ever-expanding Medicaid program. The Great Recession and the active role of the Obama administration in providing additional assistance to states and local entities is reflected in the 2010 figure, 26.4 percent. By 2015, that figure had receded slightly.

Changes in the State Revenue Structure

State fiscal systems are not static. They change over time as they adapt, albeit often somewhat slowly, to changing economic circumstances. For example, look at table 7.3, which shows the adoption of income, sales and

TABLE 7.3
The Number of States Adopting Revenue Sources in Each Decade

Decade	Income Tax	General Sales Tax	Gasoline Tax	Lottery
1900–1909	1			
1910–1919	9		4	
1920–1929	5		44	
1930–1939	17	23	1	
1940–1949	1	5	1	
1950–1959		5		
1960–1969	7	11		2
1970–1979	4			11
1980–1989				18
1990–1999				6
2000–2009				6

Source: Calculations by authors.

gasoline taxes, and lotteries by the states over time. Almost all states adopted the gasoline tax between 1910 and 1929, as the automobile became more and more prevalent and the demand for paved roads became stronger. The personal income tax became a primary revenue source in the early decades of the twentieth century; thirty-two states adopted the income tax between 1900 and 1939. Adoption of the general sales tax occurred slightly later; forty-four states adopted the sales tax between 1930 and 1969. Finally, lotteries became a common revenue source in the later part of the twentieth century as thirty-seven states established state-authorized lotteries between 1960 and 1999.[54]

One of the reasons that states seek new or altered revenue sources is because the revenue generation ability of some older sources declines over time. A case in point is the general sales tax. As noted earlier, most states tax sales on goods (products) but not on services. This was fine when most of the economic activity in the United States was goods-oriented. But over the last half-century, the economy has increasingly shifted toward the service sector. This means that less and less of the overall economic activity is captured by the goods-oriented sales tax. This is one of the reasons that so many states have increased the sales tax rate over time—to make up for the revenue "lost" to the service sector. A related problem is the development and expansion of e-commerce. Increasingly, when goods are purchased they are bought online, and states find it difficult to capture sales tax revenue from such purchases. It is estimated that by 2012 states were losing a combined $23.3 billion in sales tax revenue due to e-commerce sales. By this estimate, a typical state lost over $466 million in sales tax receipts.[55] Because a few states do not rely on a general sales tax, they obviously are not particularly affected by the shift to online purchases. But some states are affected greatly. It is estimated that California lost over $4 billion in 2012.[56] By 2016, a number of states were taking aggressive actions to force internet companies to collect state sales taxes, even in states where those companies do not maintain a physical presence.[57]

As a result of all of these changes, the relative impact of the general sales tax as a revenue source has declined over the past quarter-century. In 1977, this tax accounted for 31 percent of all state general revenue. By 2013, it accounted for 23 percent.[58] During that same period, corporate income taxes declined from about 5.5 percent to 2 percent. Meanwhile, reliance on charges and miscellaneous revenues increased from about 12 percent to 19 percent. Clearly, the relative contribution of various revenue streams changes over time. As we shall see later, the same can be said on the expenditure side—over time, spending changes. Both the supply and demand sides of state fiscal systems are in constant flux.

Local Revenues

Across the United States, the amount of revenue generated by the states is about equal to the amount of revenue generated by local governments. But all of these funds—whether at the local or state level—are authorized by the states. States determine what taxes and other revenue sources their local governments can use, the types of expenditures for which their local governments are responsible, and the relative mix of state revenues to local revenues and expenditures. Different states handle this in very different ways. In some states, the bulk of the revenue and expenditures are processed at the state level. In Arkansas, 75 percent of the revenue is generated at the state level and only 25 percent at the local level. In Vermont, almost 85 percent of the funds are state revenues. In contrast, in Florida less than half of the revenue is generated at the state level. In other words, the relative fiscal magnitude of state governments to their local governments varies quite a bit from one state to another.[59]

The ability of local governments to generate their own funds depends on what revenue tools the state allows them. Moreover, different types of local governments within a state may have different revenue sources. Counties may be allowed to impose a local sales tax but cities may not. School districts may be allowed to tax property at a higher rate than special districts. Consequently, where the figures reported are averaged for all types of local governments in all states, remember that there is in fact quite a bit of variation from state to state and type of local government.

Generally, the biggest revenue streams for local governments are the property tax, miscellaneous revenue (charges, user fees, licenses, fines), and intergovernmental transfers (direct state aid, direct federal aid, and some federal aid passed from states to local governments). Overall, these revenue streams account for 90 percent of local funds nationwide, but there are large differences in these figures from state to state. For example, two-thirds of the total local revenues in Vermont are from intergovernmental transfers, while only 10 percent in Hawaii are from these state and federal aid accounts.[60] Moreover, there are big differences by type of local government. In most states, about half of all the revenue received by public school districts is state aid—money appropriated by the state legislature and sent to local school districts. But much less state aid is sent to special districts and even less to cities or counties.

Local governments that are heavily dependent on state aid are, of course, susceptible to budget shortfalls when state revenue does not meet expectations. Again, the effects of the recent recession provide examples. In FY 2009, seventeen states reduced their aid to local governments, and in 2010 twenty states did so. Many states continued this practice when their own budgets struggled to recover; sixteen states reduced aid to local governments in FY 2011, and seventeen did so in FY 2012. By 2014, as most states economies and budgets had recovered sufficiently, only two states reduced aid to local governments.[61] Because of the wide array of state and local fiscal practices, the next discussion is based on general arrangements and trends.

Property Taxes. For most local governments in most states, the property tax is by far the largest own-source revenue generator. All types of local governments—school districts, special districts, townships, counties, and cities—make use of the property tax. The degree to which they use the property tax is determined by the state. This usually means that the state sets a maximum percentage that a particular type of local government can impose.

The actual amount of property tax paid is determined by two things: the property tax rate and the assessed value of the property. Using data on the median property tax paid on owner-occupied homes and the median home value, the Tax Foundation estimates that the typical property tax ranges from lows of 0.28 (Hawaii) and 0.43 (Alabama) to a high of 2.32 (Illinois) and 2.38 (New Jersey). By this particular metric, property owners in some states are paying rates eight or nine times greater than property owners in some other states.[62]

Local governments were hit hard in the Great Recession period because of their reliance on the property tax. One of the primary causes of the recent economic recession was the collapse of the housing market, which caused property values to decline precipitously in many areas. Home prices dropped nationwide by about 20 percent, and in states like Nevada and Arizona the drop was far more substantial. With the decline in property values, there was a significant drop in the revenue produced by the property tax. By 2010, property tax collections had suffered the largest decline in thirty years.[63]

Charges and Miscellaneous Revenues. Just as states make use of fees, charges. and fines, they permit their local governments to do so as well. In the case of some types of local governments—cities and special districts in particular—this is often a major source of revenue. In Pennsylvania, for instance, such charges account for about 45 percent of all the revenue generated by cities.[64] Many special districts (also known as special purpose districts) rely primarily on such fees and charges. Common examples include airport districts and public utility districts like water and sewer districts.[65] During the Great Recession, many subnational governments increased various user fees to help fill some of the budget holes created by declining revenues.[66]

Local Option Taxes. While these are called "local option" taxes, let us not lose sight of the fact that they are initially state-allowed. In other words, some states permit their local governments (if the local government so chooses) to impose such taxes, but other states do not allow them. Nationwide, these local option taxes represent a much smaller proportion of total local revenues. But in some states, they may account for a large proportion of local revenue—especially for cities or counties. According to the National Conference of State Legislatures, thirty-eight states allow for local option sales taxes.[67] A much smaller number of states permit local option income or payroll taxes. Where such taxes are permissible, they are usually collected at the county level, although in some states they may be imposed by municipalities (cities). Where these taxes are permitted, they may become a significant source of revenue. Compare, for example, columns 4 and 5 in table 7.1. Column 4 reports state sales tax rates, while column 5 shows the average rate for local option sales tax, where allowed. In Alabama, the sales tax jumps from 4 percent (state) to almost 9 percent when we include the local option sales tax. Similar increases occur in Colorado, Georgia, Louisiana, Missouri, New York, and Oklahoma—suggesting a heavy reliance on local option taxes in these states.

The Regressive Character of State and Local Tax Systems

As mentioned earlier, the way a state structures its overall tax system—and that of its local governments—defines several fiscal consequences. How the tax burden is spread among the citizens of the state is one of these. As any introductory textbook on macroeconomics will point out, tax structures may be progressive, proportional, or regressive. A progressive tax is one that takes a larger percentage as income rises, a proportional tax takes the same percentage from all income levels, and one that is regressive taxes people with lower incomes at a higher rate than wealthier people. The focus here is on rate, or percentage, not on the total amount the tax generates. Even a regressive tax will often mean a wealthier person is paying a greater amount than a poor person, even if the wealthy person is paying a lower percentage. For example, if Person A makes $100,000 and pays 5 percent toward taxes and Person B makes only $10,000 but pays 15 percent toward taxes, A pays $5,000 while B pays $1,500. Person A paid more in actual dollars ($5,000 to $1,500) but considerably less as a percentage of his or her income (5 percent compared to 15 percent for B). Nonetheless, the discussion about the regressive, proportional, or progressive nature of the tax structure is a common one because it is ultimately a discussion about what "share" of one's income goes to taxes and what amounts to a "fair share" across various income levels. To illustrate how the tax structures of states can affect the citizens, consider figure 7.4. Oregon and Washington are neighboring states that many people consider to be identical in policies and political cultures. But their tax structures are dia-

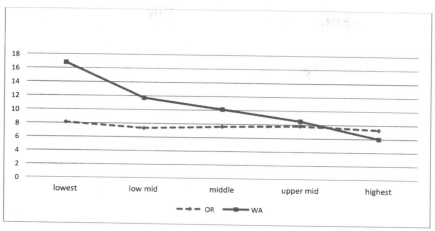

FIGURE 7.4
Comparing Tax Burdens of Income Groups in Oregon and Washington

metrically opposed and as a consequence they place different tax burdens on different economic groups within their state. Oregon has a personal income tax but no general sales tax, creating a system that is basically proportional, ranging between 7 and 8 percent for all income groups. The trend line looks very different for the State of Washington, which has no personal income tax but does have a general sales tax. There lower income groups pay a much higher percentage (16.8 percent) of their income to state and local taxes while the wealthiest quintile only pays about 6 percent. Washington's is a dramatically regressive tax structure.

The fact of the matter is that almost all state and local tax structures are regressive. The reason is that most excise taxes, licenses and user fees, and sales taxes are regressive. For example, a $100 per year automobile registration fee is a larger percent of the income of someone making $5,000 a year than it is of someone making $50,000 a year. In this case, the tax is a flat fee of $100, regardless of income. A sales tax is also regressive because it is based on the purchase of goods (consumption) rather than income. Most state and local governments rely heavily on fees, sales, and excise taxes. For the most part, the only tax that can be designed as truly proportional or even progressive is the individual income tax. Thus the degree of regressivity of a state and local tax structure is largely a matter of how much that state relies on a progressive individual income tax structure instead of a general sales tax or user fees. Table 7.4 shows the regressive nature of most state and local tax structures. The states with the most regressive tax structures are Washington, Florida, South Dakota, and Texas—all states without a personal income tax, and

TABLE 7.4
State Tax Burdens for Different Income Groups

State	Tax Burden for LOWEST Quintile (lowest 20% in state)	Tax Burden for MIDDLE Quintile (middle 20% in state)	Tax Burden for HIGHEST Quintile (highest 20% in state)	Regressivity Ranking (1=most regressive)
AL	10.2	9.5	6.1	12
AK	7.0	4.5	3.0	36
AZ	12.5	9.2	6.5	8
AR	11.9	11.4	8.3	11
CA	10.5	8.2	7.7	49
CO	8.2	8.1	6.2	32
CT	10.5	10.7	8.7	26
DE	5.5	5.3	5.2	50
FL	12.9	8.5	5.0	2
GA	10.4	9.4	7.6	22
HI	13.4	11.4	8.0	15
ID	8.5	7.6	7.3	43
IL	13.2	10.8	8.2	5
IN	12.0	10.8	7.8	10
IA	10.4	9.7	8.0	27
KS	11.1	9.5	7.2	9
KY	9.0	10.8	8.4	33
LA	10.0	9.5	7.1	19
ME	9.4	9.4	8.5	44
MD	9.7	10.3	8.4	38
MA	10.4	9.3	7.4	24
MI	9.2	9.2	7.4	29
MN	8.8	9.6	8.4	45
MS	10.4	10.6	7.1	21
MO	9.5	9.0	7.3	30
MT	6.1	6.4	5.6	47
NE	10.9	10.3	7.9	28
NV	8.4	6.6	4.3	13
NH	8.3	6.6	4.8	25
NJ	10.7	9.1	8.2	39
NM	10.9	9.9	7.5	17
NY	10.4	12.0	10.7	41
NC	9.2	9.2	7.4	31
ND	9.3	7.5	5.0	20
OH	11.7	10.3	8.3	18
OK	10.5	9.4	7.0	16
OR	8.1	7.6	7.2	48
PA	12.0	10.3	7.7	6
RI	12.5	10.5	8.4	23
SC	7.5	7.6	6.8	40
SD	11.3	7.7	5.0	4
TN	10.9	8.6	5.3	7
TX	12.5	8.7	5.7	3
UT	8.6	8.5	6.9	34
VT	8.9	10.5	8.0	46
VA	8.9	8.4	6.9	35
WA	16.8	10.1	6.0	1
WV	8.7	9.0	7.8	42
WI	8.9	10.2	8.8	37
WY	8.2	5.9	3.1	14
Mean	10.9	9.4	7.2	

Source: Institute on Taxation and Economic Policy, "Who Pays? A 50-State Report," 2015, http://www.itep .org/whopays/full_report.php. Figures represent state and local tax rates. Regressivity rank calculated by ITEP using data that include federal tax offset by state.

therefore states that rely more heavily on sales and excise taxes and user fees, all of which are regressive.[68] New York has a slightly progressive tax structure (at least when comparing the poorest and wealthiest quintiles). Several states have state and local tax structures that approach proportionality: Oregon, Delaware, Montana, and Minnesota are examples.

Fiscal Federalism: Federal Aid to States (and Localities)

Fiscal federalism is a touchy subject for the states. On the one hand, state officials (especially state elected officials) assert the independence and sovereignty and innovation capacity of their state. On the other hand, the same officials are willing to accept federal financial assistance during tough times. As mentioned earlier in this chapter, the American Recovery and Reinvestment Act (ARRA) of 2009 provided a generous infusion of federal funds to help the states weather the worst of the recession. These federal "stimulus" funds totaled about $500 billion to the states for FYs 2009, 2010, and 2011 combined.[69] Those funds were used by the states in many ways, but principal among them was to help the states pay their share of Medicaid costs and to extend unemployment benefits for longer periods than usual.[70] ARRA funds also helped many states avoid cuts (or avoid deeper cuts) in K–12 and higher education funding and to continue or start a number of infrastructure construction projects (for example, road building and other "shovel-ready" infrastructure projects). Without this additional assistance from the federal government, there is little doubt that state and local governments would have suffered even greater program cuts than they did. Of course, there was the requisite partisan posturing first. Several governors, among them Republicans Bobby Jindal of Louisiana and Mark Sanford of South Carolina, announced that their states would not accept some of the "bailout" funds. Ultimately, however, the legislatures in both states passed bills that accepted virtually all the money available to them.[71] It is hard for a state to walk away from federal money, particularly during times of great fiscal stress.[72]

Unlike the ARRA, most federal aid is ongoing, composed of annual transfers of money from the federal government to state or local governments with very specific conditions and guidelines ("strings attached") for the use of those funds. Federal grants, therefore, are not part of the state "general fund" budget but rather are part of the nondiscretionary part of the budget over which states have little control. Moreover, most federal grant-in-aid programs require that states share in the cost by using some state funds to pay for part of the program, as with the Medicaid and TANF programs discussed in chapter 5. This is known as the "match" or "cost-share" that a state must contribute. As Marilyn Rubin and Katherine Willoughby observe, "Federal funds often come with matching requirements that states must contribute a certain percentage of total funding for specified programs and particular services. Given that states must balance their budgets, if they decide to accept the federal money, they must make trade-offs between spending money for federally funded programs and other state spending priorities."[73]

Some of the programs mandated by the federal government (perhaps especially environmental and health care programs) might go unfunded in some states without the federal mandate. Overall, of the money state and local governments spend, over the last several generations a larger proportion of it has come from the federal government. And if the money comes from the federal government, it almost always comes with conditions. Accordingly, there is a reduction in state control over policy (the federal "strings" require states or local governments to do certain things).

As a result of growing concerns over the federal debt, it is likely that some types of federal aid to the states will diminish. If reductions do come to pass, they will pose additional challenges for the states and their local governments, as the programs currently funded in part by federal grants will have to be pared back, eliminated altogether, or funded by an increase in state revenues, likely necessitating an increase in state taxes. None of these are politically attractive alternatives; nonetheless, this is the reality facing state (and local) officials.

Looking back to table 7.2, we find that it shows the proportion of state revenues received through federal aid has increased, decreased, and then increased again over recent decades. But what table 7.2 does not show is how the nature of that aid has changed. At one time, the largest federal aid program was physical infrastructure needs—especially the construction of the interstate highway system. Over time, the federal aid emphasis has shifted away from infrastructure to social programs, especially health care in the form of Medicaid (see figure 7.5).

In 1960, there was no Medicaid (health care, largely for lower-income groups) program at all. Highway grants were the largest federal aid program (accounting for 43 percent of federal aid), followed by income security ("welfare," primarily Aid to Families with Dependent Children at 38 percent) and education and unemployment (8 percent). Those three functional areas accounted for almost nine out of every ten dollars of federal aid.

By 1980, federal aid was flowing to the four functional areas of health care, welfare, education/unemployment, and transportation in a roughly equal manner, and federal aid was increasing modestly for all four functional areas. As figure 7.5 shows, this trend changed dramatically by 1990. Medicaid, which had been created in 1965, had become the driving force behind the

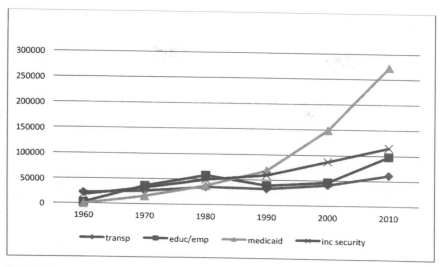

FIGURE 7.5
Federal Aid by Functional Area. Dollar figures are in constant dollars.

increase in federal aid, and by 2010 it accounted for almost half of all fiscal federalism.

To look at this point from another angle, consider that most grant money goes to one of two purposes: costs to provide for individuals and costs to build or maintain physical infrastructure. In 1960, only 35 percent of all federal aid went to payments for individuals (health care, welfare, unemployment, etc.). About half of all federal aid was for "physical capital" (that is, infrastructure).[74] By 2011, payments to individuals accounted for 64 percent and infrastructure costs accounted for only 16 percent. In other words, between 1960 and 2011 "human costs" went from about one-third to about two-thirds of all federal aid dollars. And in 2015, federal aid to individuals was 74.2 percent of all federal aid. In a half-century the broader purpose behind federal assistance to the states and their local governments had shifted from infrastructure to social services. What this suggests is that any reduction in federal aid we are likely to encounter will have a human face attached to it—meaning that the decisions about what the state should do about these programs will directly affect some citizens of the state.

While federal aid is important in all states, it is far more important in some states than in others. Figure 7.6 demonstrates this. Whereas most of our discussion of fiscal federalism reports federal aid as a percent of state *and* local revenues, figure 7.6 shows federal aid as a percent of state revenues only. The

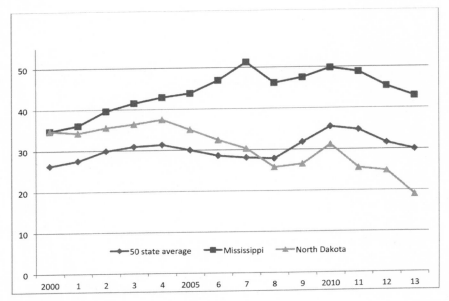

FIGURE 7.6
Federal Aid as a Percent of State Revenues

average for all states is about 30 percent (down from 35 percent three or four years ago). But note that the percentage of total state revenue from federal aid in North Dakota was only 19 percent—down significantly from earlier years (about 35 percent in 2000). In the case of North Dakota, the reduction was largely a function of the growth in the state's own-source revenues from the rapid expansion of oil revenues in the 2000 to 2014 time period. Now that the state's economic situation has changed, we might anticipate that federal aid will creep up as a percentage of North Dakota revenue.

In contrast, note the case of Mississippi. About 43 percent of all state revenue in Mississippi is currently in the form of federal aid. It is the highest percentage of any state and indicates Mississippi's dependence on the federal government. The figure is actually down a bit; in 2008, over half of all general state revenue in Mississippi was in the form of federal aid.

State (and Local) Expenditures

The first point we want to emphasize is that the services and regulatory actions performed at the local level—by cities, counties, etc.—are ultimately the responsibility of the state government. States delegate some of their governmental responsibilities to local governments because it makes sense to do so. But exactly which responsibilities they delegate and to which local governments and to what extent they are delegated are questions that are answered differently by each state. It is, in other words, a complex situation. We will try to simplify it by using the term "subnational" to refer to actions of both the state and local governments, when appropriate. Public education, for example, is largely a subnational responsibility—one shared and funded for the most part by both state and local governments. While K–12 education is delivered at the local government level, state constitutions generally hold the state government responsible for providing primary and secondary education.

As noted in chapter 5, historically the largest state and local expenditure is public education. In 1978, almost 40 percent of all subnational expenditures were for education. This includes public schools (K–12), community and vocational-technical colleges, and state universities. Expenditures in other functional areas in 1978 were pretty evenly distributed between health (12 percent), welfare and social services (10 percent), public safety (10 percent), and transportation and economic development (11 percent). A generation later, in 2014, the expenditure pattern had shifted (see table 7.5). State and local expenditures on health care increased substantially, accounting for over 20 percent of all spending for subnational governments. The only other area in which state and local governments now spend a greater share of their funds than in 1978 is public safety. This reflects an increase in spending on corrections (prisons). Relatively speaking, the biggest loser in the past thirty years is public education; its share of spending has dropped from 40 percent to 33 percent.

Still, public education remains the single largest subnational expenditure and by a substantial margin. And just to be clear, the actual total dollars spent on education have not declined; in fact, they have increased. But the relative

TABLE 7.5
Combined State and Local Expenditures,
1978 and 2014 (as a percent of total expenditures)

Functional Area	1978	2014	Increase/Decrease
Public Education	40	33	−7
Health	12	23	+11
Social Services	10	6	−4
Public Safety	10	13	+3
Transportation/Economic Development	11	8	−3

Source: General Accountability Office Report. GAO-10-899 (July 2010) and 2014 update at www.gao.gov/ fiscal_outlook/state_local_fiscal_model/interactive_graphic/about_state_local_fiscal_conditions.

position of public education compared to other functional areas—especially health care—has eroded. Most of this decline is in state support for higher education, not for K–12 schools. While public colleges and universities have seen their relative slice of the state budget pie diminish slowly for several decades, the cuts were substantial in some states during the Great Recession. Over one three-year period, the University of Washington saw its state support drop from $400 million to $200 million.[75] The University of North Carolina suffered a drop of $230 million.[76]

Expanding health care costs are a major concern, especially for state-level officials. The reason is that Medicaid costs continue to absorb an ever-increasing share of the state budget.[77] Medicaid costs to the states have increased an average of 7 percent per year over the past decade—that means the costs basically doubled in ten years, prompting one New Mexico legislator to describe Medicaid costs as a "runaway train."[78] Indeed, the most recent estimate (2015) is that Medicaid is the single largest expense now for state governments (25.6 percent), surpassing K–12 spending (19.8 percent).[79] Moreover, Medicaid costs increase during an economic downturn. As more people become unemployed and lose job-related health care insurance, they become eligible for health care benefits through Medicaid. So the demand for Medicaid benefits increases but the supply of state revenue to fund those benefits decreases (because the unemployed pay less in taxes). It is, in other words, a pro-cyclical effect. For example, the Medicaid caseload in Colorado grew by 19 percent as the Great Recession took effect.[80]

Another increasingly significant expenditure for subnational governments is their contribution to public employee pension funds. As the National Conference of State Legislatures notes, "State pension funds have been impacted by underfunding of obligations and by the severe economic recession."[81] Historically, retirement packages for many state and local employees included "defined benefit" plans, meaning that the recipient would receive a specific, defined, annual retirement benefit based on their years of service and the salaries they earned. These benefits (pensions) are paid from funds state and local governments maintain. In most instances, retirement funds rely on income from three sources: contributions from the public employee, direct appropriations from the state or local government budget, and revenue generated by investments of pension funds. Today, many of these pension funds are underfunded; they do not contain enough money to meet their projected obligations as "baby boomer" public employees begin to retire. This problem was caused in part by the Great Recession, which caused pension fund investments to perform poorly. But it is also the case that many states opted to skip their required contributions, using that money instead to fund other priorities. The public employee pension problem is especially acute in Connecticut, Illinois, Kentucky, and New Jersey, but nine other states are also seriously underfunded.[82] The Pew Center on the States has referred to this as "the trillion dollar gap" and it is a looming demand side (expenditure) problem for many states.[83] Kentucky's situation is particularly serious. Years of underfunding the pension account by the state legislature, coupled with a $50 million decline in the value of the state's investment portfolio because of the 2015 decline in the stock market, has left Kentucky with only 19 percent of the assets needed to fully fund its future pension commitments.[84]

One result of this situation is a movement to change the way public employee pensions are going to be funded in the future. Many states are instituting "defined contribution" plans for the newly hired, in which the employee and employer both contribute to a retirement account that the employee controls. Once the state makes its contribution, however, it is no longer on the financial hook in the manner it is with a traditional "defined benefit" plan. The financial risk is transferred completely onto the employee. Some states have developed "hybrid" pension plans that combine features of both defined contribution and defined benefit plans and shares the risks.[85]

Conclusion

In this chapter we have discussed a number of variables that, in combination, bode ill for state fiscal systems. Balanced budget rules and heavy reliance on income and general sales taxes as revenue sources mean that state fiscal systems tend to be pro-cyclical. To exacerbate the situation, economic downturns trigger a higher demand for state social services (unemployment benefits, health care, and the like). Furthermore, federal aid to the states is likely to diminish in the future as the national government grapples with its own daunting fiscal challenges. As two public finance experts note, "While the federal government has recently provided antirecession assistance to states and localities in the short term, escalating deficits in the short and long term will sap the flexibility and capacity of the federal government to play its time-honored role as the equalizer in public finance."[86] Meanwhile, many states have underfunded public employee pension plans at the same time that their baby boomer workers are beginning to retire.

To compound their dire situation, many states have infrastructure systems that are rapidly deteriorating. Recently, the American Society of Civil Engineers graded the quality of American infrastructure—roads, highways, bridges, and levees, etc.—as "D+."[87] Much of the responsibility for dealing with the sorry state of the infrastructure—estimated to cost some $4 trillion over the next decade—will likely fall to the states. As one report states, "Over the last two years state and local governments have come to realize that the federal government isn't coming to the rescue. The cavalry isn't coming."[88]

Interestingly, some Republican governors and legislators—usually extremely reticent to discuss tax hikes—have pushed to raise gasoline taxes or automobile license fees as a way to generate money for road and highway upgrades.[89] Notably in 2015, Republicans in Iowa and Washington agreed to gas tax increases to fund transportation projects. In 2016, Republicans in other states—Oklahoma and Kansas are prime examples—opted to raid their transportation budgets to plug budget shortfalls in the general budget.

More generally, a recent report by the federal Government Accountability Office stated, "GAO simulations of long-term fiscal trends in the state and local government sector . . . have consistently shown that state and local governments face long-term fiscal pressures. Absent any policy changes, the state and local government sector faces a gap between expenditures and receipts in future years. Closing this gap will require state and local governments to make policy changes to assure that receipts are at least equal to expenditures."[90]

It will be necessary for states to tackle these issues head-on. "States' rights" also means "states' responsibilities." It may also mean "opportunities for the states." Given the extent of federal deficits and given that most federal aid now and in the future will have to be spent on health care, now is the time for states to think about their roles and responsibilities in the other policy arenas. This includes the way in which states allow their local governments to address problems at the community level.

A report from the Urban Institute notes that any balance between state revenues and expenditures is increasingly tenuous and some of the problems facing the states—such as increased Medicaid costs, aging populations, and potential cutbacks in many federal aid programs—do not lend themselves to simple solutions. As two political scientists recently described it, state and local governments are facing a "fiscal ice age" in which "a given level of tax revenue purchases a considerably lower level of current services."[91] States will face painful decisions. As the report states, "This challenge is not new. What is new is the unwillingness to acknowledge the dilemma that leads to recurring budget showdowns even as the economy recovers. Eight states could not agree on a budget by the time their fiscal year started in July 2015. Many of them were in the same position last year and are likely to be in the same position next year."[92] Indeed, as the headlines at the beginning of this chapter demonstrate, the problem has not gone away. And it may become a chronic feature of American political life.

Notes

1. http://www.miamiok.com/article/20160322/NEWS/160329882.

2. http://www.wsj.com/articles/illinois-budget-standoff-nears-one-year-mark-1464427802.

3. http://www.theatlantic.com/politics/archive/2016/04/kansass-never-ending-budget-mess/479400/.

4. http://www.nola.com/politics/index.ssf/2016/02/louisiana_is_in_a_budget_mess.html.

5. http://www.fox10tv.com/story/27814457/gov-bentley-alabama-in-a-budget-crisis.

6. http://www.wtae.com/news/pennsylvania-sets-new-budgetday-mark-in-historic-gridlock/37898632.

7. http://www.nytimes.com/2016/04/10/us/alaska-faces-a-clear-budget-deficit-without-an-evident-solution.html?_r=0.

8. On Pennsylvania, see Karen Langley, "Pennsylvania's Budget Impasse Comes to an End: 'We Need to Move On,'" *Pittsburgh Post-Gazette*, March 24, 2016.

9. http://triblive.com/news/allegheny/10157118-74/million-district-budget.

10. Sophia Tareen, "Awkward: Illinois Governor Sued by Wife's Non-Profit," *St. Louis Post-Dispatch*, June 9, 2016.

11. See, for example, Irene Rubin, *The Politics of Public Budgeting*, 7th ed. (Washington, DC: CQ Press, 2014).

12. Phil Kabler, "West Virginia Heads into Special Session to Close Budget Shortfall," *Tribune News Service*, May 12, 2016, http://www.governing.com/topics/finance/tns-west-virginia-budget-session.html. The senator quoted is Mike Hall.

13. Another way to think about this is that the calendar year is divided into four quarters and these quarters are often important reporting periods for businesses and economic analysis (for example, "second quarter sales were up by 5 percent"). Only Texas does not operate off of one of the four economic quarters.

14. The National Bureau of Economic Research (NBER) has determined that the Great Recession actually began in December of 2007 and bottomed out in June of 2009.

15. National Conference of State Legislatures (NCSL), "Update on State Budget Gaps: FY 2009 & FY 2010," Denver: National Conference of State Legislatures, February 20, 2009, 2.

16. These and subsequent figures are from the Center on Budget and Policy Priorities, "Largest State Budget Shortfalls on Record."

17. NCSL, "Update on State Budget Gaps: FY 2009 & FY 2010."

18. Pamela Prah, "States Balance Budgets with Cuts, not Taxes," *Stateline*, June 15, 2011, http://www.pewstates.org/projects/stateline/headlines/states-balance-budgets-with-cuts-not-taxes-85899375037.

19. http://www.usatoday.com/news/nation/2009-05-04-fed-states-revenue_N.htm.

20. Pew Charitable Trust, Fiscal 50: State Trends and Analysis, "Federal Funds Provide 30 Cents of Each Dollar of State Revenue," February 25, 2015. It should be

noted that different reports cite different figures for a variety of reasons. The most important difference is that some calculate federal aid as a percent of state and local revenues and some report it as percent of state revenues only. Because states receive more federal aid than do local governments, the "percent of state revenue" figure is always higher than the "percent of state and local revenue." For example, while federal aid comprised 35.5 percent of state revenue, it comprised only about 26 percent of state and local revenue.

21. http://www.ncsl.org/research/fiscal-policy/state-experiences-with-annual-and-biennial-budgeti.aspx.

22. With the exception of the last four years of the Clinton administration, the federal government spent more than it received in every year since 1970. In other words, the federal government has run a deficit in 90 percent of its budgets over the past forty years.

23. John Kincaid, "The Constitutional Frameworks of State and Local Government Finance," in *The Oxford Handbook of State and Local Government Finance*, ed. Robert D. Ebel and John E. Petersen (New York: Oxford University Press, 2012), 62–63.

24. See David M. Primo, *Rules and Restraint: Government Spending and the Design of Institutions* (Chicago: University of Chicago Press 2008), chap. 5.

25. See Carl E. Klarner, Justin H. Phillips, and Matt Muckler, "Overcoming Fiscal Gridlock: Institutions and Budget Bargaining," *Journal of Politics* 74 (2012): 992–1009.

26. "What's Open, What's Closed: Your Guide to the Shutdown," *Star-Tribune*, July 12, 2011, http://www.startribune.com/politics/statelocal/124952649.html.

27. See W. Mark Crain, *Volatile States* (Ann Arbor: University of Michigan Press 2003), especially chap. 8. For an alternative point of view, see Thad Kousser, Mathew D. McCubbins, and Ellen Moule, "For Whom the TEL Tolls: Can State Tax and Expenditure Limits Effectively Reduce Spending?" *State Politics and Policy Quarterly* 8 (2008): 331–61.

28. Katharine Bradbury, "State Government Budgets and the Recovery Act," Public Policy Briefs, No. 10-1, February 17, 2010, Federal Reserve Bank of Boston, 3.

29. http://www.tennessean.com/story/news/politics/2016/05/20/gov-bill-haslam-signs-hall-income-tax-cut-repeal-into-law/84044810/.

30. David Brunori, *State Tax Policy: A Political Perspective*, 2nd ed. (Washington, DC: Urban Institute Press, 2005), 53.

31. Brunori, *State Tax Policy: A Political Perspective*, 54.

32. Michael Leachman and Michael Mazarov, "State Personal Income Tax Cuts: Still a Poor Strategy for Economic Growth," Center for Budget and Policy Priorities, May 14, 2015, http://www.cbpp.org/research/state-budget-and-tax/state-personal-income-tax-cuts-still-a-poor-strategy-for-economic.

33. These are the state sales tax rates and do not include any additional sales taxes levied by local governments.

34. http://www.taxadmin.org/assets/docs/Research/Rates/mf.pdf; https://www.tobaccofreekids.org/research/factsheets/pdf/0222.pdf.

35. http://time.com/4037604/colorado-marijuana-tax-revenue/.

36. http://www.bloomberg.com/news/articles/2015-10-23/washington-expects-pot-sales-tax-revenue-surge-to-1-billion.

37. http://taxfoundation.org/sites/taxfoundation.org/files/docs/TaxFoundation-FF497.pdf; Prah, "States Balance Budgets with Cuts, not Taxes."

38. Mike Maciag, "How States' Dependence on Corporate Taxes Has Declined," *Governing*, January 6, 2016, http://www.governing.com/topics/finance/gov-state-corporate-income-tax-revenues.html.

39. http://www.statejournal.com/story/16933140/long-term-growth-of-severance-tax-unlikely.

40. http://www.wvgazettemail.com/news/20160307/with-coal-and-gas-down-west-virginia-faces-budget-quandary/.

41. http://www.adn.com/politics/2016/06/29/walker-budget-vetoes-include-capping-permanent-fund-divdends-at-1000/.

42. See, for example, http://www.reuters.com/investigates/special-report/usa-northdakota-bust/.

43. http://www.ncsl.org/research/transportation/registration-and-title-fees-by-state.aspx, as of March 27, 2016.

44. http://www.ghsa.org/html/stateinfo/laws/seatbelt_laws.html, as of June 2016.

45. Donna Leinwand, "Cities, States Tack on More User Fees," *USA Today*, March 18, 2009, http://www.usatoday.com/news/nation/2009-03-17-user-fees_N.htm; Katherine Barrett and Richard Greene, "The Risks of Relying on User Fees," *Governing*, April 2013.

46. Cletus C. Couglin, Thomas A. Garrett, and Ruben Hernandez-Murillo, "The Geography, Economics, and Politics of Lottery Adoption," *Federal Reserve Bank of St. Louis Review*, May/June 2006. Also see Frances S. Berry and William D. Berry, "State Lottery Adoptions as Policy Innovations: An Event History Analysis," *American Political Science Review* 84 (1990): 395–414.

47. Lee Davidson, "Utahns Buy 19% of Idaho's Lottery Tickets," *Salt Lake City Tribune*, April 6, 2012, http://www.sltrib.com/sltrib/news/53862915-78/lottery-idaho-utah-sales.html.csp.

48. These figures, as well as state-specific figures discussed in the text, are based on information from the National Conference of State Legislatures, "Chart of Lottery Payouts and Revenue, By State," http://www.ncsl.org/issues-research/econ/lottery-payouts-and-state-revenue-2010.aspx

49. See http://www.americangaming.org/sites/default/files/uploads/docs/sos/aga_sos_2012_web.pdf.

50. See http://www.indiangaming.org/info/NIGA_2009_Economic_Impact_Report.pdf.

51. For state liquor stores, see http://www.nabca.org/States/States.aspx.

52. Chester Dawson, "Shale Boom Helps North Dakota Bank Earn Returns Goldman Would Envy," *Wall Street Journal*, November 16, 2014.

53. The Morrill Land Grant Act (1862) is usually noted as the first actual example of fiscal federalism, transferring federal lands to states for the establishment of land grant colleges.

54. Another six states adopted lotteries between 2000 and 2009.

55. http://www.ncsl.org/research/fiscal-policy/collecting-ecommerce-taxes -an-interactive-map.aspx.

56. http://www.ncsl.org/research/fiscal-policy/collecting-ecommerce-taxes -an-interactive-map.aspx.

57. Richard Rubin, "States Set Up Fight Over Web Sales Tax," *Wall Street Journal,* February 23, 2016.

58. See State and Local Government Finance Data Query System, the Urban Institute-Brookings Institution Tax Policy Center, http://www.taxpolicycenter.org/ taxfacts/displayafact.cfm?DocID=528&Topic2id=90&Topic3id=92; http://www.tax policycenter.org/briefing-book/what-are-sources-revenue-state-governments.

59. See Ronald Fisher and Andrew Bristle, "State Intergovernmental Grant Pro- grams," in *The Oxford Handbook of State and Local Government Finance,* ed. Robert Ebel and John Petersen (New York: Oxford University Press, 2012), especially Table 9.2, 218–20.

60. This summary is based on data in Table 8-15, "Variations in Local Dependency on State Aid, 2007–2008," in *Vital Statistics on American Politics 2011–2012,* ed. Har- old Stanley and Richard Niemi (Washington, DC: CQ Press, 2011), 322.

61. Presentation by Scott Pattison, Executive Director of the National Association of State Budget Officers (NASBO) on July 30, 2014.

62. http://taxfoundation.org/blog/how-high-are-property-taxes-your-state.

63. The Pew Charitable Trusts, "The Local Squeeze" (Washington, DC, 2012), 8, http://www.pewstates.org/research/reports/the-local-squeeze-85899388655. Also see Federal Funds Information for the States, "State Policy Reports," 30, no. 10 (July 2012) and Lucy Dadayan, "The Impact of the Great Recession on Local Property Taxes," State University of New York at Albany: The Rockefeller Institute, July 2012.

64. Susan Landes, "Financing Recreations and Parks," Commonwealth of Pennsyl- vania (2005), 10, http://www.dcnr.state.pa.us/brc/publications/Pubs/Finance_Hand book.pdf.

65. Perhaps our favorite such case is from the State of Washington. State law (Chapter 36.95 of the Revised Code of Washington) allows for the creation of "Tele- vision Reception Improvement Districts," which may be financed by the imposition of an annual fee of up to $60 per television on households and hotels/motels. See RCW 36.95.100. There is at least one such district in operation, in the municipality of Okanogan.

66. Barrett and Greene, "The Risks of Relying on User Fees."

67. See http://www.ncsl.org/issues-research/budget/local-option-taxes.aspx.

68. Tennessee currently taxes income on dividends. That tax is scheduled to disappear in 2022. See http://www.tennessean.com/story/news/politics/2016/05/20/ gov-bill-haslam-signs-hall-income-tax-cut-repeal-into-law/84044810/.

69. See Congressional Budget Office, "Actual ARRA Spending Over the 2009-2011 Period Quite Close to the CBO's Original Estimate," www.cbo.gov/publication/42682.

70. Not all of these funds went directly to state and local governments, as some were directed to small businesses and qualifying individuals. Moreover, ARRA yielded at least an additional $200 billion in tax reductions to individuals and

corporations, making the "value" of the total stimulus package in excess of $700 billion.

71. There were at least half a dozen governors (all Republicans) who announced they would refuse ARRA funds that extended unemployment benefits, arguing that certain strings attached to these funds would obligate their state to offer extended benefits in the future. Ultimately, the funds were accepted in most of these states.

72. But it does happen from time to time. For an explanation of the causes of such refusals to accept the federal funds, see Sean Nicholson-Crotty, "Leaving Money on the Table: Learning from Recent Refusals of Federal Grants in the American States," *Publius* 42 (2012): 449–66.

73. Marilyn Rubin and Katherine Willoughby, eds., *Sustaining the States: The Fiscal Viability of American State Government* (Boca Raton, FL: CRC Press, 2015), 10.

74. The remainder (17 percent) is categorized as "other." See OMB, "Fiscal Year 2013 Analytical Perspectives," Table 18-2, "Trends in Federal Grants to State and Local Governments," http://www.whitehouse.gov/sites/default/files/omb/budget/fy2013/assets/spec.pdf.

75. Josh Goodman, "The Year School Budget Cuts Went Straight to the Classroom," *Stateline*, June 14, 2011, http://www.pewstates.org/projects/stateline/headlines/the-year-school-budget-cuts-went-straight-to-the-classroom-85899375039.

76. Peter Harkness, "Public Universities Reach Tipping Point After Years of Decreased Education Funding," *Governing*, June 12, 2012, http://www.governing.com/topics/education/gov-public-universities-reach-tipping-point.html.

77. Note that we refer to state spending, not state and local combined. Medicaid funds are part of the state appropriations process.

78. Rachel Brand, "Medicaid: The 800-Pound Gorilla," *State Legislatures* (October/November 2011), 15; Dan Boyd, "State Medicaid Costs Called a 'Runaway Train,'" *Albuquerque Journal*, October 28, 2015, http://www.abqjournal.com/666735/state-medicaid-costs-a-runaway-train.html.

79. The National Association of State Budget Officers (NASBO), "State Expenditure Report," Washington, DC: NASBO, 2015.

80. Center for Colorado's Economic Future, "Issue Brief: Colorado's State Budget Tsunami," University of Denver, July 2009, 6.

81. NCSL, http://www.ncsl.org/issues-research.aspx?tabs=951,69,140.

82. Michael Cembalest, "The ARC and the Covenants, 2.0: An Update on the Long-Term Credit Risk of US States," *Eye on the Market*, J. P. Morgan, May 19, 2016.

83. The figure declined to $968 billion by 2013. See http://www.pewtrusts.org/en/research-and-analysis/issue-briefs/2015/07/the-state-pensions-funding-gap-challenges-persist.

84. Liz Farmer, "As Pension Prospects Worsen, Kentucky Lawmakers Spar Over Worst-Funded Plan," http://www.governing.com/topics/finance/gov-kentucky-budget-pension-reform.html.

85. See "Hybrid Public Pension Plans," Pew Charitable Trusts, April 2015.

86. Timothy Conlan and Paul Posner, "Federalism Trends, Tensions and Outlook," in *The Oxford Handbook of State and Local Government Finance*, ed. Robert Ebel and John Petersen (New York: Oxford University Press, 2012), 98.

87. http://www.infrastructurereportcard.org/.

88. John Schoen, "Rebuilding America Will Be Harder than it Sounds," *CNBC*, May 17, 2016, http://www.cnbc.com/2016/05/17/rebuilding-america-will-be-harder -than-it-sounds.html.

89. http://www.governing.com/topics/transportation-infrastructure/is-this-the -way-states-can-sell-tax-hikes-for-transportation.html.

90. http://www.gao.gov/fiscal_outlook/state_local_fiscal_model/interactive_ graphic/about_state_local_fiscal_conditions.

91. D. Roderick Kiewiet and Mathew McCubbins, "State and Local Government Finance: The New Fiscal Ice Age," *Annual Review of Political Science* 17 (2014): 105.

92. Norton Francis and Frank Sammartino, "Governing with Tight Budgets," September 2015, http://www.urban.org/research/publication/governing-tight-budgets.

8

Why States Matter Now

I N THE PREVIOUS CHAPTERS, we have made the case that states continue to matter in the American federal system. They are important because many significant policy decisions are made at the state level. They are important because federal policy is often administered through state agencies. They are important because states are often innovative policymakers, in some cases moving well in advance of the national government. They are important because they offer a greater role for the individual citizen through the instruments of direct democracy. They are important because the states are the electoral source of all national elected officials. They are important because they generate and spend billions of dollars on their own and determine how local governments operate. As Thomas Gais, director of the Rockefeller Institute of Government, points out, "A lot of people don't realize that state and local governments carry out the great bulk of domestic policies in the United States. The federal government administers some big domestic programs such as Social Security, Medicare, SSI and a few others. For the most part, however, when you're talking about the domestic programs, state and local governments make them happen. Out of eight people working for governments in the United States, seven of them are on the state and local payrolls."[1]

While the public and the media may be slow to understand this trend, interest groups have recognized and responded to it. As one public policy expert notes, there is a "fundamental shift underway in lobbying, as interest groups switch their focus from Washington to the states."[2] As evidence, he cites a recent report that the number of organizations with lobbyists declined by 25 percent in Washington, DC, but increased by more than 10 percent in the states.[3] One government relations firm that represents a variety of clients in the states says that gridlock at the national level has caused many organizations to shift their focus and they are "taking a renewed interest in state government relations."[4]

Unified government at the national level has become a rare occurrence.[5] In the thirty-six-year period between 1980 and 2016, the president's party has held a majority in both houses of Congress only nine years. Remarkably, during this period we had divided government at the national level *75 percent of the time*, punctuated only briefly by instances of unified party control. While one party may capture both the presidency and Congress for one or two electoral cycles, as the Republicans did in the 2016 election, it is unlikely that unified control can be sustained for long at the national level. Separated powers with different electoral institutions, along with polarized parties and a nonrandom distribution of ideological preferences geographically, means that currently it is difficult to sustain a governing majority at the national level in the United States. In other words, gridlock at the national level is likely to occur more often than not, at least for the foreseeable future. As we noted in chapter 2, under this scenario the states become the default option.

States in an Ever-Evolving Federal System

The American experiment with federalism was just beginning as the eighteenth century was ending. It was a new political system for a nascent nation and there was much uncertainty about exactly how the new arrangement would work in practice. For the nineteenth century, historians and political scientists often characterize the arrangement that developed as "dual federalism," meaning that each level of government had its own sphere of operation, and the national level did not intrude much into what was considered the state sphere. This characterization is, of course, a simplification. In fact, there was considerable disagreement about the proper roles to be played by each level.

As we noted in earlier chapters, the New England states resisted some of the federal government's actions surrounding the War of 1812, as illustrated by the Hartford Convention. John C. Calhoun of South Carolina ardently defended slavery and states' rights and was a central figure in the 1832 Nullification Crisis. He argued that states not only had the right to nullify odious federal laws, but that they also had the right to secede from the Union. By 1861, southern efforts to leave resulted in the Civil War. More than 600,000 soldiers died in that conflict—more not just as a percentage of the population, but also in raw numbers, than any other war in American history.[6] Perhaps "duel federalism" is a more apt description of the period than "dual federalism."

During the latter half of the nineteenth century and continuing into the twentieth century, the nature of the relationship between the national and state governments changed. Some of the changes were wrought by the European wave of immigration prior to World War I, the rapid population growth, and the transition from a rural to an urban society brought on by industrialization. Recall that at the beginning of the twentieth century the U.S. population stood at about 100 million. By the close of the century, it was about 300 million. In 1900, a majority, about 60 percent, of Americans still lived in rural areas. By the close of the century, about 80 percent lived in urban and suburban areas. A huge transformation of American society had occurred. Many local governments, especially cities, adapted and expanded their service and regulatory functions.

Meanwhile, after two world wars and a severe economic depression, the national government emerged as a much stronger and more visible presence. Thus both the national and local levels of government adjusted to modern times. Meanwhile, many states languished. Still geared toward a rural society, many of them resisted making the transition. One journalist lamented "the shocking depth to which state government has sunk in the United States."[7]

As the country was urbanizing, many legislatures remained dominated by rural interests, largely due to lingering malapportionment. An observer proclaimed that "state legislatures may be our most extreme example of institutional lag. In their formal qualities they are largely nineteenth century organizations and they must, or should address themselves to twentieth century problems."[8] Thus two political scientists note, "Over the course of a century, the state legislatures evolved from the wellsprings of American government into political backwaters."[9] The president of the U.S. Conference of Mayors in 1949 wrote that "American cities are under the control of unsympathetic state legislatures dominated by agricultural oligarchies."[10]

By mid-century, then, there was growing pressure to "do something" about state governments generally and about state legislatures in particular. The American Political Science Association commissioned a study and the Council of State Governments created committees to make reform recommendations.[11] Several other organizations aimed at modernizing state governments became active. One of these organizations was the National Municipal League, which had become frustrated with what they viewed as unsympathetic views of cities and their problems from their own states.

Consequently, at roughly the same time as the legislative "reapportionment revolution," there began a concerted effort to upgrade and modernize the institution of state government. California was at the forefront of this movement, but others followed quickly. The Eagleton Institute of Politics at Rutgers University provided an institutional locus, often with funding from benefactors like the Carnegie Corporation and the Ford Foundation. The Eagleton Institute provided commissioned analyses of state legislatures in at least eight states. Meanwhile, many states pursued their own reform agendas; commissions to review and recommend changes to state legislative practices were created in Pennsylvania, West Virginia, Iowa, Illinois, Idaho, Oregon, and Washington.[12] As we discussed in chapter 4, similar efforts were made on behalf of the executive and judicial branches. Moreover, numerous states transformed their fiscal systems during the last few decades of the twentieth century. By 1980, states had emerged as stronger and more capable partners in the federal system, leading to "the resurgence of the states."[13] Their metamorphosis has been called a "quiet revolution," a "resurgence," and "a phoenix-like resurrection of federalism."[14]

Getting Beyond "Zero-Sum Games" and the "Alabama Syndrome"

Reemergence of the states is not a topic that is well understood. First, there is the proclivity to view developments in federalism as a zero-sum game. As Alison LaCroix states, "The debate is nearly always framed in terms of a binary confrontation" in which either the national government wins or the states win.[15] We have tried to show that federalism in today's world is much more complicated than that simple characterization. It is not just about the states versus the national government. In today's polarized political world, it is often one party dominating policymaking at one level and the other party controlling policymaking at the other level. Under these conditions, federalism becomes complicated by partisan concerns.

Second, even today, despite the irrefutable progress made by states as policymaking and administrative units over the past forty-five years, there is a lingering tendency to judge states by their lowest common denominator. This phenomenon has been called "the Alabama syndrome" and refers to the reluctance of the federal government decision makers in the 1960s to give any latitude to state administrators in administering new federal policies like Medicare or the "War on Poverty" for fear of what a "George Wallace would do" with that sort of power.[16] For some, that period still colors their perception of the relationship between the national government and the states. As one expert on the subject wrote, "The tenacity and violence of southern resistance to changes in race relations gave federalism a very bad name."[17]

Clearly, not all states are the same. We have sought to document that fact in this book. Some states are leaders and some states are laggards on any given policy. Perhaps we are reluctant to embrace an expanded role for the states precisely because we lack confidence in some states to "do the right thing," whatever we perceive that to be on any given policy.

Most people are inconsistent in their views of the proper federal-state relationship. Both Republicans and Democrats are guilty on this score. People will favor a national or state approach depending on the particular issue, the relative position of the national government and any given state on that issue, and their own opinion on it. Politicians take varying positions on what federalism "ought" to look like as an "expedient tool," according to David Brian Robertson, who points out that "federalism has been used by and against Republicans as well as Democrats, liberals as well as conservatives and innovators as well as those who resist change."[18] Simply stated, partisans want decisions made by the level of government they currently control. When in 2006 Congress was debating a constitutional amendment banning same-sex marriage, 56 percent of gay marriage opponents thought it was an issue for the federal government to decide. When in 2015 the Supreme Court was on the verge of issuing a decision making same-sex marriage legal across the nation, 72 percent of gay marriage opponents thought it was a matter best left to the states.[19] So federalism gets something of a black mark against it because everyone seizes on the policies that some states produce that they do not prefer. We are all for greater policymaking independence for the states except when we disagree with the policies they produce. When it comes to federalism, we are all hypocrites.

States and the Task Ahead

As one federalism expert notes, "The most appealing reason for courts to enforce limits on Congress and to preserve the role of autonomous states is the prediction that states will in fact experiment with new policies, looking for new ways to serve the public good."[20] This comment, of course, harkens back to Justice Brandeis's "laboratories of democracy" argument. The notion may be particularly pertinent today for several reasons. First, the federal deficit will almost certainly require cutbacks in federal aid, especially outside the health care area. Second, changes in technology and communication are such that states are aware of the policy choices undertaken by other states. Policymakers and administrators in one state talk to their counterparts in other states. They are aware of the policy options available, especially as some associations, interest groups, think tanks, and others provide such information to state policymakers. The executive director of the National Governors Association put it this way: "You have all these policies going on in the states.

They've got K–12 education to run, a university system, and incredible challenges in health care and criminal justice. So we're trying to share ideas, solutions . . . and to analyze what's working and what's not working."[21] Finally, there is a strong argument to be made for allowing states some policy latitude, as it is clear that states still differ in terms of political culture and policy preferences. The party realignment, or sorting, that began in the 1960s and 1970s is complete, and many states appear to be "more red" or "more blue" today as fewer states are experiencing divided government. As Ann Althouse succinctly states, "There are times for the national government to stand back and let policies emerge at the lower level of decision making."[22] This appears to be one of those times.

Not too long ago, the respected British newsmagazine *The Economist* published a special report on how the states were leading the way in search of innovative policies to reinvigorate the United States. The article was aptly titled "Let 50 Flowers Bloom" and noted that "America's 50 states are consciously and vigorously competing to find the best formula for regulation and taxes and introducing sweeping reforms to that end. . . . Whether or not Congress puts aside its fiscal vendetta long enough to help with any of this, progress is being made around the country."[23]

The challenges facing state governments and their local governments are great. The biggest challenge will be the financial one, as many states are likely to face, in the words of one observer, "prolonged fiscal austerity."[24] Alice Rivlin, a former head of the federal Office of Management and Budget (OMB), argues that the combination of the current federal deficit and the aging of the population results is a long-term structural imbalance that is unsustainable.[25] As federal budget problems continue, there will be irresistible incentive for national policymakers to push the cost of administering programs down to the state level. Indeed, this has been happening for some time. The National Conference of State Legislatures estimated that the administration of George W. Bush offloaded over $100 billion in program administrative costs onto the states. Such unfunded or poorly funded mandates may help the federal government's budget, but it creates major fiscal problems for the states.

Increasingly, state officials will have to make hard choices between paring back or eliminating programs or raising taxes and fees. In a recent review of American federalism, the authors observed that "mounting concern about federal debt, partisan politics, and legislative gridlock at the federal level has also contributed to the need for states to step up and take matters into their own hands."[26] Demography and economics are conspiring to force the states to the policy fore.

The Public's Responsibility

Given all this, the first task of the public citizen is to be better informed of the role that states play. While states remain essential partners in the American federal system, they are not often presented as such. For one thing, from the media's point of view, there is rarely a natural state constituency. News is usually viewed as being either national or local in scope.[27] Over time, there are fewer and fewer reporters covering the "state capitol beat."[28] A recent study found that between 2003 and 2014 the number of full-time newspaper reporters assigned to the nation's statehouses declined by 35 percent.[29] Another analysis observes, "State governments have more power and more money than ever before. . . . Everyone—political parties, academics, trade organizations, labor unions, corporations—has discovered this. Everyone, that is, except the press."[30]

Even when there is coverage from the state level, it is almost always just about a particular state. In this sense, there is very little comparative reporting occurring in regard to the states. This is understandable because most consumers of the news are only interested in what is happening in their own state—if they are interested at all![31] But without a comparative perspective, we miss most of the trends in state policymaking and we miss the bigger picture of the changes in the federal relationship. There are, however, a few excellent sources of comparative state political news available, such as *Governing* magazine and stateline.org. Unfortunately, these sources are not well known to the general public. They should be. One gains a greater appreciation for the vitality of the states through such venues.

It is only through a comparative framework that we can truly appreciate the advantage of a federal system. The public needs to understand that states only matter if they have the freedom to try a variety of approaches to solving public problems and that they have the ability to do so within the political and cultural context of each state. There are limits to such variation, of course. In a compound republic, both individual rights and states' rights have a place. "States' rights" is an easy phrase to toss about, especially when one is frustrated with the national government. But with rights also come responsibilities for all the citizens of the state, not just the citizens who form the majority. There is a cost to having the states continue to matter as we enter a period of austerity. It may be a cost in the form of reduced services or the elimination of entire programs in some instances. It may be a cost in the form of higher state and local taxes in order to replace federal aid. It will likely be both.

An important task for the citizen is to understand there are hard choices ahead and the value of having a variety of policy options explored. It is essential that we recognize there are real policy consequences to state elections.

States with unified Republican control will make different decisions than states with unified Democratic control. States with divided control will likely make still different decisions. States matter, and who controls the governing apparatus of the states matters. Understanding this basic fact and understanding their role in determining who governs is perhaps the most important of all tasks for citizens.

Notes

1. "Institute Q&A," The Nelson Rockefeller Institute of Government, University of Albany, New York, September 2010.

2. Donald Kettl, "Lobbyists Leave Capitol Hill for the States," *Governing*, June 2016, http://www.governing.com/columns/potomac-chronicle/gov-lobbying-states -washington.html.

3. Kettl, "Lobbyists Leave Capitol Hill." The report is from The Center for Public Integrity, "Amid Federal Gridlock, Lobbying Rises in the States," https://www .publicintegrity.org/2016/02/11/19279/amid-federal-gridlock-lobbying-rises-states.

4. Mike Macaig, "Louisiana's Budget Crisis Empowers an Unusual Group," *Governing*, July 2016, http://www.governing.com/topics/politics/gov-louisiana-budget .html.

5. Shanna Rose and Cynthia Bowling, "The State of American Federalism 2014–15: Pathways to Policy in an Era of Party Polarization," *Publius* 45 (2015): 351–79.

6. Anne Leland and M-J Oboroceanu, "American War and Military Operations Casualties: Lists and Statistics," Washington, DC: Congressional Research Service Report 7-5700, February 26, 2010.

7. Robert S. Allen, "The Shame of the States," in *Our Sovereign State*, ed. Robert S. Allen (New York: Vanguard Press, 1949), xiii.

8. Alexander Heard, "Introduction—Old Problem, New Context," in *Our Sovereign State*, ed. Allen, 3.

9. Stephen Ansolabehere and James Snyder, *The End of Inequality: One Person, One Vote and the Transformation of American Politics* (New York: Norton, 2008), 88.

10. Quoted in Allen, "The Shame of the States," xxii.

11. See the discussion in Peverill Squire, *The Evolution of American Legislatures, Colonies, Territories, and States, 1619–2009* (Ann Arbor: University of Michigan Press, 2012), 291–97; and Belle Zeller, *American State Legislatures* (New York: Thomas Y. Crowell, 1954).

12. Jon Teaford, *The Rise of the States* (Baltimore: The Johns Hopkins University Press, 2002), 199–200; Squire, *The Evolution of American Legislatures*, 297–307.

13. Ann O. Bowman and Richard Kearney, *The Resurgence of the States* (Englewood Cliffs, NJ: Prentice Hall, 1986).

14. Carl Van Horn, ed., *The State of the States* (Washington, DC: CQ Press, 1989), 1–12; Teaford, *The Rise of the States*, chap. 8.

15. Alison LaCroix, "How the Noisy Debate Over States' Rights Distorts History and the Intent of Federalism," http://voices.washingtonpost.com/political-bookworm/2010/03/how_the_noisy_debate_over_stat.html. Also see Alison LaCroix, *The Ideological Origins of American Federalism* (Cambridge, MA: Harvard University Press, 2010).

16. There are numerous references to the "Alabama syndrome," but it is generally attributed to James L. Sundquist, *Making Federalism Work* (Washington, DC: Brookings Institution, 1969), 271. Also see Ira Sharkansky, *The Maligned States*, 2nd ed. (New York: McGraw-Hill, 1978), 7; Kimberly Johnson, *Governing the American State: Congress and the New Federalism, 1877–1929* (Princeton, NJ: Princeton University Press, 2006), 159; and John D. Nugent, *Safeguarding Federalism: How States Protect Their Interests in National Policymaking* (Norman: University of Oklahoma Press, 2009), 221.

17. Martha Derthick, *Keeping the Compound Republic* (Washington, DC: Brookings Institute Press, 2001), 148.

18. David Brian Robertson, *Federalism and the Making of America* (New York: Routledge, 2011), 9.

19. Aaron Blake, "Gay Marriage Opponents Are Suddenly All about States' Rights. Wonder Why," *Washington Post*, June 11, 2015.

20. Ann Althouse, "Vanguard States, Laggard States, Federalism and Constitutional Rights," *University of Pennsylvania Law Review* 152 (2004): 1745–827.

21. Louis Jacobson, "New Head of Governors Group Talks Future of States," *Governing*, March 28, 2016, http://www.governing.com/topics/politics/gov-scott-pattison-national-governors-association.html

22. Althouse, "Vanguard States, Laggard States," 1746.

23. "Let 50 Flowers Bloom," *The Economist*, March 16–22, 2013, 16.

24. Virginia Gray, "The Socioeconomic and Political Context of States," in *Politics in the American States*, ed. Virginia Gray, Russell Hanson, and Thad Kousser, 10th ed. (Thousand Oaks, CA: CQ Press, 2013), 26.

25. Alice Rivlin, "Rethinking Federalism for More Effective Governance," *Publius* 42 (2012): 390.

26. Shama Gamkhar and J. Mitchell Pickerill, "The State of American Federalism 2011–2012: A Fend for Yourself and Activist Form of Bottom-up Federalism," *Publius* 42 (2012): 378.

27. Nugent, *Safeguarding Federalism*, 215–16.

28. Alan Rosenthal, *The Decline of Representative Democracy* (Washington, DC: CQ Press, 1997); Peverill Squire and Gary Moncrief, *State Legislatures Today: Politics Under the Domes*, 2nd ed. (Lanham, MD: Rowman & Littlefield, 2015), 211–13.

29. http://www.journalism.org/2014/07/10/americas-shifting-statehouse-press/.

30. Jennifer Dorrah, "Statehouse Exodus," *American Journalism Review* (April/May 2009), www.ajr.org/article.asp?id=4721.

31. Nugent, *Safeguarding Federalism*, 216.

Index

abortion laws, 124–128, 133

Advantage 2020, 161

Affordable Care Act (ACA), 24, 30, 39, 103, 128–130

Alabama: 2009 budget shortfall, 190; court clerks, 94; ethics problems, 96; fiscal calendar, 189; Great Depression era budget problems, 36; judicial campaign costs, 152; legislative turnover, 88; local option sales taxes, 206; Medicaid eligibility, 130; quadrennial legislative sessions, 58; preemption laws, 46; primary election calendar, 154; property tax range, 205; religiosity, 10; same-sex marriage, 124; single-member district majority rule, 149; Temporary Assistance for Needy Families (TANF) policies, 131; tobacco purchasing age, 118; veto power, 64

Alabama Constitutional Revision Commission, 64

Alabama syndrome, 226

Alaska: abortion laws, 126; automatic voter registration, 157; budget problems,184; federal aid, 34; gasoline tax, 198; gun control laws, 116; IRV vote, 150; local sales taxes, 195; marijuana laws, 117, Medicaid eligibility, 129–130; no general sales tax, 195; no income tax, 194; primary voting rules, 154; severance taxes, 198–199; Temporary Assistance for Needy Families (TANF) policies, 131; tobacco purchasing age, 118; women and minority judges, 94

Alien and Sedition Acts of 1798, 30

Althouse, Ann, 228

American Law Institute, 126

American Legislative Exchange Council (ALEC), 35, 91

American Political Science Association, 225

American Recovery and Reinvestment Act of 2009 (ARRA or federal stimulus money), 190–191, 209–210

welfare policies, 128–132; higher education, 113–115; home schooling, 112–113; infrastructure problems, 209–211; innovation leaders, 105; leadership pools, 145–146; marijuana laws, 117; miscegenation laws, 121–122; morality policies, 103, 121–128; noodling laws, 134; partisanship of, 103, 120, 159–161, 224; pension liabilities, 164, 214–215; police powers, 115–121; policy diffusion, 105, 117–118; policy-making capacity, 41–42, 77–78; policy responsiveness, 4, 132–133; political cultures of, 11; political party systems, 146–147; presidential elections, 167–172; primary election rules, 153–156; prisons, 118–121; redistricting practices, 158–161; relations with local governments, 9, 23, 44–47; religiosity, 10, 103; revenue systems, 7, 193–203; same-sex marriage laws, 72–73, 121–124; school choice, 81–82, 110–113; tax and expenditure limitations (TELs), 192; texting bans, 105; three strikes laws, 119–120; tobacco laws, 117–118; voter eligibility rules, 156–158; welfare policies, 35–36, 128–132, 210–213

state bureaucracies: education level of administrators, 86; employment levels, 86; demands on, 86; growth of, 64–66, 86; minority administrators, 86–87; policy-making capacity, 85–87; silver tsunami and, 87; women administrators, 86–87

state courts: campaign costs, 151–153; capacity of, 91–95; clerks, 94; education level of judges, 92; elections to, 70–71, 151–153; decision-making rules, 69; evolution of, 67–68; merit plan, 71; minority judges, 94; number of judges, 95; organization of, 68–69;

professionalization of, 94–95; salaries of, 92; selection of judges, 69–72; women judges, 94

state governments: compared with private businesses, 82; constitutional design of, 56, 73; growth of bureaucracy, 64–66, 86; media coverage of, 229; policy domains, 73–74; policy innovations, 102–103; public opinion on, 8; relations with local governments, 9, 23, 44–47; school funding, 106–109; separation of powers, 56–58, 73

state governors: education levels, 80–81, 84; good-time Charlies, 78; media coverage of, 79; minorities as, 84; policy-making capacity, 78–85; previous experience, 81–83; salaries, 83–84; terms of office, 59–62, 64, 84–85; staff, 85; veto powers, 62–64, 79–80; women as, 84

state legislatures: 2010 elections, 159–162; capacity of, 87–91; days in sessions, 58–59, 90; education level of members, 87; evolution of, 57–59; media coverage of, 229; minorities, 87; multi-member districts, 149; partisan composition of, 159–161; professionalization of, 8, 59, 89–91; reapportionment revolution and, 7–8, 88, 158, 225–226; recall elections, 162–163; redistricting, 158–161; salaries, 66, 89–90; single-member districts, 148–149; staff, 90–91; term limits and, 88–89, 166–167; turnover rates, 88–89; women, 87

stateline.org, 229

state's rights, 7

Stewart, Jon, 133

Suffolk County, New York, 68

tax and expenditure limitations (TELs), 192

taxes and revenues, 193–203; corporate income taxes, 198–199; e-commerce

About the Authors

Gary F. Moncrief is University Distinguished Professor of Political Science Emeritus at Boise State University. He received his undergraduate degree in political science from the University of California, Santa Barbara and his PhD degree from the University of Kentucky. He is the coauthor or editor of six books, including *Reapportionment and Redistricting in the West* (2012) and *State Legislatures Today: Politics under the Domes* (second edition, 2015). He is a frequent speaker at training workshops for state legislators and staff around the country. Although retired from his tenured faculty position, he continues to teach graduate seminars in the School of Public Service at Boise State University.

Peverill Squire is professor of political science and holds the Hicks and Martha Griffiths Chair in American Political Institutions at the University of Missouri. He received his AB, MA and PhD degrees from the University of California, Berkeley. Professor Squire's research centers on American politics with an emphasis on legislatures. He has authored *The Rise of the Representative: Lawmakers and Constituents in Colonial America* (2017) and *The Evolution of American Legislatures: Colonies, Territories and States, 1619-2009* (2012); coauthored *State Legislatures Today: Politics under the Domes* (second edition, 2015), *101 Chambers: Congress, State Legislatures, and the Future of Legislative Studies* (2005), and *Who Runs for the Legislature?* (2001); and coedited *Legislatures: Comparative Perspectives on Representative Assemblies* (2002). He teaches undergraduate courses on American state government and American legislatures and graduate courses on legislative institutions, the evolution of American legislatures, and American state politics.